Streetwise™

CUSTOMER-FOCUSED

SELLING

Books in the Streetwise™ series include:

Streetwise™ Customer-Focused Selling
Streetwise™ Do-It-Yourself Advertising
Streetwise™ Hiring Top Performers
Streetwise™ Independent Consulting
Streetwise™ Managing People
Streetwise™ Small Business Start-Up

Streetwise™

SELLING

Understanding customer needs,
building trust, and delivering solutions . . .
the smarter path to sales success

Nancy J. Stephens

with Bob Adams

Adams Media Corporation
Holbrook, Massachusetts

An Adams Streetwise® Publication. Adams Streetwise® is a registered trademark of Adams Media Corporation.

Published by Adams Media Corporation
260 Center Street, Holbrook, MA 02343

ISBN: 1-55850-725-6

Printed in the United States of America.

J I H G F E D C B

Library of Congress Cataloging-in-Publication Data
Stephens, Nancy J.
Adams Streetwise customer-focused selling : succeed in sales by putting your customer first / Nancy F. Stephens & Bob Adams.
    p.   cm.
Includes index.
ISBN 1-55850-725-6 (pbk.)
1. Selling. 2. Customer services. 3. Consumer satisfaction.
    I. Adams, Bob, 1955-   . II. Title.
        HF5438.25.S736   1997
    658.8'12–dc21   97-30375
                                CIP

Inside photos: Photodisc™ Images ©1996, PhotoDisc, Inc. and BodyShots™ ©1994.
Cover photo: Jan van Steenwijk. Cover background photo Superstock.

This publication is designed to provide accurate and authoritative information with regard to the subject matter covered. It is sold with the understanding that the publisher is not engaged in rendering legal, accounting, or other professional advice. If legal advice or other expert assistance is required, the services of a competent professional person should be sought.
—From a *Declaration of Principles* jointly adopted by a Committee of the American Bar Association and a Committee of Publishers and Associations

This book is available at quantity discounts for bulk purchases.
For information, call 1-800-872-5627 (in Massachusetts, call 781-767-8100).

Visit our home page at http://www.adamsmedia.com

TABLE OF CONTENTS

TABLE OF CONTENTS

SECTION TWO: PREPARATION MAKES THE DIFFERENCE

TABLE OF CONTENTS

TABLE OF CONTENTS

SECTION THREE: ANATOMY OF THE SALE

TABLE OF CONTENTS

TABLE OF CONTENTS

TABLE OF CONTENTS

TABLE OF CONTENTS

SECTION SIX: THE EXTRA EDGE

TABLE OF CONTENTS

TABLE OF CONTENTS

FOREWORD

Customer-Focused Selling is an advanced sales process that requires an ability to assess situations accurately, implement personal judgment, build long-term relationships, create mutual satisfaction, and connect as a true business partner in the sales decision-making process.

Customer-Focused Selling is a shift from traditional selling techniques of manipulation, tactics, and scripting to an advanced ability to truly connect to your customers. "Connecting" means involving the customer in all aspects of the sale. It means knowing your customer's business, their goals and objectives, and then positioning your product or service as part of their company's success.

Customer-Focused Selling means working from the same side of the table to create results for the customer. Sales go up because you are not pushing "stuff," you are solving problems and creating results. Customer-Focused Selling emphasizes the intangible side of every sale—your products and services, the real value to the customer, and what you personally bring to the table.

Customer-Focused Selling requires salespeople to understand where they are coming from, to leverage their strengths, to learn new skills, and to take full responsibility for managing the sales process and sales results. It's your job in selling to fully understand your customers and how you can help them before you sell them anything. With Customer-Focused Selling, you are in the driver's seat at all times. You have a clear understanding of where you are in the sales process and what it will take to advance the sales. Gone are the days of hoping for the business, wondering if you'll get the order, wishing for a good deal; with Customer-Focused Selling, you create the business with methods that work. The rewards of being Customer-Focused are increased commitment, loyalty, referrals, and, of course, increased sales! Customer-Focused salespeople are top producers because they are connected to their customers beyond the scope of their product or service, and beyond their competition. The key to your success with Customer-Focused Selling is understanding

FOREWORD

the dynamics of what happens during a sales decision-making process and how you can positively influence every decision.

Customer-Focused Selling helps you differentiate yourself from the crowd of competitors first by the collaborative approach you'll take and finally by the business results you'll create. Your customer will view you as a true business partner, an integral part of their success, not as a vendor or supplier. Your customers will see you as one of the "secret weapons to success," part of their team, not a simple salesperson. The relationships between customer and salesperson is powerful, and it is your job to grow that relationship so that both sides win big.

— NANCY J. STEPHENS

CHAPTER

1

ANYONE CAN SELL

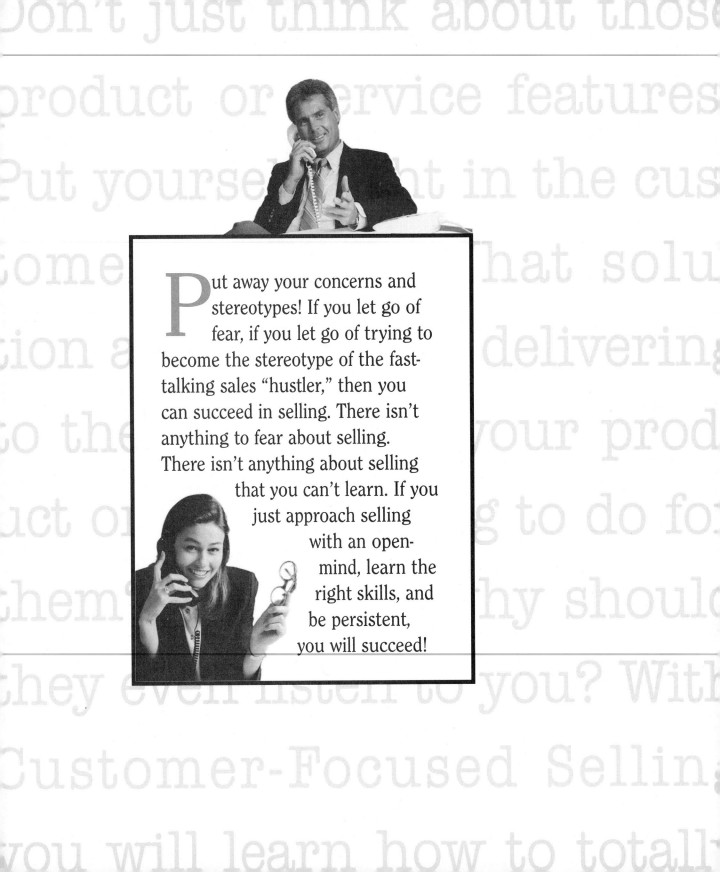

Put away your concerns and stereotypes! If you let go of fear, if you let go of trying to become the stereotype of the fast-talking sales "hustler," then you can succeed in selling. There isn't anything to fear about selling. There isn't anything about selling that you can't learn. If you just approach selling with an open-mind, learn the right skills, and be persistent, you will succeed!

ANYONE CAN SELL!

I f you can read this, then you can sell!
Selling is just like any other relatively simple skill: You can learn this skill, and it isn't as difficult as it might appear at first!

LETTING GO OF FEAR.

When you rode a bicycle for the first time, you might have been afraid of falling and getting hurt on the hard pavement. When you swam for the first time, you might have been afraid of forever disappearing under the water. But once you tried riding a bicycle or swimming, you found out that these activities weren't as death-defying as they might have appeared! You found that if you fell off your bicycle, you didn't break into pieces. You found if you swam in shallow water, you didn't disappear under the water, never to be seen again. Similarly, you'll find that even if everything goes completely wrong on some of your early sales calls, you can pick yourself up and go on to make a great sales presentation on the very next call!

PRACTICE AND TECHNIQUE.

With riding a bicycle and swimming you probably learned the basic techniques fairly quickly, and with a little practice, you probably became quite comfortable on a bicycle or in the water. And so it can be with selling. If you learn a good technique and practice, you'll be very comfortable selling in no time at all!

THE BIGGEST OBSTACLE IS ATTITUDE.

If you think you can't sell, then it becomes much more difficult to succeed. But why think this? It's simply not true. Anyone can sell. How do I know this? Because my first sales attempts were miserable! At first I thought I might never be able to make it through

> If you learn a good technique and practice, you'll be very comfortable selling in no time at all!

ANYONE CAN SELL!

the day, let alone make a successful career of it. But I kept going...and I soon learned that not only could I sell, but that it could be a lot of fun and very rewarding. And I've seen plenty of other people, too, who thought they would never be able to sell, become truly great salespeople.

WHY SO MANY PEOPLE WRONGLY BELIEVE THEY CAN'T SELL.

Especially if you've never done selling, the word "salesperson" probably brings to mind an image of a fast-talking used-car sales huckster pulling every trick and gimmick possible to talk customers into buying a product they don't really want at a price they can't afford! To be sure, there are some salespeople out there who do use fast talk and gimmicks to sell. But you don't have to! There is absolutely no need to use fast talk and gimmicks to succeed at sales.

CUSTOMER-FOCUSED SELLING STARTS AND ENDS WITH INTEGRITY!

In fact, I'm going to show you how to use exactly the opposite approach—complete integrity and an honest and open attitude of helping the customer—to show you not only how you can succeed in sales, but how this approach is by far the most powerful sales approach of all. I'm not talking about just appearing to help the customer, just appearing to be his or her friend. I'm talking about feeling for the customer, and doing for the customer, just the way you would want the salesperson helping you if you were the customer.

CUSTOMER-FOCUSED SELLING IS BY FAR THE EASIEST SALES APPROACH.

You're going to see that Customer-Focused Selling is the easiest way to succeed at sales. You will learn how the customer and the customer's needs and wants can actually help *pull you* through the sales process. You will learn how to work in tandem with the customer instead of against the customer. It sounds simple. And it is simple.

The Deadly Myth Of "The Naturally Born Salesperson"

Forget the myth of the naturally born salesperson. It isn't true. And it's a myth that's destroyed a lot of sales careers.

I've known a lot of salespeople, and I've yet to meet a person who's confided in me that he or she was an absolute, instant smash hit in selling! Instead, I constantly meet lots of really successful salespeople who tell me the same story—of how they built their sales abilities over a long period of time, combining both skill-building and practice.

BUT FEW PEOPLE START OUT WITH CUSTOMER-FOCUSED SELLING.

Why don't more salespeople use Customer-Focused Selling? It is the most effective way to sell. Customer-Focused Selling is also the easiest way to sell. So why doesn't everyone start out with it? Because especially when you first start selling, you are first focused on yourself, not on the customer! You're thinking: "Will I get the appointment? Will they listen to me? Will I convince them to buy? Will I get the sale? Will I succeed at this?"

After thinking about themselves, new salespeople tend to give second priority to focusing on the product or the service they are selling. "Let me tell you about my great product." "Our service is much better than any other because."

CUSTOMERS REALLY DON'T CARE ABOUT YOU.

Customers care about themselves. They might at some point actually begin to like you. But no matter what you do, they are going to like themselves even more. They want to make their own business or career succeed more than they want you to succeed. You don't want to try to compete with them. You don't want to try to get them to buy from you just because they like you, because they are going to always like themselves more. This doesn't mean you shouldn't be likable...it just means that YOU should not be the center of your sales effort.

CUSTOMERS REALLY DON'T EVEN CARE ABOUT YOUR PRODUCT OR SERVICE.

Customers care about how your product or service may provide solutions for them. Beyond achieving their own solutions, customers really don't care about your product or service. They are much more interested in figuring out how to meet their own business objectives than in hearing about lots of product features. But they do want to know how your product is going to deliver a solution to their needs.

> Beyond achieving their own solutions, customers really don't care about your product or service.

ANYONE CAN SELL!

CUSTOMER-FOCUSED SELLING MEANS PUTTING YOURSELF IN THE CUSTOMER'S SHOES.

Don't just think about those product or service features. Put yourself right in the customer's shoes. What solution are you really delivering to them? What is your product or service going to do for them? And also, why should they even listen to you? With Customer-Focused Selling you will learn how to totally focus on the customer; how to adopt the customer's perspective; how to build the customer's trust; how to get the customer to not just be willing to listen to you, but to *want* to listen to you, and even to pull you right through the entire sales process.

CUSTOMER-FOCUSED SELLING IS YOUR FASTEST ROUTE TO SALES SUCCESS.

Even if you've never sold before, the fastest way you can succeed in sales is with Customer-Focused Selling. Now, to be sure, you could close this book right now, make some sales calls, and maybe land some sales. But your ability to really succeed at sales in a short period of time is going to be a lot greater if you invest just a little time to go through this book and learn the Customer-Focused Selling Approach. You are going to have to practice Customer-Focused Selling to really master it. You're going to have to try really hard to keep reminding yourself to keep the customer's perspective foremost in your mind. But you'll find that once you've developed the habit of Customer-Focused Selling, sales success will be at your doorstep.

I'm sure you've met people who seem that they are naturally born salespeople. People who seem to make sales and develop relationships with potential buyers with seemingly no effort at all. But I assure you that at least earlier in their selling careers these sales stars had to learn how to sell. And frankly, you might be surprised that many of these people who appear to be gliding through the sales process are actually very carefully following techniques they have carefully honed over a period of years. You might be surprised to hear that these sales stars get very excited and sometimes anxious about the sales process, just like you! But usually they have learned how to channel their excitement and anxiety into a positive energy that helps push them forward.

You, too, can learn how any anxiety or excitement you feel about the sales process can be focused in a positive manner to push the sales process ahead. And it will be a lot easier and more natural by using Customer-Focused Selling. Because by really adopting and believing in Customer-Focused Selling, you are going to see each sales prospect as an opportunity to help your customers reach their solutions—and by doing this you will also achieve your own success.

Why is the myth of the "naturally born salesperson" so deadly?

This myth scares people out of sales. It makes them wrongly think that they may not "have what it takes to succeed at sales" even though it's just not true. Because anyone can be a huge success at selling if they learn and practice Customer-Focused Selling.

This myth stops people from even trying to learn the techniques they need to excel at sales.

Another problem with this myth is that it focuses totally on the salesperson. What you need to be focusing on is the customer, and also the dynamics with the customer. Are you focusing on them? Are you gaining their trust? Are you helping them?

Furthermore, this myth perpetuates the worst selling approaches. It perpetuates the stereotype of the fast-talking huckster who can and would sell anything to anybody whether or not they even need or can benefit from it. This is the exact opposite of Customer-Focused Selling. Customer-Focused Selling is based on the premise of helping your customers find solutions, not selling them what they don't need.

2

WHAT'S WRONG WITH THE OLD SELLING APPROACHES?

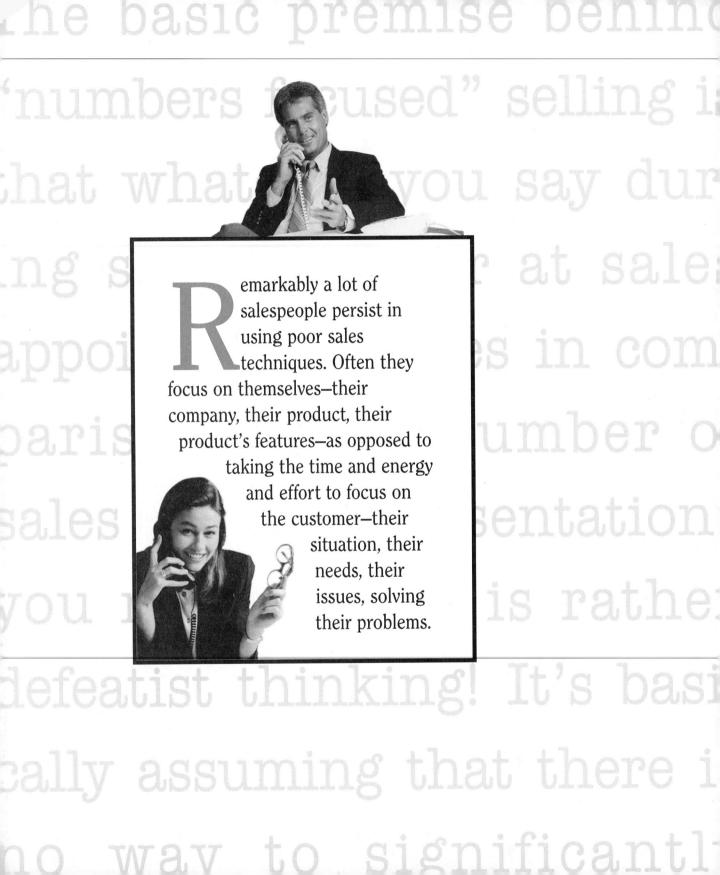

Remarkably a lot of salespeople persist in using poor sales techniques. Often they focus on themselves—their company, their product, their product's features—as opposed to taking the time and energy and effort to focus on the customer—their situation, their needs, their issues, solving their problems.

WHAT'S WRONG WITH THE OLD SELLING APPROACHES?

The old selling approaches are based upon an assumption that you and the customer are working at cross purposes. The old approaches focus on getting the customer to "buy" your product or service and for you to "sell" the product or service. Much of the sales process focuses on product or service features or competitive comparisons.

On the other hand, Customer-Focused Selling has both you and the customer focusing on the same objective: providing a solution for the customer.

In the old selling approaches you focus very directly on getting the customer to buy your product or service. The sales process often represents an exchange of gunfire between two battleships. You fire a volley of reasons to buy, such as great product or service features, or today's special offer. Then the customer fires back a volley of objections and reasons not to buy the product or service. Meanwhile, each of you is constantly trying to figure out what information the other is providing you that is really meaningful, or even true. For example, the buyer wonders, "Which of these product attributes are meaningful in helping me to achieve my objectives, and are these performance claims accurate or just meaningless exaggerations?" And the salesperson wonders, "Which of these objections are substantive, and which are just his or her way of saying that they don't feel like really considering buying my product today?"

In Customer-Focused Selling, on the other hand, you focus overwhelmingly on how your product or service may be able to provide added value to the customer. Together with the customer, you search for the value added.

> The sales process often represents an exchange of gunfire between two battleships.

WHAT'S WRONG WITH THE OLD SELLING APPROACHES?

WHAT'S WRONG WITH PRODUCT-FOCUSED SELLING, PERHAPS THE MOST COMMON SALES APPROACH?

In this approach the salesperson's central focus is on product or service features. For example, a presentation might begin like this: "Our new industrial engine has 270 horsepower, 12 cylinders, 18 valves, and a 24-month guarantee."

A basic problem with this approach is that the buyer may not care! All too often the sales rep starts selling features without even finding out what the concerns of the buyer are. Does the buyer care how many horsepower or how many cylinders the engine has? Just because the last customer cared about the horsepower doesn't mean that this customer will.

An even more serious problem is the buyer may not even be listening! People who make buying decisions often hear one sales rep after the next roll off product features and attributes. Maybe an hour before, another sales rep began her presentation with "Our new industrial engine has 275 horsepower, 14 cylinders, 16 valves, and a 30-month guarantee."

> Buyers hear one rep after the next roll off lists of product features and attributes.

EACH PRODUCT HAS ITS SELLING POINTS.

Even when you know beyond any doubt that your product or service has better features overall, other sales reps selling products or services that are inferior can always find some true, positive selling points about their product. For the buyer it can all lead to a lot of confusion and frustration and just plain be tiring to listen to one sales rep after the next trumpet their product's features.

Another problem with selling focused on the product is that it doesn't lend itself well to building rapport and trust with the buyer. It lacks constructive interactivity.

EVEN A DISCUSSION OF BENEFITS MAY STILL BE A LONG WAY FROM CUSTOMER-FOCUSED SELLING.

Even when you link benefits to product or service attributes, this still can be a long way from Customer-Focused Selling. For example,

WHAT'S WRONG WITH THE OLD SELLING APPROACHES?

you may do a wonderful job of explaining how a product feature of an industrial engine may mean a 5 percent fuel savings for your prospective customer. But your customer may not really care about fuel economy. He or she may be may preoccupied with reliability concerns. Or maybe they are more concerned about the possibility of lease financing, or the service guarantee. Customer-Focused Selling will lead you to the heart of the customer's concerns, which is different from focusing on a general presentation of product attributes or benefits.

WHAT'S WRONG WITH FOCUSING ON "MY COMPANY" OR "MY BACKGROUND"?

This approach is often used in selling services, but sometimes salespeople from product companies use it as at least part of their sales pitch.

The big problem with this approach is that it takes the focus 180 degrees from where it should be–the customer. As the salesperson or perhaps as the small business owner, you are probably proud as punch of your company and can't wait to tell prospective customers about it. But prospective customers don't want to hear you brag about your company. They want to be able to brag about their own company–and they want your help to be able to do it! If they trusted you, they would rather tell you about their company and their issues so you could help them.

Another problem with talking up your company and your background is the risk of being thought of as someone who is more focused on continuing to build your company and your own accomplishments, as opposed to helping your potential customers build their company. You risk being seen as someone who really doesn't care about the prospective customer, but only wants to make the sale.

Perhaps the biggest risk of all with the "my company" or "my background" approach is that prospective customers just aren't going to really listen to anything you have to say. They might not throw you out of the office immediately or slam down the receiver, but they are likely to "tune out," focus away from you, and start thinking about how they can politely end the conversation.

> Prospective customers don't want to hear you brag about your company. They want to be able to brag about their own company—and they want your help to be able to do it!

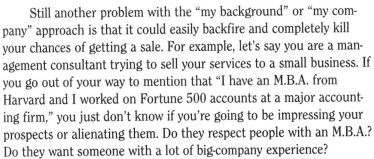
WHAT'S WRONG WITH THE OLD SELLING APPROACHES?

> One of the fastest ways to alienate your prospective customer is to start bashing your competitors or their products.

Still another problem with the "my background" or "my company" approach is that it could easily backfire and completely kill your chances of getting a sale. For example, let's say you are a management consultant trying to sell your services to a small business. If you go out of your way to mention that "I have an M.B.A. from Harvard and I worked on Fortune 500 accounts at a major accounting firm," you just don't know if you're going to be impressing your prospects or alienating them. Do they respect people with an M.B.A.? Do they want someone with a lot of big-company experience?

There may be an appropriate time in building a sales relationship to talk about your company. But try to avoid initiating sales presentations with talk about your company or your professional background; try to wait for signals from prospects that they are interested in hearing about your firm, and keep the focus on the customer, not on you or your company.

WHAT'S WRONG WITH SELLING AGAINST THE COMPETITION?

One of the fastest ways to alienate your prospective customer is to start bashing your competitors or their products. Even if you are completely right, customers don't enjoy hearing negative things about other firms. Saying negative things can ruin any ability to build trust. Are you going to trust someone who has lots of negative things to say about their competitors? Probably not.

Even if the negatives you are tempted to point out about your competitor's products or services or business are completely true, don't do it. Even if the customer knows these negatives are true, don't remind him or her. You're not going to build trust by saying negative things about your competition!

Chances are that the customer knows the negatives about your competitor's product, service, or business better than you do.

You also need to be especially careful about making any negative reference about any product or service the customer has previously bought—because by doing so you are indirectly criticizing his or her judgment.

WHAT'S WRONG WITH THE OLD SELLING APPROACHES?

In fact, under certain circumstances, you may even want to build trust by saying positive things about your competitors or even referring some business to them! Today many astute salespeople and businesses as a matter of policy refer some business to their competition when they think it might be in their customer's best interests. A common example may be when you know you can't meet a customer's scheduling requirements. What these companies are doing is putting their customer and their relationship with their customer ahead of making another sale today.

WHAT'S WRONG WITH THE "BE MY BUDDY" SELLING APPROACH?

One of the classic sales stereotypes is the slap 'em on the back, let's tell another joke and have another beer, "good ole' boy" sales style, the focus being on building a close friendship with your buyers to ensure their undying loyalty.

These days—if there ever were these days—are completely gone! No buyer wants to think of himself as buying from you just because you're his or her friend or buddy. In fact, today's buyer often won't even give favoritism to close relatives.

This doesn't mean you shouldn't nurture a friendly relationship with a potential or current customer. But it should never be your primary selling focus. And you should only build a relationship with the attitude that it will help your customers reach better solutions with their business, not that it will give you a selling advantage.

In building a friendly relationship with a buyer, you should tread slowly. Buyers are defensive and quickly shrug off a salesperson who is too overtly friendly, especially at the early stages of building a business relationship.

So especially in your first contacts with potential buyers, keep the small talk short, and be sure that you quickly progress to a business discussion focused on helping your customers build their business.

> No buyer wants to think of himself as buying from you just because you're his or her friend or buddy.

WHAT'S WRONG WITH THE OLD SELLING APPROACHES?

> Salespeople fall into the trap of arguing out objections.

WHAT'S WRONG WITH SELLING FOCUSED ON "OVERCOMING OBJECTIONS"?

A lot of sales managers make a big deal about having a list ready for their neophyte sales trainees with a brilliant response to every objection under the sun. For example:

Customer says: "I can't afford it."

You respond: "You can pay in twelve installments."

Customer says: "I'll think about it until tomorrow."

You respond: "The sale ends today."

Customer says: "I'll have to ask my wife."

You respond: "Does your wife make all the decisions?"

The basic problem with this sales approach is that it's like trying to win an argument with someone who has the exact opposite viewpoint. You are too unlikely to convince the prospect to buy from you, even if all of your responses to their objections are perfectly rational.

Salespeople fall into the trap of arguing out objections when they try to close the sale before the customer has really decided to buy the product or service. Customers will find one objection after the next if they are not completely comfortable with making the purchase.

On the other hand, if you follow a Customer-Focused Selling approach, you will have a much better idea of when the customer is ready to buy and when is an appropriate time for you to finalize your sales agreement. The customer is more likely to clearly see how the product or service delivers a solution to his or her needs.

"Overcoming objections"-based selling creates a rift and undermines trust. Even if you manage to get the customer to verbally agree to the sale after you have argued through a lot of objections, the customer might very well cancel the sale or not become an ongoing customer. But if your sales approach is built on openness and trust and building rapport, such as Customer-Based Selling is, you are more likely to get to a solid close and build a productive, ongoing relationship.

WHAT'S WRONG WITH THE OLD SELLING APPROACHES?

WHAT'S WRONG WITH SELLING FOCUSED ON "THE PERFECT CLOSE"?

Too many salespeople waste too much effort in an endless search for the "perfect close": the few magical words that will trick the customer into thinking they will have to buy the product or service.

But any sales process that is focused on tricking or manipulating customers to a decision they really don't want to make—you don't want to have anything to do with. Selling like this, you'll never build relationships, you'll never build referrals, you'll never feel good about selling, and you'll never come close to achieving your peak selling ability.

There are all kinds of closing techniques, such as the Benjamin Franklin Close, the Puppy Dog Close, the Assumptive Close, and the Choice Close, just to name a few. But today's customers often see right through these closing techniques. Most of today's customers—businesspeople and consumers alike—are much more aware when they are being hit with a high-pressure close and much more resistant to it. High-pressure closes are more likely than ever to lose the sale and completely break your chance of landing the customer as they are to win the sale. And the more sophisticated and hence probably the more desirable the customer, the more likely you will be to lose the sale.

Many salespeople find closing very difficult. And it's no wonder: With most sales techniques it's difficult to get customers to feel comfortable to make a firm decision to buy from you. But with Customer-Focused Selling, closing the sale has never been easier. In fact, the customer is often going to close the sale for you. Why? Because the whole sales process revolves around trust. And you're not just an "outsider" waving products and sales points at the buyer. Instead, you're "inside" with the buyer, exploring with him or her how you can deliver a solution that will solve the customer's needs.

Now, even with Customer-Focused Selling, you may have to give some attention to helping the customer with the step of making a final decision that you offer the best solution. But "the close" should

> Too many salespeople waste too much effort in an endless search for the "perfect close."

> High-pressure closes are more likely than ever to lose the sale.

WHAT'S WRONG WITH THE OLD SELLING APPROACHES?

never be the overwhelming focus of the sales process. Helping the customer find the solution is the direction most of your energy should be expended in.

Even if you've had some success with manipulative closing techniques, I assure you that you will be much more successful if you drop all manipulative techniques entirely, and move completely—100 percent—to Customer-Focused Selling.

WHAT'S WRONG WITH SELLING FOCUSED ON "TODAY'S SPECIAL"?

Selling isn't always easy. And there's nothing wrong with telling a prospective customer about any legitimate sales incentive that will help make the product or service more attractive to that customer.

The problem is the timing and the amount of emphasis you place on the incentive. No matter how generous the "extra" sales incentive is for the customer, you should keep your primary focus on how the product or service is going to deliver a solution for the customer. Even if you are offering a 50-percent-off sale or a "buy one, get one free" offer or a thousand-dollar factory rebate check, you first should show the customer how you are going to deliver a solution for him or her.

Then at the appropriate time you can use the incentive to help move the sales process to the agreement stage. No one ever bought anything just because it was on sale. They had at least some interest in what the product or service would do for them.

It's usually very easy and quick to explain to the customer the value of a sales incentive—"that's a one-thousand-dollar factory rebate check." But to carefully develop with the customer exactly how the product or service will be the very best possible solution for his or her needs may take some time. So you need to give the overwhelming emphasis to your approach solving the customer's needs, even when you also have a juicy sales incentive to offer.

> No matter how generous the "extra" sales incentive is for the customer, you should keep your primary focus on how the product or service is going to deliver a solution for the customer.

WHAT'S WRONG WITH THE OLD SELLING APPROACHES?

WHAT'S WRONG WITH SELLING FOCUSED ON FEAR?

People don't like to think about bad things. And if they don't have to, they won't!

If your sales pitch is based on the fear that if a business doesn't buy your product that the competition will trounce on them, you may find it difficult to get prospective customers to listen to your pitch. Wouldn't you rather hear a salesperson paint a picture of how a new product or service would take your business to great new heights, than hear how a product will simply help you avoid getting beaten up by the competition? Wouldn't you be more likely to trust a salesperson who explains how your business may prosper as opposed to the salesperson who tries to convince you that your business is on the verge of collapse?

I'd even recommend that for selling life insurance, you focus on the positive. Don't dwell on the chances that your prospect will die and leave his family destitute! That's basically insulting him or her and building a gulf between you and your prospect. Instead, consider painting the picture of the strong feeling of confidence the individual will have knowing that his or her family is protected by life insurance. By focusing on the flip side of fear—the feeling of being secure because you have purchased the service or product—you will build a more positive rapport with your client and also will build trust.

In Customer-Focused Selling you never want to try to use negative emotions such as fear to motivate a prospect to buy. It's manipulative. And it's just mean. To really succeed in selling, you want to do your customers a positive service, not just by selling them a good product or service that really meets their needs, but also by making the sales process as honest, open, and positive an experience as it can possibly be. The customer will feel better. You'll feel better about yourself. And in the end, you'll make more sales.

> I'd even recommend that for selling life insurance, you focus on the positive.

WHAT'S WRONG WITH THE OLD SELLING APPROACHES?

WHAT'S WRONG WITH THE "SOFT SELL" APPROACH?

The classic soft sell—just leaving the customer with some information and letting them get back to you if they are interested—does have integrity, but it is rarely effective. And just as it's not effective for you, it's not effective for the customer either. Usually your customers are not going to seriously consider buying your solution unless you help show them how it might be able to help them.

Customer-Focused Selling, on the other hand, allows you to provide added value during the sales process by working with your customers to find a solution for their business or personal needs. In Customer-Focused Selling you, the salesperson, can bring tremendous value to your customers by helping them. In the classic "soft sell" approach the salesperson adds little value to the sales process.

The classic "soft sell" approach is selling with integrity. But you're not doing the complete job. You're not really thinking and working as hard as you could be to help your customers find a better solution to their needs. In the classic "soft sell" approach you are not even finding out exactly what the customers' needs are. But in Customer-Focused Selling you are delivering high value added to your customers by identifying their needs and determining how you might be able to help deliver a solution.

> Your customers are not going to seriously consider buying your solution unless you help show them how it might be able to help them.

WHAT'S WRONG WITH THE OLD SELLING APPROACHES?

WHAT'S WRONG WITH "NUMBERS FOCUSED" SELLING?

The basic premise behind "numbers focused" selling is that whatever you say during sales calls or at sales appointments pales in comparison to the number of sales calls or presentations you make.

This is rather defeatist thinking! It's basically assuming that there is no way to significantly improve the *quality* of your sales visits, so you are locked into focusing endlessly on increasing the *quantity* of sales visits. In a way it ties in with the myth of "the naturally born salesperson": Why bother to give much effort to improving your sales abilities because you can't really change them.

This is basically nonsense. You can almost always improve the *quality* of your sales visits, and you can dramatically increase your ability to close each sale. If you are able to switch to Customer-Focused Selling, you will experience a huge increase in the amount of sales you complete.

But many salespeople get locked into the habit of following one of the traditional, relatively ineffective sales approaches. Habits are hard to break. And for these people it may seem easier to just make more sales calls rather than to break their old habits. On the other hand, with just a little work, they could fully adapt Customer-Focused Selling and improve their ability dramatically to close each sale.

> Many salespeople get locked into the habit of following one of the traditional, relatively ineffective sales approaches.

3

CUSTOMER-FOCUSED SELLING

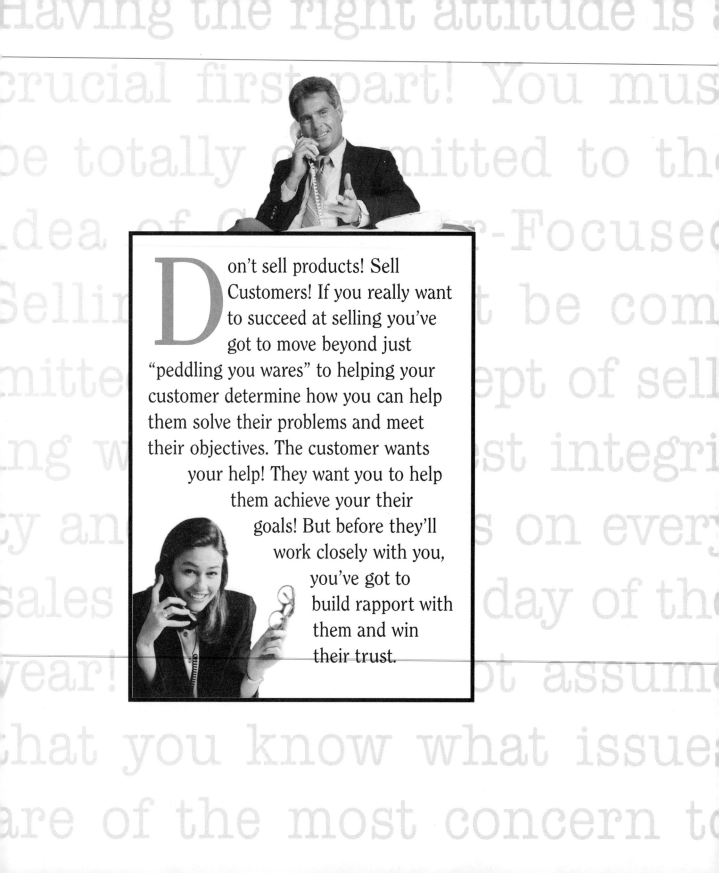

Don't sell products! Sell Customers! If you really want to succeed at selling you've got to move beyond just "peddling you wares" to helping your customer determine how you can help them solve their problems and meet their objectives. The customer wants your help! They want you to help them achieve your their goals! But before they'll work closely with you, you've got to build rapport with them and win their trust.

CUSTOMER-FOCUSED SELLING

Customer-Focused Selling is not just an adaptation of existing selling techniques to focus more on the customer. Instead, it's a whole new approach that can barely even be called "selling."

Take any sales techniques you have used in the past—and don't adapt them. Instead, throw them out!

Don't even think of this approach as "selling the customer." Think of it instead in terms of helping customers to find solutions that will help them achieve their objectives.

Leave *your* objectives, *your* sales goals, and *your* quotas at the door. Instead, adopt the mindset that you are there as an "inside" consultant to help your prospect with the tools (the products or services) you have available.

Don't focus on sales techniques. Focus on helping the customer.

Forget about trying to find the perfect sales introduction.

Forget about trying to polish the perfect sales presentation.

Forget about trying to find the perfect response to the most likely objections.

Forget about trying to find the perfect close.

Instead focus on how you are going to help your customer!

Don't focus on your product or service. Focus on the customer's needs

Customer-Focused Selling means turning off the spotlight that shines on your great products or your terrific services!

I know you can't wait to show them to the customer! I know you can't wait to explain to the customer how you think your products or services will help your prospect's business! I know you can't wait to highlight your competitive advantages! But you're going to have to wait! If you want to sell the best way possible, you are going to have to wait before turning the focus to your products or services.

Be an inside consultant.

CUSTOMER-FOCUSED SELLING

Instead, you first need to shine the spotlight on the customer! You need to find out what the customer wants. What the customer cares about. What objectives the customer is trying to achieve.

HOW CAN YOU HELP YOUR CUSTOMER FIND ADDED VALUE?

You need to be totally focused on and immersed in helping your customer. You need to focus toward how you can deliver as much benefit as possible toward the customer's objectives. And as business today becomes more complex, a salesperson needs to be able to explore and address the many different concerns of buyers.

In selling to retailers, for example, I see salespeople overwhelmingly assuming that the buyer is completely preoccupied with how well the salesperson's product will sell. But often the retailer's concerns are more complex. They may also need to determine how the product will affect their overall product mix; how it will impact their monthly open-to-buy budget; what co-op advertising funds may be available; how reliable the restocking schedule will be; and so on and so forth.

REALIZE THAT EACH CUSTOMER IS UNIQUE!

Even if you are selling a commodity, each customer has different concerns. Even if you and your competitors are each selling "widgets" that are exactly identical products sold at exactly the same prices, each customer will likely have very different concerns and issues that are important for that customer in achieving his or her objectives! One customer, for example, may be mainly concerned about payment terms; another may be primarily concerned about shipment schedules; and another may be most concerned about the reliability of your suppliers.

In selling services, customer concerns tend to be even more varied.

The Highest Integrity

Think, act, and be of the highest integrity

Getting customers to just think you are helping them misses the point of Customer-Focused Selling. Customer-Focused Selling is based on *wanting* to help the customer.

There is nothing more powerful for convincing a client that you want to help them than the real thing. To truly succeed, you must be convinced that being fully honest and up-front with your customer is your best approach.

Never hide information. Never exaggerate the truth. Be consistent in this approach with every customer, every call, every day.

CUSTOMER-FOCUSED SELLING

DETERMINE EACH CUSTOMER'S PECULIAR CONCERNS AND NEEDS.

Why go into a customer meeting with a preset sales presentation? Why decide in advance which selling features you are going to emphasize?

To be sure to save your customers time, you should do as much advance research as you can about the customers' business before you meet with them. In the chapter "Precall Planning," you will find exercises that will also help you prepare to meet with a customer. But most of the crucial information about the customer's concerns and objectives you will have to hear from him or her. Remember, you will never hear what the customer's unique concerns and objectives are unless you visit that customer with an open mind—and don't assume that one customer necessarily has exactly the same concerns or issues as other customers in similar situations.

ESTABLISHING RAPPORT AND BUILDING TRUST ARE CRITICAL.

Before you can start working with customers to find out their concerns and objectives, you must first establish a good rapport and build trust.

Having the right attitude is a crucial first part! You must be totally committed to the idea of Customer-Focused Selling. You must be committed to the concept of selling with the highest integrity and nothing less on every sales call on every day of the year! You must not assume that you know what issues are of the most concern to your customer until you have spoken with him or her.

Just having the right attitude—feeling in your soul that you are there to help your customer, not just to make another sale—will go a long way to help you establish rapport and build trust. You will feel better about yourself, you will feel positive about being there calling on the client, and you will have a higher level of confidence in yourself.

Repeat Business And Referrals

A Customer-Focused Selling approach, coupled with complete integrity, is the absolutely best path to building trust and to establishing a successful long-term relationship with the customer.

Today's buyers are more astute than ever before, and they usually know, even before the first sale is made, what kind of salesperson you are. If you're the kind of person who's totally focused on getting that sale no matter what, the buyer can usually sense it. On the other hand, if you're of the rarer breed who is truly customer-focused, the customer will sense that, too. And you will dramatically increase your chances of getting repeat business with that account.

CUSTOMER-FOCUSED SELLING

Getting lots of referrals

Many of the truly outstanding salespeople build their business on referrals. Getting lots of referrals takes another level of selling than just getting the sale. Sure, now and then you will be able to pry a referral or two out of a customer who isn't even pleased with your sales approach, but you're going to get a heck of a lot more referrals if you leave the customer with the feeling that you really looked out for him or her during the sales process, not just for yourself.

As in the closing of the sale, there are techniques you can learn to generate referrals, but the best way to generate referrals is to develop not just satisfied customers but also ecstatic customers—and that's what you will get when you use Customer-Focused Selling.

Having the right attitude is crucial! But what you do and say the first few minutes of the sales call also send very strong signals to the buyer. Later in this book we give sample dialogues of effective versus ineffective examples of "ice-breaker calls," "setting the right tone," and "building trust."

While what you do and say these first few minutes are crucial, you can't follow a canned presentation. You can't fall into a routine pattern that might *sound like* a canned presentation.

THINK OF THE CUSTOMER AS A NEW FRIEND YOU ARE TRYING TO HELP.

You might want to think of your customer as a new friend—perhaps someone introduced to you by a mutual friend—who asked you to help this person consider how your products or services might be of help.

While you may think of the buyer as a friend, it's important to emphasize "*new* friend." You don't want to sound or appear overly familiar too quickly, or you will not appear sincere in your desire to help your customer find solutions.

ASKING QUESTIONS IS A CRUCIAL PART OF DETERMINING THE ISSUES AND CONCERNS OF YOUR CUSTOMERS.

Asking questions is also an important part of building trust with your customers and showing that you really care about their concerns.

But you don't want to ask too many questions too early, or turn the sales meeting into an interrogation session.

EFFECTIVE LISTENING IS IMPORTANT, TOO.

Too many salespeople talk too much. In fact, a powerful expression I would suggest you remember that I have heard other salespeople mention is: "Shut up and start selling." It's true. The more you get your customers to talk, the more you are going to help them find the right solution, and the more you are going to sell. At most sales meetings you should spend more time listening than talking.

CUSTOMER-FOCUSED SELLING

Listening is more than just letting other people talk. You put energy into listening to absorb all they are saying. Observe their tone and body language.

You also need to indicate that you are listening carefully. Make regular eye contact and verbally acknowledge from time to time that you are intently listening.

Especially on important or complex issues, you occasionally will want to quickly summarize for the customer what you heard him or her say. This is the best way to guarantee that you and the customer are on the same wavelength.

> Sell needs, not products.

RESIST THE TEMPTATION TO START "SELLING" WITHOUT ADDRESSING NEEDS.

Being committed to the product or service you are selling, it is difficult to stop from "selling" your wares before you are finished exploring with buyers what their concerns and issues are. But you must hold back.

If you start "selling" your product before you and the buyer have explored his or her needs, you risk sounding just like another salesperson who doesn't care if he or she helps the buyer or not. Even quick references to "what your product can do" or especially "why it's better than the competition" will undermine your attempts to show buyers that you are on their side.

Depending on the product or service and the customer, you may take just a couple of minutes to explore the buyer's needs. Or it may take a series of meetings. Generally, you want to take as much time as you can to carefully work with the customer to identify his or her issues and concerns before you start getting into how your product may help.

KEEP YOUR PRESENTATION CUSTOMIZED TO THE ONE CUSTOMER.

You may very well have a slick dog and pony show that's lots of fun to present to customers. Maybe it's a video, a computer program, or just a four-color catalog. Think twice before you make a generic presentation.

CUSTOMER-FOCUSED SELLING

Customers don't want to hear about how great your company is or how wonderful your products are. They want to have their particular concerns answered.

Today, customers are overflowing with information. And they are overflowing with high-tech, slick presentations.

What you can offer is a presentation that addresses their concerns and issues—and ONLY their concerns and issues.

Keep your presentation to the buyer interactive. Not multimedia interactive, but two-way-conversation kind of interactive. Encourage questions and comments, even if you are presenting to a group.

Remember, you are trying to help these people solve a problem; you are not competing for an award for the slickest presentation.

HELP LEAD YOUR CUSTOMER TO A SOLUTION.

Usually it will be fairly easy for you to determine how one of your products or services may be able to help the customer, now or in the future. If you are not sure how you can help, don't be afraid to say so during the sales presentation. Your candor may go a long way to building trust. But if you try to pretend you are sure you have a solution when you don't, you could lose the sale anyway. If you need more time to try to come up with a solution, tell the customer, and at least give him or her a time when you will be back with a progress report.

Think "Gaining Agreement."

DON'T THINK OF CLOSING THE SALE; THINK OF "GAINING AGREEMENT."

"Closing the sale" sounds like something you do *to* somebody. But "gaining agreement" is something you do *with* somebody.

In Customer-Focused Selling, since you will have been talking about solutions almost since the beginning of your sales relationship, gaining agreement is not the big, traumatic step that is often the case with traditional selling processes.

Instead, by handling the "agreement" process like reaching a consensus between two business partners—not like signing a peace treaty between two warring armies—you can further build and reinforce a solid customer relationship.

CUSTOMER-FOCUSED SELLING

NOTHING SAYS MORE CLEARLY WHAT YOU'RE ALL ABOUT THAN FOLLOW-UP AFTER THE SALE.

Once the agreement is inked and the money has changed hands, how you act as a salesperson will make all the difference regarding any future business with this buyer and referrals.

A lot of really great salespeople and really great customer-oriented firms, from car dealers to department stores, regularly follow-up with their customers *after* the sale is done. And especially after a big transaction, a customer waits and wonders curiously: "Was that salesperson genuinely on my side? I'll guess I'll find out for sure when I see how they act after the deal is signed!"

Even if it is a one-shot sale and the customer is unlikely to generate direct referrals, you may be surprised to find out how quickly you can build a super-positive reputation with a little follow-up work.

PUT YOURSELF IN YOUR CUSTOMER'S SHOES.

Wouldn't you rather have a salesperson call on you who genuinely wants to help you find solutions for your business, than a salesperson who is just going to blast canned product sales pitches at you?

Wouldn't you rather deal with a salesperson who explores solutions with you, instead of one who tries to close the sale prematurely, and who meets every one of your objections with an argumentative response?

Wouldn't you rather deal with a salesperson who is trying to sell you the best product or service for your needs, than one the seller can make the most money on?

Today's buyers have more salespeople to choose from, so be sure they choose you!

As so many markets are becoming hypercompetitive, with companies aggressively trying to match one another's features and prices, buyers often are able to choose among an array of competing products. And if the products and prices are similar, the salesperson may often be a deciding factor in which firm they decide to do business with.

> Put yourself in your customer's shoes.

CUSTOMER-FOCUSED SELLING

Today's buyer is increasingly sophisticated—not just sophisticated about products or services, but also more sophisticated about selling styles. Today's buyer wants and increasingly demands sales reps who are customer-focused. So if you want to ensure your success in today's and especially tomorrow's marketplace, the best way is to adopt a totally Customer-Focused Selling approach today!

The one thing Customer-Focused Selling can't do

Hand-in-hand with the myth of the naturally born salesperson is the myth that a great salesperson should be able to sell anything, to anybody, anytime. This myth also perpetuates the false concept that you must be a fast-talking huckster to succeed in sales. Nothing is farther from the truth!

Customer-Focused Selling does not help you sell anything, to anybody, anytime. The basic premise of Customer-Focused Selling is that you are helping your customers, not hurting them. That you are helping them find better solutions, not tricking them.

Customer-Focused salespeople would not even want to sell ice to Eskimos.

This is really the heart of the difference with Customer-Focused Selling. It isn't just a technique, it's also an attitude. And nothing is stronger than the attitude and feeling that you are out to help people.

By walking away from the wrong sale, you'll sell a lot more in the end.

Sometimes you will come across a customer who really can't benefit from your product or service. If you're selling a reputable product or service it probably won't happen very often. But when it does, don't sell to that customer. Don't compromise your integrity. Maybe it's a customer you'll be able to sell another product to another day. Maybe someday that person will be in a different job or position, where you will have a great solution. Maybe you'll never be able to sell to that person, but maybe he or she can give you a referral.

The sale you walk away from will strengthen you tenfold.

Even if you never have a chance to sell to the customer again and never get a referral, you will make more money in the long run. Why? Because you will know you did the right thing. And every other time when you are selling to somebody, you will know that you are selling with integrity. You'll have more positive energy, and you'll be more convincing. Sure, you'll lose a few sales here and there, but you'll be a much, much stronger salesperson.

C H A P T E R

4

KNOWLEDGE
IS
POWER

From finding the right customers at the right time, to building rapport with customers, to making yourself an invaluable resource, the power of knowledge can leapfrog you ahead! Today's customer is not going to put up with a lot of baloney or sales puffery. But if you can pass on even a little knowledge that is *relevant* for the customer, you will significantly increase your value to the customer and be able to stand out in a positive way from all the other competitors.

KNOWLEDGE IS POWER!

Put the power of knowledge to work for you! Knowledge combined with a Customer-Focused Selling approach can produce tremendous results. Because now, you are going to be proactively involved with the customer in delivering solutions, not just talking up your product's features.

To be able to help customers find solutions, you are going to have to develop a strong level of trust and rapport with them. And one of the best ways to be able to do this is to have knowledge—not just knowledge of your product lines or services, but also knowledge of the competition, the industry, and your customer. If your customers find out that you don't have a solid knowledge base, they aren't going to give you the chance to work side by side with them to develop solutions to their issues.

But if you can show your customers that you can offer information and insights they might not be aware of, you may have tremendous added value for those customers.

Even if you can't find any new information to offer a potential buyer, if you come across as intelligent and well informed, the customer is going to find it much easier to feel comfortable working with you.

As the world becomes more and more one big, global economy, as distinctions between or among industries continue to blur, and as many markets are becoming hypercompetitive, companies are often quickly matching one another's features and prices. So the ability of the salesperson to deliver knowledge to the customer takes on an increasingly important dimension. In some cases the knowledge of the salesperson, and the ability to help the customer find solutions may be the most important competitive selling advantage a salesperson has; in fact, in a few cases it may be the *only* sales advantage!

> You can develop a strong level of trust.

KNOWLEDGE IS POWER!

Why Knowledge Is Power for Customer-Focused Selling

- Knowledge helps you find prospects to call.

- Knowledge helps you determine which prospects are most worthwhile to focus on.

- Knowledge can immediately distinguish you from other salespeople and let a prospective customer know that you might really be able to help him or her.

- Knowledge helps you build rapport with and gain trust from your customer.

- Knowledge helps you ask appropriate questions in defining the customer's issues, concerns, and objectives.

- Knowledge helps you apply judgment in determining which product or service may best provide a solution for your customer.

- Knowledge helps you articulate how your products may help your customer.

- Knowledge makes you aware of your product strengths versus those of competing alternatives (but never bash the competition).

- Knowledge helps you paint a picture for the customer of how your products and services and your company may continue to provide solutions for the customer in the future.

- Knowledge makes you a valuable reference person your customers will want to turn to and listen to for industry information.

- Knowledge will increase the possibilities for repeat contact with customers.

- Knowledge that helps customers will increase your number of referrals.

- Knowledge will improve your ability to network.

KNOWLEDGE IS POWER!

With the information explosion, buyers have more and more information at their fingertips. In a second they can tap into the World Wide Web and find huge amounts of information. But there is so much information available, the difficulty is in quickly finding out what information is useful and what is not. As a salesperson you must be careful not to waste your buyer's time providing information they are likely to have already. But if you can provide even a little information that will be of use to the buyer, you will have a lot of extra value to the buyer and a huge competitive advantage.

KNOWLEDGE HELPS YOU FIND PROSPECTS TO CALL.

The more you know about your products, your competitors, your industry, and your customers' industries, the easier it's going to be to find prospects. Perhaps there are niche markets where your product currently is being sold that you are not aware? Perhaps your competitors are making inroads in a new market? Perhaps a competitor is discontinuing a product line, leaving their customers more open to your products?

The more knowledge you have in general, the more likely you may be to stumble upon ideas of new prospects to call or new approaches for current prospects, and the more likely you will be to find new business before your competition does.

KNOWLEDGE HELPS YOU DETERMINE WHICH PROSPECTS ARE MOST WORTHWHILE TO FOCUS ON.

Finding and chasing prospects each take lots of time and energy. And time is one of your most precious resources. Knowledge can help you direct your time more efficiently.

For example, if you hear that one of the prospective customers that you have been spending a huge amount of your time on is on the edge of bankruptcy or about to be absorbed into a larger firm, you may decide to spend much less time on this account.

If you find out that one prospective customer is on a sharp downward sales trend and another has just announced huge growth plans, you may decide to reallocate your time spent pursuing each of these accounts.

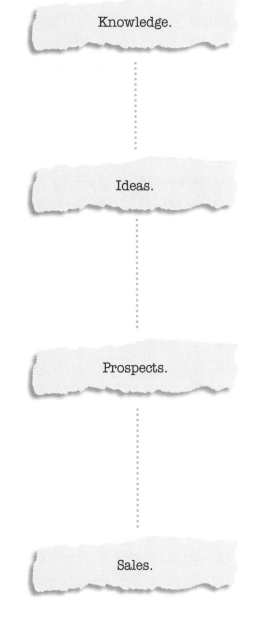

Knowledge.

Ideas.

Prospects.

Sales.

KNOWLEDGE IS POWER!

Changes in customers' product mixes and business strategies may sharply affect their interest in buying or in continuing to buy your product. Today, when business is changing so fast, if you don't keep up with the news, you could find yourself spending huge amounts of time pursuing business that existed yesterday but that may be gone today.

KNOWLEDGE CAN IMMEDIATELY DISTINGUISH YOU FROM OTHER SALESPEOPLE AND LET A PROSPECTIVE CUSTOMER KNOW THAT YOU MIGHT REALLY BE ABLE TO HELP HIM OR HER.

One of the most difficult challenges of selling is initially gaining rapport with your customer and building trust. The days of breaking the ice with bad jokes are gone. Talking about the weather–not again!

Probably the very best way to break the ice with a customer is with some relevant and interesting comment or two about the industry. It keeps the small talk business-focused so you're showing the customer that you are not there to waste his or her time. The customer will probably have some genuine interest in the talk. And, perhaps best of all, it shows the customer that you know something about the industry and that you might very well be able to help provide him or her with a useful solution.

At the same time, though, don't become overbearing in a rush to show off your knowledge. Don't offer a comment that the customer might find offensive. And don't say anything negative about a competitor.

KNOWLEDGE HELPS YOU BUILD RAPPORT WITH AND GAIN TRUST FROM YOUR CUSTOMER.

Customer-Focused Selling demands that you build rapport with and gain trust from your customer. You need your customers to share their concerns and objectives with you and work with you to find appropriate solutions. To get your customers to "open up" with you, you need to make it clear that you are intelligent and knowledgeable,

> Knowledge helps build rapport.

KNOWLEDGE IS POWER!

that you may be able to help them, and that you are not there to waste their time.

Not just having lots of knowledge, but also having knowledge that your customer is interested in is important in proving to buyers that you may have value to them. And the more readily and easily you share this information with the buyer, the easier it will be to build trust.

For example, let's say you are a real estate broker trying to get a house listing from a prospective seller. If you tell the prospect "I will do a market survey of your house if you sign a listing agreement with me," you will not build as much trust as if you say, "I estimate the market value of your house to be between $310,000 and $315,000, and I'd be happy for no charge to do a market survey to ascertain this."

Sharing information builds trust.

KNOWLEDGE HELPS YOU ASK APPROPRIATE QUESTIONS IN DEFINING THE CUSTOMER'S ISSUES, CONCERNS, AND OBJECTIVES.

If you're not knowledgeable, it's all too easy to ask a question or make a comment that immediately kills the chance of building a close relationship with the customer. Does the customer want to work closely with someone who appears not to know what he or she is talking about? Of course not.

On the other hand, if because of your knowledge, you can ask questions that are even a little more insightful than the buyer might expect, you can rapidly build respect and gain trust.

KNOWLEDGE HELPS YOU APPLY JUDGMENT IN DETERMINING WHICH PRODUCT OR SERVICE MAY BEST PROVIDE A SOLUTION FOR YOUR CUSTOMER.

Okay—so maybe there are a few selling situations where more knowledge will not help you to deliver better customer solutions, but I suggest that there are very, very few of these situations.

KNOWLEDGE IS POWER!

For example, let's take a fairly simple sales situation. A salesperson for a company that stocks vending machines is trying to convince a new company to allow a vending machine to be put on its premises for the first time. A competitor is offering the same machine; its products sell for exactly the same price; and the company can choose from exactly the same product mix to stock the machine. But the salesperson for the first company also offers knowledge—she can share with the customer information from studies that show what products employees would prefer to have stocked in the vending machine. So her knowledge adds extra value to her company's product, and in this situation, the *only* competitive difference.

> Knowledge helps you turn features into solutions.

KNOWLEDGE HELPS YOU ARTICULATE HOW YOUR PRODUCTS MAY HELP YOUR CUSTOMER.

Knowledge helps you show your customer not just how your products or services function, it also helps you articulate how it can add value. For example, rather than just saying "our new industrial engines each offer 20 percent more horsepower," you may be able to say "our new industrial engines will allow you to produce the same capacity at your Chicago plant with seven less engines and an estimated 15 percent fuel savings; in addition, you will free up three thousand square feet of factory floor space."

KNOWLEDGE MAKES YOU AWARE OF YOUR PRODUCT STRENGTHS VERSUS THOSE OF COMPETING ALTERNATIVES (BUT NEVER BASH THE COMPETITION).

Knowledge helps you determine which of your features are strongest in comparison to competitors' and hence which features you may want to highlight. But you want to be sure to do this within the context of Customer-Focused Selling. You want to give overwhelming emphasis first to working with the customer to find a solution. But because of your knowledge you will know what your strongest features are and how these can turn into benefits and solutions for your customers. So when exploring how you can help the customer, you

KNOWLEDGE IS POWER!

Never pass on proprietary information.

At times it will be tempting—but don't do it! If you do pass on such information, you and your company may be subject to lawsuits. And your reputation will go down the tubes. No one will trust you. Word of an unscrupulous sales rep passing along inside information travels fast.

However, you can put together proprietary information and use it to talk about the industry in general. This does not mean that you can say, "One of your competitors, whom I will not name, just ordered 312,000 units of this product," or "One of your competitors just picked up these three new customers...." If this information is made public, fine—then it's fair game. But what you could say is, "Industry orders are looking good this month and new customers are being lined up at a very fast pace."

What is considered proprietary and what is not may vary from one industry to the next. To avoid trouble, you should check with your company on their particular guidelines on what information is deemed proprietary and what is not.

Generally, proprietary information is information particular to a specific company that you have learned about through your dealings with that company that is not yet public information and could harm the company if made public. Nonpublic sales figures, nonpublic financial information, information about customers, and information about unannounced products—all such information is deemed proprietary.

Remember, Customer-Focused Selling requires selling with integrity at all times.

will want to emphasize how you can best deliver solutions based on your particular product features.

KNOWLEDGE HELPS YOU PAINT A PICTURE FOR THE CUSTOMER OF HOW YOUR PRODUCTS, SERVICES, AND YOUR COMPANY MAY CONTINUE TO PROVIDE SOLUTIONS FOR THE CUSTOMER IN THE FUTURE.

Today, companies everywhere are slashing the number of vendors they buy products and services from. Many corporations are slashing their number of vendors by as much as 90 percent to save on transaction costs. Individuals, too, are giving increased preference to one-stop shopping—for example, buying a wider array of financial

KNOWLEDGE IS POWER!

products from either a bank, a brokerage house, or an insurance firm, but not necessarily from all three.

What this means for you, the salesperson, is that even to get that first sale you must often show that you are going to be a great provider of solutions not just for this one situation but in the future as well.

Companies and individuals, too, are changing direction and refocusing their efforts faster than ever. Companies are changing strategies, shedding divisions, merging, and consolidating. Individuals now don't just change jobs more often, they also change careers more often. One or both spouses go in or out of the work force and are increasingly likely to shift to and from full- or part-time work and to and from an entrepreneurial venture.

Knowledge is especially important when it comes to how your products or services are going to be of value in providing solutions in the future, because in providing solutions you must be able to project how your product or service will interact with other products or services in the future. How might they interact better in the future than competitors' products?

You need to have a particularly solid knowledge of what direction key complementary products or services are headed in, as well as key suppliers. Let's say you sell personal computers; you need to know as much as you can about what the future holds for microchips—a key component. Let's say you sell rental car usage to corporations; you need to know what the future holds for key complementary services such as airlines and hotels.

> Fresh and relevant knowledge shows you are attuned to your customer.

KNOWLEDGE MAKES YOU A VALUABLE REFERENCE PERSON YOUR CUSTOMERS WILL WANT TO TURN TO AND LISTEN TO FOR INDUSTRY INFORMATION.

Fresh knowledge or intelligence that you can pass on to a customer or a prospect can go a long way to building a relationship: It keeps you in a customer's mind, it builds appreciation, and it shows that you are attuned to issues that affect that customer.

KNOWLEDGE IS POWER!

For example, passing on a copy of an article or piece of information that is fresh and relevant for a customer will almost certainly be highly appreciated.

If, when you meet with a customer, the customer remembers gaining some particular intelligence from you—or just an intelligent overview of the current industry situation—that customer is not only more likely to meet with you again, but also more likely to approach each meeting with a positive, productive mindset.

KNOWLEDGE WILL INCREASE THE POSSIBILITIES FOR REPEAT CONTACT WITH CUSTOMERS.

Perhaps even more so than getting the initial order, knowledge will help you get repeat business. The more the buyer appreciates your knowledge and the more you can customize your knowledge to benefit the buyer, the more you will turn your knowledge into value added for the customer.

KNOWLEDGE THAT HELPS CUSTOMERS WILL INCREASE YOUR AMOUNT OF REFERRALS.

Being a solid source of information can dramatically increase the amount of referrals. It will increase the willingness of buyers to give you names of other prospects when you ask for them. It will make it more likely for buyers to spontaneously suggest you to other possible customers. It also will give you a better idea of which prospective customers you most want to try to get referrals to.

KNOWLEDGE WILL IMPROVE YOUR ABILITY TO NETWORK.

The more knowledge you have, the easier it will be to network within your industry and outside your industry. And, of course, the more you network, the more information and knowledge you will acquire. Fresh knowledge gives you a great reason to contact other people in your network, and it also positions you as an intelligent, business-focused individual.

> Knowledge gives a great reason to call the buyer

KNOWLEDGE IS POWER!

Knowledge also gives you ideas on how to network better. You can find out about meetings and associations and the more obscure trade shows. You can find out about events or venues where you can meet other salespeople who sell noncompetitive products to your same customer base—perfect people for networking and sharing prospective leads with.

Never pass on proprietary knowledge. Salespeople often have lots of access to proprietary information. An obvious example is the size of competitors' orders or the names of customers' clients.

KNOWLEDGE YOU NEED:

PRODUCT OR SERVICE KNOWLEDGE

- Your level of knowledge can really set you apart from the competition.

I know this sounds obvious. But there are huge variances in the amount of familiarity salespeople have with their own products and services.

Too many salespeople spend too much time focusing on sales techniques and not enough time learning indepth about their own products and services. And most serious prospective customers are hungry for in-depth information on the particular aspect of a product or service that may be relevant to their needs. This is information that customers usually can't readily access someplace else.

So many buyers prefer to deal with product managers, technical people, or executives because all too often the sales reps have only a cursory knowledge of their own product lines. Sure, they might know every product. And they certainly know all kinds of information about pricing. And they probably know all the key features. But do they really understand the subtleties of each feature? Do they understand all the different ways in which each feature can benefit the customer? Do they understand the minor features?

KNOWLEDGE IS POWER!

- **There's a lot more to products than the top one or two features.**

  Especially when you are selling solutions, you need to focus on everything you bring to the customer, not just the one or two biggest product features.

  For example, with a product business, color, size, quantity, delivery schedule, reliability of supply, packaging, shipping capability, electronic information exchange, and ability to integrate your supply with the customer's operation are just a few of the elements that may be extremely important for your customer.

  With a service business, available staffing, scheduling, reliability, and performance measures may be extremely important for your customer.

- **Intangible features**

  The successful ability to sell the intangible part of the product or service is often the mark of a truly talented salesperson. Intangibles may include company background, expertise, commitment to excellence, service ethics, standards of doing business, and ability to create long-term relationships.

BENEFITS TO CUSTOMERS OF USING YOUR PRODUCTS OR SERVICES.

Thoroughly understanding and being able to clearly articulate the benefits of your products or services to customers are integral to Customer-Focused Selling.

You must also learn to clearly convey benefits to your customers in instantly meaningful ways. For example, the power of one of your products has doubled. This is new product information. Now people using this product can work 25 percent faster. That is the benefit. But it might be a lot more powerful to state the benefit in terms the customer can instantly comprehend the significance of; for example, "Because this product is faster, all of your workers will save fifteen hours per month of work."

> Knowledge helps you sell the intangible aspect of the product.

KNOWLEDGE IS POWER!

OVERALL KNOWLEDGE ABOUT YOUR COMPANY

- Product brochures
- Technical reports
- Internal company departments (technical, customer support, product development, marketing, research)
- Discussions with other sales reps in the company
- Customer surveys
- Customer feedback and observations
- Any published articles or reviews of the company's products or services

KNOWLEDGE OF COMPETING PRODUCTS AND SERVICES

- **You also need to know the tangible and intangible features of your competitors' products and services.**

Where do your products and those of each of your competitors fit in the marketplace? Are they high-priced or low-priced? High-quality or value-oriented? Custom or mass-produced? State-of-the-art or "classic" in design? Determine the parameters of competition in your industry and then peg where your products and those of each of your competitors are. Set up a chart. The importance in selling is not just where you come out on the chart but also knowing just where you stand. By having this knowledge you will know how best to help your customers find solutions using your products.

OVERALL KNOWLEDGE OF COMPETING FIRMS

- **Your competitors will be better than you at some areas, the same in others, and worse in still others.**

The key here is to have an accurate assessment of what your competitors' strengths and weaknesses are. Let's say they are a big, established, successful firm and you are a small new competitor. You need to be cognizant of this because you can bet that salespeople from the other company are likely to use this against you in their sales pitches. (And remember, just because you don't specifically bash the competition doesn't mean that competing sales reps won't be bashing your firm and products.)

> Know the competition.

KNOWLEDGE IS POWER!

Step one is to know where your competition may be coming from. Step two is to use the newness to your advantage—for example you might stress that your company emphasizes innovation, new ideas, and the flexibility of a smaller structure and go on to explain specifically how this can help the potential customer. (You can do all of this without directly saying anything negative about the larger competitor.)

KNOWLEDGE OF HOW YOUR COMPETITION IS PERCEIVED IN THE MARKETPLACE BY CUSTOMERS

- **It is important to understand how your customers view your competitors.**

  They might see them as expensive or cheap, as flexible or stringent, as large or small, as effective or ineffective, as "hot" or as "has-beens." Whatever the perception, it's part of your due diligence to figure out how the competitors are viewed by the customer base.

  Sources of competitive information:
  - Competitors' Web sites
  - Competitors' public financial reports
  - Competitors' product sheets and catalogs
  - Industry publications
  - Trade associations
  - Business publications
  - Newsletters
  - Customer input

Know how customers perceive your competitors.

KNOWLEDGE ABOUT YOUR INDUSTRY AND ABOUT YOUR CUSTOMERS' INDUSTRY

- **What makes up all the facets of your industry and your customer's industry?**

  When you consider your industry make sure that you're looking at the full circle of those within and touching your industry. Within and related to your industry will be a combination of customers, suppliers, vendors, distributors, consultants, professional service providers, trade organizations, and the range of local to international

KNOWLEDGE IS POWER!

affiliations. In selling you need to gather information from all available sources and disseminate how the various areas impact you, your company, and your customers.

What are the biggest changes that your industry and your customer's industry will face in the near and distant future?

Is this the year that a structural shift at one level of the industry or a technological advancement will have wide-reaching impact, or will things be pretty much the same? In this changing world you constantly need to be watching for the big or small industry changes that will make a significant difference for you or your customers. The worst place to sell from is the "catch-up" mode, when you weren't aware of an upcoming change until your competitor already used it to successfully sell against you.

Short-term change as well as long-term change needs to be paid attention to—especially as more and more companies and individuals are looking to build long-term relationships with suppliers. Make sure that you are good at asking questions within your industry and within related industries. Questions you can ask are "What's new in your area?" or "What are you focusing on the next six months?"

Sources of information about customers' industry:
- World Wide Web
- Industry consultants' long-term reports
- Investment bankers' industry reports
- Industry publications
- Trade associations
- Business publications
- Newsletters
- Customer input

CHAPTER

5

FINDING
NEW
CUSTOMERS

There are lots of techniques for finding new customers—some of which tend to be more effective than others. Generally the best leads are going to be those leads that you are closest to—such as word-of-mouth leads that you personally hear about directly from other people. Often the best salespeople use many different techniques for finding leads—but what really sets them off from the pack is their attitude about finding leads—they are always, always, always trying to talk up their business and find new leads even during nonbusiness hours.

FINDING NEW CUSTOMERS

T he best way to get business is to get repeat business from current customers by doing absolutely everything you can possibly do to find solutions for them and serve their needs. The next best way to get business is to get referrals from your current customers, which you can also get by taking terrific care of those current customers and by asking for referrals. So by using a Customer-Focused Selling approach you will greatly increase your chances of getting both repeat business and plenty of referrals.

There is a small minority of very talented salespeople who actually get all of their new business from referrals from satisfied customers. Hopefully someday you might be in this situation—but in the meantime there are plenty of great ways you can get plenty of good leads.

THE BEST AND WORST WAYS TO FIND LEADS.

The worst way to generate leads is through completely unqualified lists, such as phone books, because it means that you have no relationship with the prospect, no targeting criteria, and virtually no information about the lead. The next better tier would be brokered lists—better because you can buy them based upon criteria that you designate. The next tier, and often significantly more effective, are lists that you carefully create yourself. And the very best leads are word-of-mouth leads when you are referred to a lead through a personal contact.

Keep in mind, however, that there are many salespeople who have been successful at finding customers using just one of these methods—and there are even more salespeople who have been successful at using several of these methods. There are no hard-and-fast rules about what is going to work for you. But generally, the more personalized and targeted the lead is to you, the more likely you are to be successful.

> The very best leads are word-of-mouth leads.

FINDING NEW CUSTOMERS

GETTING NEW CUSTOMERS IS 90 PERCENT ATTITUDE.

If you think you are going to devote just a few minutes each day to thinking about finding new leads and not thinking about it at all the rest of the week, you'll be lucky to survive, let alone succeed. To really succeed in sales you have to *want to* think about finding new leads all the time. You might reach the point when you should be so fortunate that your customer base consists largely of long-term customers—but even so, you need to continue thinking about new customers to continue to grow and even maintain your number of clients.

> To really succeed in sales you have to *want to* think about finding new leads all the time.

SUCCESSFUL SALESPEOPLE THINK ABOUT FINDING NEW LEADS ALL THE TIME.

Successful salespeople think about finding new leads all the time. And I don't just mean all the time when they are at work. I mean all the time. They think about finding leads when they're commuting back and forth to the office. They think about finding leads when they're at the airport. They think about finding leads when they're at a cocktail party. They think about it when they're at their club or association meeting. And they think about it when they're at weddings and birthday parties.

It might sound like a lot of work, but that's not how really successful salespeople feel about finding leads. They seem to see it as a sport or a game. They are always curious to find out if someone they meet might possibly have any interest in their product or service. And they seem to love to find the chance to interest someone in whatever they sell. They make a point of telling everyone they meet what they do, and you always get the feeling that they really enjoy their work and take a lot of pride in the products and services they sell.

FINDING NEW CUSTOMERS

ANYONE CAN DEVELOP A FULL-TIME ENTHUSIASM THAT HELPS FIND SALES LEADS.

I notice that successful salespeople will enthusiastically talk about their product or service with you, even when they find out that you are absolutely not a prospective customer. And I also notice that the more pleasant and enthusiastic salespeople are when talking with me (as long as they are not overbearing), the more I will strain to think if I can possibly think of a referral or lead idea for them. They don't necessarily ask for the lead, and if they did I probably wouldn't think so hard about trying to provide one. But I, like everyone else, enjoy talking with people who are bright, upbeat, and enthusiastic about their work.

You don't need to be a naturally born salesperson to be able to talk about your product or service to casual friends and new acquaintances. But you do need to make the effort. And you do need to have a lot of passion for your product or service and your ability (even if it's potential ability when you're just getting started) to deliver solutions to customers. And you need to develop enthusiasm and positive energy. You might think it's something you either have or don't have, but that's simply not true. There are plenty of people who grew into adulthood downbeat and dry, but over a period of time were able to develop an enthusiasm they never lost. A lot of it is attitude. If you can think positive and act positive, you will be perceived as positive. You will begin to succeed. And the more you succeed, the easier and more natural it will be to show enthusiasm and to think positive.

> The more pleasant and enthusiastic salespeople are when talking with me, the more I will strain to think if I can possibly think of a referral or lead idea for them.

WHAT'S THE SECRET FORMULA FOR FINDING NEW CUSTOMERS?

Over the years I've asked a lot of very successful salespeople how they find their leads—waiting someday to hear the one magic formula that may be broadly applicable. But I'm constantly disappointed. The usual response I get begins with a pause while the salesperson thinks for a while . . . followed by usually a list of at least several different types of sources. There is no magic formula.

> The one magic formula.

FINDING NEW CUSTOMERS

THE MOST SUCCESSFUL SALESPEOPLE USE LOTS OF DIFFERENT METHODS TO FIND CUSTOMERS.

My point isn't that different salespeople selling different products have each found one particular sales method to be overwhelmingly successful. My point is that usually highly successful salespeople often employ many different methods to find customers, although they tend to put more emphasis on personal referrals and other "hot" word-of-mouth leads. They always seem to be open to new ideas, suggestions, or possibilities. They seem to never quite be satisfied with their sales progress and often are trying new methods to find leads–dropping other methods or sources that are proving to be less successful.

As previously discussed, successful salespeople usually do everything possible to talk up their products and services with every casual acquaintance they meet every day. They seem to place extra emphasis on any lead they can possibly get through a personal referral–even from a very casual acquaintance. But they also use lots of other methods to find leads.

> Highly successful salespeople often employ many different methods to find customers.

PUTTING TOGETHER YOUR OWN LISTS OF LEADS.

The more time you can spend refining and carefully targeting the people who are most likely to be interested in buying your product, the less time you will have to spend trying to sell people who have no interest. In putting together lists of possible business prospects you can find collections of reference books at your library. Each reference work will have different criteria for including businesses. You can also buy CD-ROMs at computer stores that list virtually every business in the country–although they typically only list the SIC (industry) code and perhaps the estimated annual sales or number of employees instead of giving any description. You also can go on the World Wide Web to find information on most larger and midsize firms. Many industry associations have lists of firms in their industry that you may be able to purchase, and most trade magazines do an annual issue that ranks firms in their particular field.

> Spend the time to target qualified prospects.

FINDING NEW CUSTOMERS

There's lots of information available, and it is worth quite a bit of time to sort through it carefully to put together as carefully pruned a list of prospects as you possibly can. If you are selling a product that might be applicable for a broad range of businesses or consumers, such as printing services or paper products or office supplies, you should try carefully focusing your effort on one customer segment at a time. So if you are selling office supplies you might want to put together a list of fifty banks to call, or if you are selling life insurance you may want to put together a list of fifty lawyers. Then keep careful track as you go through the sales process as to how successful you are with each group that you are targeting. If a particular kind of customer or a particular kind of lead source proves particularly promising, use that again and again until results fall off.

> Track your success with each target group.

BUYING LISTS OF LEADS.

You can also buy lists of names from mailing list brokers and other companies that compile information on companies and individuals. Check the Yellow Pages in the metro areas (also usually available in your local library for distant cities) for names to call. If you want phone numbers be sure to specify this, because most mailing lists are sold to businesses doing direct mail, not telemarketing or direct sales.

There are many different ways to buy the same names. You could buy the names of everyone who lives in a certain zip code. You could buy the names of subscribers to a particular magazine who live in a particular city. You could buy the names of computer manufacturing firms with sales between $10 million and $50 million located in California. You can also get mailing list brokers to merge lists for you and provide you with all of the names or only the names that show up twice. So, for example, you may be able to buy the names of business executives who subscribe to three particular magazines.

Although mailing lists can be purchased for just a few cents per name, there is usually a minimum charge of at least several hundred dollars, although it varies quite a bit from one mailing list broker to the next.

FINDING NEW CUSTOMERS

You can get mailing lists on disks or printed out on sheets of paper on note cards (easy for phone contacting), or on pressure-sensitive labels (ready to be attached to envelopes).

Most mailing houses sell mailing lists for one-time use only, and lists are "seeded" (with disguised addresses or phone numbers that actually lead back to the mailing list owner) so be sure to comply with the terms of the contract.

Always test-contact a small list of names before you go wild spending a lot of money on a big list.

Also, beware that some mailing lists are sold and used often. Business executives and doctors, for example, are flooded with phone calls. I know the owner of a small business who received ten phone calls on one day just from stockbrokers at one brokerage house.

Generating Leads Lists in the Home Alarm Industry

In the alarm business, the most likely scenario is selling to people who either have an existing home or who are building a home. If they're building a home, it's a great time to get customers to buy an alarm system because the walls are open and they can put the wires in at almost no additional cost.

So now you have two potential and separate markets. One is for existing homes, which covers virtually anyone in the phone book. But it's not the best list because you don't know who has an alarm or who has money for an alarm. It's an okay list but certainly not a good place to start, as it's too broad.

You then turn to the second segment, the new housing market, and of course everyone selling alarms has thought of this as well. You have to think, "Okay, I can't be in there too late. How could I ever find out about these people early on?" Well, guess what? Everybody doing building has to obtain a building permit in the town hall. That's

public information. Go into the town halls and do some homework. Hopefully you've been working this target segment all along, and although you do uncover prospects, you also encounter considerable competition.

What you should be doing is building a list of a customer base that has a need in a particular market. And then you build one in another market and another market.

Reviewing your product services and needs, you rethink the main thrust of your product line: security. And it dawns on you that widows, isolated after the death of their spouses, may for the first time in their lives be faced with the dread of living alone. In your community you can contact the council on the aging and other places where you could go and introduce yourself and your services. At local hospitals, could you be on a referral list? You have to start to think creatively. How are you going to access these people?

BE CREATIVE IN GENERATING LISTS OF POTENTIAL CUSTOMERS.

This is a common situation and one where you have to step back and review your knowledge and insight of your customer base and needs. You can almost always use this effort to identify some creative ways to find new potential accounts.

Don't think of it as starting from scratch. Instead, use this as an opportunity to look creatively at some other avenues for compiling your own listings. You could certainly always look at purchasing a list, but first look at developing your own.

In developing your own list, you want to think about who the buyers of this product are, how you get their names and numbers, and where you can get them. Don't underestimate your local library, town hall, chamber of commerce, or business groups. There are numerous places you can go to for information on potential customers.

SORT THROUGH YOUR LISTS TO DETERMINE THE "HOT" PROSPECTS.

Hot is determined by biggest need. So you need to have some criteria built into your information-gathering that are signals that tell you when people need your product or service. Always try to develop lists that are need-based, not hope-based. Then segment them into tiers. In most cases it's going to take getting on the phone with three or four good qualifying questions that introduce who you are and that gather some key information that will help you figure out a customer's degree of interest.

Now, if they're obviously hot, then of course you're going to try to schedule an appointment. If you find out on the phone that they're not building that house for another twelve months, good. You've already set the stage for the next step, which is, "Well, let's touch base in six months."

This process prioritizes your list as you build it. You know you've got five hot ones, you've got fifty that are mediocre, and you've got three hundred that are okay. And your list should keep moving up. The three hundred should then either go to the warm list, the hot list, the keep-'em-posted list, or the dead list.

> Tier your lists.

FINDING NEW CUSTOMERS

Still thinking about offering increased security to potential customers, you now consider single professional business owners. Being professionals, they'll likely travel more than the average person and frequently leave their homes unattended. Where are they? Perhaps you can buy a professional singles club list. Many organizations will sell you an inexpensive label list, and that should be enough to get the ball rolling.

Your development lists should give you lots of people to call all day long. You should never find yourself saying, "Whom do I call today? What do I do? Oh, my gosh, I don't have a networking meeting until next Thursday, and that's not going to bring me anything for three months."

Find creative ways to compile prospect lists and keep working them!

GETTING PRIORITIZING INFORMATION.

Ask open-ended questions.

If you know how people make decisions for your product or service, ask questions that are not intrusive. "Do you have a need for this?" or "When do you want to do this?" usually does not work. You want to say that you have some information: "I understand from the building permit that you're building a house. As you probably know, the best time to look at alarm systems is when you're building a house. What I was curious about, could you give me a little information on what your time frame is on this? What's your process on this? What's your perspective on this?"

You want to get them talking, and what they're going to say is, "I could care less" or "I'm more concerned with what the doorknob looks like." Or they're going to say, "It's a big issue. There's no fire department in this town, and if I don't have an alarm into a central station, our house could burn down." Well, you just got the answer you were seeking without putting them on the spot.

The problem with too many qualifying questions is that they tend to be closed-ended. Keep the qualifying questions open-ended because you don't want to set up their answer. You don't want a yes or a no. You want information, and within that information you will likely find the yes, the no, the maybe, or the gray area.

FINDING NEW CUSTOMERS

Gathering as much information as you can from the prospective customer, positions you for either today, tomorrow, or down the road with that client.

Everyone is a potential customer, and you really want to keep that attitude. It may not be today, this minute, but perhaps at some future time they'll be a potential customer for you.

FOLLOW THE COMPETITION.

Try to figure out where your competition is selling, and pursue these accounts. It is so often so difficult to locate fresh, qualified prospects that you are much better off going after an account even if you know your competition is solidly entrenched there.

GET YOUR COMPETITION TO REFER YOU BUSINESS.

It might sound crazy to you, but a huge amount of business today is generated when one supplier who feels they either can't handle a job or aren't best suited for it recommends a competitor. This is happening more and more today as more sales reps are focusing on serving their customers as well as they can, even when it means recommending that some work may be better done by competitors.

For example, let's say a commercial printer does 90 percent of the printing work (primarily catalogs and product brochures) for a small manufacturing firm. The commercial printer is then asked to print a hundred copies of a single-page party announcement. Because the commercial printer's presses are designed for longer runs, the commercial printer would have to charge the manufacturer three times what a small copy shop would charge—so the sales rep for the large commercial printer refers the job to a small copy shop. There are many small copy shops nearby, but the sales rep refers the job to a particular shop because he recently met a sales rep from that shop who seemed intelligent and who spoke convincingly of the capabilities of his small shop.

So when you meet sales reps from competing firms, don't necessarily shy away from them. Give them your card and tell them what kind of work your firm does best.

Some Ways to Find Leads for New Customers

- Friends and relatives
- Acquaintances
- Networking
- Creating your own target lists
- Buying lists of prospects
- Following the competition
- Getting referrals from competitors who are not ideally suited for a particular job
- Local business associations and groups
- National trade association and professional groups
- Nonprofessional groups
- Alumni or alumnae
- Trade shows
- News and feature articles
- Seminars
- Speaking engagements
- Media publicity

FINDING NEW CUSTOMERS

LOCAL BUSINESS ASSOCIATIONS AND GROUPS.

If you're selling products to local businesses, try to join or attend activities at every group you can. Some groups you may not be able to join as an individual may have some activities that are open to the public. Also try to find people who belong to these associations and see if they will pass your cards around.

NATIONAL TRADE ASSOCIATIONS.

Particularly if you are selling nationally, you will want to consider joining or participating in the national trade association or professional groups. At the least, you should find people like yourself you can network with and bounce off ideas. Many trade and professional associations have local chapters. You can find a listing of many professional associations on the World Wide Web at www.careercity.com.

JOIN EVERY RELEVANT GROUP YOU HAVE TIME FOR.

If you're trying to find leads among consumers, you may want to join every possible group that may have members who are good prospects. If your target consumers tend to live in certain communities, you may want to consider moving to that town.

DON'T FORGET ABOUT THE ALUMNI OR ALUMNAE FROM YOUR ALMA MATERS AND OTHER GROUPS.

Some sales reps have built their livelihood just selling to alumni or alumnae from their college or other schools. There is some immediate trust in this kind of sales situation. And by focusing all your efforts on one group, you are more likely to develop some positive word-of-mouth and to increase your chances of getting referrals.

TRADE SHOWS.

Trade shows are terrific sources of leads. Today, perhaps because of the availability of more high-tech means of communication, fewer deals are actually closed at trade shows, but they remain one of the most important venues for finding leads. Some buyers who are

Join every group you possibly can!

FINDING NEW CUSTOMERS

already being called on regularly by sales reps from larger firms are particularly interested in what smaller firms have to offer at trade shows. Some trade shows are very inexpensive to attend; others are quite expensive and sold out long in advance.

There are very inexpensive alternatives. For example, if your firm is not renting a booth at a trade show, you can often attend anyway individually—for a small fee.

Also don't overlook smaller, regional, and local trade shows. These shows are often very inexpensive, and buyers may have more time to spend with possible new sources of supply.

NEWS AND FEATURE ARTICLES.

One of the problems with many lead sources, especially for smaller companies and individuals, is that often you cannot learn much more than their name and address. This is one reason why following news and feature articles is valuable.

For selling to local businesses you should pay particular attention to local business journals. They tend to focus on local firms more than major newspapers do. And the smaller the publication, the less likely you'll face competition from other firms calling the same buyer.

For selling to national firms, you want to follow-up with the trade press very carefully.

For selling to individuals, keep track of the "Who's News" section of as many relevant publications as possible.

A lot of this information, of course, is increasingly available on the World Wide Web.

KEEP EXPERIMENTING AND COMPARING NOTES WITH OTHERS.

It could be that in your particular situation the best method for finding prospects is very different from all the methods I just outlined! But whatever methods are working for people in your situation, find out what they are. Don't be shy about asking salespeople at your firm or at similar firms what methods of finding leads is working for them.

> Don't overlook smaller, regional, and local trade shows.

FINDING NEW CUSTOMERS

And regardless of what method you decide to try, test it in a small way first to see if you get results. If you don't, move on to another method fast.

Most of all, never stop trying to find new leads. Remember, the key to finding new leads lies in your attitude of the "endless search," and of spreading enthusiasm about your products or services and your ability to provide solutions to customers.

CHAPTER

6

GETTING
IN
THE
DOOR

Most salespeople tend to fall in the habit of pitching their product too fast and too hard over the phone. They'd be a lot more effective if they backed off and focused more on building rapport and developing a true two-way dialogue with prospects. This kind of Customer-Focused approach takes more energy, a strong positive attitude, and will power to focus on the other person— but it is a heck of a lot more likely to be successful!

GETTING IN THE DOOR

G etting appointments might at first seem like a daunting task. But with a Customer-Focused Selling approach, it's one heck of a lot easier. Add in great voice tone, a little bit of enthusiasm, and a few choice words—and presto! Cold-calling becomes a manageable job that anyone can excel at!

CUSTOMER-FOCUSED ATTITUDE.

You're not calling to "sell" the customer. You're calling to try to help the customer. You're calling to help the customer find solutions. You have products and services that might have significant value added for the customer. These products don't necessarily have to be even markedly or marginally better than a competitor's. As long as the products or services have value and utility for a customer, you can, and should feel great about helping customers better reach their goals by buying your products.

If you approach the cold call with the perspective of "I'm going to 'sell' a product to someone," this conjures up images of trying to persuade someone to buy something he or she really doesn't want. This is why it is important to think of the cold call as trying to "help" the customer find solutions. And if you have totally adopted a Customer-Focused Selling approach, it is a lot easier to envision yourself "helping" the customer and not "selling" the customer—because this is truly what you will be doing!

So before every call, envision yourself "helping" a potential customer.

It is so deeply ingrained in our culture that a salesperson should be "selling" a customer rather than "helping" a customer, you may benefit by reminding yourself before every call that your purpose first is to help that customer.

So why don't customers always seem to want your help?

Getting Through Voice Mail

In a real cold call, there's a good chance they're not going to call you back ever, so just keep trying. But don't leave too many messages. One message a week for two or three weeks is plenty.

But in a "warm" call, when the calls are referrals, not complete cold calls, you usually get the call back. This is all the more reason why Customer-Focused Selling works. Because if you make your customers so happy that you can generate lots of referrals, then it's going to be a lot easier to break out of voice-mail jail!

I know not everyone is at the point when they can just count on referrals. And I know a lot of people are frustrated by voice mail. I hear again and again, "I've called ten times and I always get voice mail. I think they always leave it on." But then a few days later I hear, "You won't believe it—on the twenty-second call, the customer actually picked up the receiver." This happens all the time in the business world. People in decision-making positions are often simply not available to take phone calls. They might be in meetings, traveling, at appointments, or on another phone call. The more important a decision-maker you are trying to reach, the more difficult it will be to find that person quietly sitting in his or her office, waiting for your call. So if you really want to get through, then make lots of dials.

Of course, you can always work on improving the message you leave, too—but be very careful about leaving more than a couple of messages on voice mail. With someone you haven't done business with before, keep your message brief, concise, compelling, and not hokey. Make it as personalized as possible. "This is [so-and-so]. Our business is expanding quickly in your area. I just wanted to be sure you were familiar with our latest [xyz] product, that has proved particularly useful at [xyz] firms. You can reach me at this number…"

Our society teaches us to say "no." Say "no" to strangers. Say "no" to any salesperson. Be skeptical of every new idea. Don't waste any time considering it.

Human nature is not only to say "no" to any new idea–but also to remain closed minded to it.

Human minds like nice, simple, established patterns. Human minds don't like to think about adopting new options, new ideas, new solutions, new products, or new services. This requires thinking, and thinking requires energy.

A core job of a salesperson is to get a customer to think.

One of the biggest benefits that you, the salesperson, bring to a customer is that you get the customer to think. You get the customer to consider new options, new ideas, new solutions, new products, and new services.

You're trying to get the customer to make a careful, informed choice.

> You're trying to help the customer make an informed choice.

But to do so you most overcome the natural human tendency to say "no" and remain closed to new ideas. So even though as a Customer-Focused salesperson your ultimate job is to help the customer, you still need to persist to a reasonable degree even when the customer shows no interest in carefully finding out all the information about your product or service and evaluating it.

You're not trying to get your customers to buy something they don't want. You are only trying to get them to thoroughly evaluate your product or service and consider how it might add value for them.

But you do need to overcome the first human reaction to say "no" and not try anything new.

SEPARATE COLD-CALLING TIME FROM LIST-BUILDING AND INFORMATION-GATHERING TIME.

Don't confuse cold-calling to get an appointment with randomly calling to build a list of prospects or calling to get information. Before you call a company to make a sale, you want to know the name of the decision-maker you should be calling. Especially in selling higher-value goods or services, you will probably want to call other people

GETTING IN THE DOOR

Working with Gatekeepers

Make sure you don't launch into your sales pitch with the wrong person. Too many salespeople go through their sales pitch with the receptionist or the assistant instead of the real decision-maker.

Instead, use the gatekeeper as your ally. Get his or her name. I might say when I call back, "Hi, Joan, it's me again. I'd love to talk with [whomever] about this project. If you were I, what would you suggest I do?" She may respond, "The only time they're in here is Friday morning. You call then and I'll make sure the call gets through."

Try to make that gatekeeper part of your time. Not every salesperson shows respect to gatekeepers, and if you do, you will often quickly make a very favorable impression. I might go on to say, "Let me put something in the mail so you can give them an agenda of what we're going to talk about."

in the company to try to get more information before you call the decision-maker.

Separate your calls to build lists and to gather information. For example, set aside certain times to call to gather information and certain times to call to try to get appointments. It is much easier to build momentum and get into the pace of cold-calling if you make a bunch of these calls at the same time, ideally at some regularly pre-established time.

SEPARATE APPOINTMENT-GETTING FROM SELLING.

Clearly distinguish from the outset what the purpose of your call is. Are you calling to set up an appointment? Are you calling to try to sell over the phone? Are you calling to simply determine if there is enough interest to send out a sample of your product or service?

The first few words are important.

They may seem routine to you. But the first few words on the phone are very important.

Typically you will want to start a sales call by identifying yourself and asking a very simple question to get the other party talking, most commonly by asking, "How are you today?"

Don't put the customer on the defensive.

Other approaches for the very first few words of the call, such as rushing into a detailed sales pitch, can send the recipient of your call into a very defensive posture, closing their mind to the remotest possibility that they will consider whatever you are presenting.

THE INITIAL TONE AND PACE OF SPEECH ARE OFTEN MORE IMPORTANT THAN THE WORDS.

Talk to your customers the way you would like to be talked to. (Think customer-focused!) Keep your tone enthusiastic but not overbearing. Remember, they were probably engaged in another activity when you called, not breathlessly waiting for you to phone them. So

How to Keep Going at Cold Calls

Break the cold-call tension.
Everyone feels some tension with cold calls. But you can make it a lot easier on yourself. Accept it as a natural feeling—don't try to fight it. Even experienced people feel some degree of anxiety when making cold calls.

Call in batches.
Have several prospects to call in one sitting. Don't pause between calls during batches. This will help ease the tension, because you know that if you don't "hit" on the first call, there are still a bunch of others to try.

Get into a cold-calling rhythm.
One of the hardest things about cold calling is making the first call of the day or the first call after being away from the phone. So schedule a specific time to begin your calls, and stick with it. And by calling in batches you will get into a rhythm with the conversation, one call helping put you in a "selling" frame of mind for the next call.

No single call is a make-or-break situation.
You're not going to sell every call. Don't view each call as a make-or-break situation. Sink into it when you are on the phone—get into the customer's viewpoint—but if you are clearly blown off, forget the call and go on to the next one.

Build momentum from successful calls.
When you do have success on the phone, don't let this success hamper your further progress either. For example, if you line up an important appointment you've been trying to get for days, don't let it stop or slow down your work for the rest of the day as you celebrate. Instead, take advantage of the momentum of this call and plow into as many more calls as you can as soon as you can.

GETTING IN THE DOOR

especially with the first couple words (such as your name and the name of your company), talk slowly so they will understand you.

So often, customers don't hear the caller's name or the name of the company and hence don't get pulled into the conversation; they find it easier to hang up on a person whose name they didn't hear; and they are less likely to build trust if they didn't clearly understand the name of the company.

DOES YOUR VOICE SMILE?

Would you rather talk with someone who sounds depressed or bored, or with someone who sounds upbeat and interesting? Make your voice sound not just enthusiastic but warm and inviting as well. How important is this? It's crucial. Practice with friends. Call your coworkers in the office. Better yet, call yourself—call your answering machine and listen to yourself on tape. Make sure your voice is the voice you would want to buy from if a salesperson were calling you.

Smile on the phone.

DOES THE PROSPECT SEEM PARTICULARLY RUSHED OR PREOCCUPIED?

If the customer sounds preoccupied, you may want to ask if there is a better time for you to call. Maybe the customer is preoccupied. If so, you probably aren't going to be able to get very far—not now, anyway. Or maybe the customers just want you to know that they really aren't feeling particularly receptive to your call. At least by asking "Is there a better time?" you are acknowledging that you understand the customer is sounding less than positive and that you are thinking of his or her perspective, not just yours.

MAKE AN "INTEREST-BUILDER" STATEMENT QUICKLY.

Immediately after exchanging a couple of words with the customer (such as "I'm fine today, thank you"), you need to get down to business and make an interest-building statement. Don't try to spend too much time in small talk first. The sooner you get to the interest-building statement, the more receptive the prospective customer will be to listening to it.

GETTING IN THE DOOR

Plan out a specific interest-builder statement before you call. Don't try to ad-lib it. Write a very, very short attention-getting sentence or two, the shorter the better. The longer you go on in a monologue, the greater the chance the other party will lose interest. Remember, you are doing Customer-Focused Selling, so you need to focus on keeping the customer involved first as opposed to being concerned how many positive product features you are able to list.

In fact, the best interest-building statements don't even mention product or service features.

Everyone Sometimes Has Rough Prospecting Calls; What's More Important Is How You React to Them

No one handles every call perfectly—not even seasoned pros.

Don't be hard on yourself for not being great on each call. Don't be surprised, especially if you've just started, occasionally to even get tongue-tied or break into a stutter. Even if you've been selling for years, don't be surprised to occasionally say absolutely the wrong thing or even to suddenly not be able to say anything at all! Whatever you say, or don't say, try to keep going during the call. Even a phone call that you absolutely maul may still be salvageable. And even if the call is not salvageable, forget it and go on. Everyone has some lousy phone calls.

Every salesperson has bad calls, bad days, and bad weeks.

Sales is not a steady, constant, upbeat curve. If it were, it wouldn't be half the challenge it is. You need to acknowledge that in sales you will often get the feeling, when you don't get an appointment or don't get the sale, that you made a mistake—you did something wrong. ("If only I had just . . .") Well, forget about it! Learn from your "mistakes," but don't dwell on them. And accept that no matter how hard you try, you are not going to be perfect, either getting appointments or making sales—nobody is! This in an imperfect, difficult, fast-moving process. Strive to be great—but don't beat up on yourself for being human.

What matters more is how you recover from bad calls and bad days.

You need to acknowledge that even when you do everything right, you are going to have bad calls, bad days, and sometimes bad weeks. What is going to determine your ultimate success is how you recover from a bad call or a bad period of calling. Do you berate yourself for it? Do you wonder if you should be doing something different? Or do you acknowledge that everyone who sells has bad calls and just go on to the next one?

GETTING IN THE DOOR

Here are some examples of interest-building statements:

BUILD INTEREST BY REFERRAL.

This is the strongest interest-builder. You might want to add, if appropriate, what you accomplished for the person who referred you to this prospective customer, or a customer in a roughly similar situation.

Example: "Susan Jenkins suggested that I call you. We have had complete responsibility for maintenance of her computer systems, and she's been quite pleased with the results."

BUILD INTEREST WITH COMMONALITY.

A commonality statement particularly helps build trust. Often, however, unless you both belong to a fairly tightly knit group, you will quickly need to move on to another interest statement or to beginning your presentation of how you may provide a solution to the prospect.

Example: "I see that you belong to the Southtown Business Association. I joined when I moved to town last year . . ."

BUILD INTEREST BY QUALIFYING AT THE SAME TIME (IF YOU . . . , THEN . . .)

This kind of statement signals to the customer that you are going to take a Customer-Focused Approach and that you are going to provide a certain kind of solution. At the same time, if the prospect has no interest in the kind of solution you are offering, then you will find out quickly without spending any more time.

Example: "If lowering the cost of your courier services is something that is of interest to you, I may be able to help."

BUILD INTEREST WITH NAMES THE PROSPECT WILL RECOGNIZE.

More powerful than dazzling the prospect with the names of the most visible companies that your firm worked with, is mentioning the names of competitors. For individuals it is more effective to mention people the prospect may personally know, rather than celebrities they may recognize only from media coverage.

Spark their interest.

GETTING IN THE DOOR

Example: "I've recently completed some work with Smithtown Shoestores and East City Shoes, and I may be able to help you, too!"

BUILD INTEREST WITH SUCCESS STORIES.

Remember, customers are more interested in results and solutions than the product features that helped achieve them.

Example: "We helped Washington Wholesale increase their sales 30 percent in the first month alone."

BUILD INTEREST WITH SUCCESS INDICATORS.

Success indicators help build trust and credibility extremely quickly.

"Our buildings have won three national awards for design excellence."

Build interest by mentioning customer benefits.

Be sure to focus on the benefit to the customer, not just the product feature.

"Customers using our copiers have averaged fewer than two days of downtime per year."

BUILD INTEREST BY FOCUS.

Statements of this type are particularly powerful for service firms.

"Our bank specializes in helping midmarket businesses like yours."

Don't get into a long-winded product pitch.

Keep it a conversation! Not a lecture! You need to keep the customer involved in the conversation or you will lose his or her interest. At the beginning of the call, try to keep your side of the conversation to short, single sentences at most.

LISTEN CAREFULLY TO WORDS, TONE, AND INFLECTIONS.

If prospects seem particularly interested in a point you made, then elaborate on it—or better yet, engage them in a conversation about it. If they don't seem interested in points you have made, either try another point or ask a question to try to determine what might pique their interest.

Prospecting Calls

Question: At your level, aren't most sales made in person?

Nancy Stephens: I actually make a lot of sales over the phone because I work all of the United States, Canada, Mexico, and Europe.

Question: I usually think of telemarketers as people who call at dinnertime: Am I right?

Nancy Stephens: Yeah, and annoy you! Telemarketing is usually prospecting and selling over the phone. I first get my leads (usually by referral), then I sell over the phone. I approach the firm over the phone, maybe send out a detailed information packet by overnight courier, and then call them back as soon as the next day or two and close the sale.

GETTING IN THE DOOR

Should I Make Lots of Calls or a Few, Targeted Calls?

Ideally you want to make lots of carefully targeted calls. When you first get started in sales you probably aren't going to have referrals, and it may take you a while to develop really good lead sources. So you've got to go out and make things happen—which will mean making lots of calls. An advantage of making lots of calls when you're starting out is that you can get a lot of solid experience under your belt. Learn to take rejection in stride and generally get more comfortable on the phone.

At the same time, you always want to be thinking not just how you can get more leads, but also how you can get better leads. And I strongly encourage you to develop personal referrals as much as possible. Networking as described later in this book is a great way to jump-start personal referrals.

THINK CUSTOMER-FOCUSED AND GO WITH THE FLOW.

Develop empathy for your customers as you start to talk with them. Try to "feel" what they are feeling. Follow their signals of interest from their responses.

But remember, most people at first are "no"-minded.

So try not to give up when your customers indicate in anything less than emphatic terms that they are not interested. Try another interest-builder or ask them a question. Keep a friendly, nonconfrontational tone.

VIEW OBJECTIONS AS REQUESTS FOR MORE INFORMATION.

When prospects say they are not interested, especially early in the phone call, it almost always means they don't have enough information to be interested. More particularly it means they don't appreciate how your product or service can provide a solution for them, or they aren't confident that your product will provide the solution or results you are promising. Be patient and understanding when prospects raise objections, but unless they are emphatic, keep trying to convince your prospects that you have a product or service that may help them.

KEEP TO YOUR OBJECTIVE—DON'T TRY TO CLOSE PREMATURELY.

Remember, if you called to set up an appointment, stay with this objective. Don't try to close the sale. As soon as your prospects show enough interest so you think they will agree to see you in person, go for it—set up the appointment. Don't risk the appointment by trying to keep on selling when they are already willing to see you for an appointment. Save additional talk for the in-person visit.

LEAVE THE DOOR OPEN EVEN IF YOU DON'T GET THE APPOINTMENT.

Even if you can't get an appointment on this phone call, try to leave the door open so you can make a smooth follow-up call. For example, you could say:

"Tom, I hear what you are saying. I'll tell you what. I'll just send you the literature anyway and give you a chance to take a look at it."

"Linda, I'll call you back closer to the time when you're working on the new budget."

"Thanks for talking with me today. I'll give you a chance to reflect on this solution further. Then I'll call you next time I'm in this area."

COLD-CALLING APPROACHES.

Frank Bingham sells for Open Page, a firm that sells pagers for both regional and national use. He is calling on Hampton Real Estate, a regional real estate firm and franchisee of a national chain. Frank reaches Katherine Bates, the receptionist. The objective of the call is to get the buyer to commit to a special trial rate of $49 per unit for a three-month period. Naturally, the paging company would then like to retain the contract. In the ineffective approach, Frank pushes too hard and fails to get by the receptionist. In the effective approach, he knows who he needs to reach and gets to speak to her directly.

THE INEFFECTIVE APPROACH

Kathy: Good morning. Hampton Real Estate, this is Kathy. How may I help you?

Frank: Hi, this is Frank Bingham. How are you today?
Kathy has heard this many times before.

Kathy: Fine.
Frank comes on strong.

Frank: That's great. Kathy, I'd just like to take a few moments of your time to tell you about a special we're running on pagers this month. Does your company use pagers?
Kathy is reluctant to supply much information.

Kathy: I really couldn't say. Maybe our sales reps . . . .

Frank: That's great. Well, Kathy, if your company signs up a minimum of four sales reps this week, then we'll give you the

What's the Best Time of Day to Call?

It depends entirely on the kind of clients and prospects you call on. There are many businesses where if it's a small business, they're busy and out all day long, but they come in at the crack of dawn. So you might catch them at six or seven in the morning and never again—except perhaps at the very tail end of the day. Or you might have a different kind of business where they're tied up in meetings from the minute they walk in the door until noon or two o'clock in the afternoon. So if you don't get the person you are trying to reach, and you can get a receptionist or assistant, you should ask when the best time is to reach that person.

So you need to work on your customer's schedule, not on your schedule.

GETTING IN THE DOOR

first three months of service at a terrific price. How does that sound?

Kathy: Thanks anyway, but we're all set. Good-bye. (Hangs up.)

THE EFFECTIVE APPROACH

Kathy: Good morning. Hampton Real Estate, this is Kathy. How may I help you?

Frank: Good morning, Kathy. May I please speak with Julie Ross?

Kathy: One moment, please.
We hear the phone ring and then Julie picks up.

Julie: Julie Ross.

Frank: Hi, Julie. This is Frank Bingham calling from Open Page. I understand that your company uses pagers to stay in contact with your agents. Is that right?

Julie: Yes, that's true.

Frank: Do you have a minute?

Julie: Well, things are pretty hectic around here. What can I do for you?

Frank: I promise to be brief. Last week I sent you a letter describing our introductory offer for companies such as yours. Did you get a chance to review it?

Julie: You know I get so much mail in here I really can't remember.

Frank: The letter describes our realtor success program, which gives you three months of pager service at a discount of 40 percent. We also waive the fee for the pagers themselves. To take advantage of the realtor success program, all you have to do is sign up three of your realtors.

Julie: What happens after three months?

Frank: Our service is fully guaranteed and you have no commitment whatsoever to continue after three months. We'll review at that time to see if you'd like to continue the service. Can I send out three beepers today?
[She's interested. This is now a potential sale.]

Julie: Well, it sounds interesting. We've just added some new realtors for the spring market. Tell me a little bit more about the models you carry . . .

> Decision-maker identified on previous call.

GETTING IN THE DOOR

COMMENTARY:

Remember to first determine who is the individual who buys your product or service. An introductory letter has already been sent and gives an ideal starting point of reference from which to begin the introduction. Frank is immediately able to begin describing the three-month offer and thus avoids the dangerous "Are you interested in . . ." yes-or-no scenario. From there he is able to get the conversation to productively focus on explaining his beeper service and has created interest in his product, which he will then follow-up.

INFORMATION-GATHERING APPROACHES.

In this scenario, Earl Crocker sells for Tri-County Supply, a paper products company. He is calling on Neely Temporary Services, a busy temporary employment agency. His objective is to gather information to gain a later appointment. This cold call should not be used to sell products. He is confronted by Doreen, the receptionist who acts as a gatekeeper and is trained to discourage salespeople. In the ineffective scenario, Earl does not bother to get information; rather he simply leaves material. In the effective scenario, he learns who is in charge of signing off on purchasing paper products.

THE INEFFECTIVE APPROACH

Earl: Hi. I'm Earl Crocker from Tri-County.

Doreen: Hi. (She pays very little attention.)

Earl: Is the office manager in?

Doreen: She's not available right now.

Earl: Do you know who you order your paper products from?

Doreen: No, I'm afraid I don't.

Earl: I'd like to leave some samples of our product line. Where should I put them?

Doreen: Sure. Put 'em up there on the counter.

Earl: Thanks. I'll stop by in a few weeks.

Watch Out for the Bite of the Big Fish!

While you certainly want to spend more effort on the larger accounts, don't forget the smaller ones. I've seen lots of people early in their sales careers put 100 percent of their efforts into the big accounts and then, when they've missed, they've starved for a year or so.

Beware of the trap of getting a taste of the big ones and forgetting the small ones. Keep your effort proportional—and not 100 percent on the very biggest. Don't gloat over yesterday's sale.

Successfully landing a big fish early in your career may spell the end of it. For example, I was giving a training program last week and I sat down for lunch with a woman who told me, "I'm here for sales training." I asked how it was going with sales, and she told me that she made a single huge sale right out of the gate but had not made a single sale since then. I've seen this happen again and again. She stumbles on one big sale. Thinks she's grandiose, floats on that, and doesn't take the time to learn the skills and get out and sell. She'll be out of the business before she knows it.

Remember, if you're talking about yesterday, you're not doing enough today. It's history. I don't care how good it is. Gloat if you must for five minutes, then get on with it. It was yesterday, it doesn't matter. It's all business. It's all selling.

Earl leaves after putting a few items, a catalog, and his card on the counter. After he walks out, Doreen throws the materials in the trash can.

THE EFFECTIVE APPROACH

Earl: Hello, I'm Earl Crocker with Tri-County Supply. I see you're pretty busy so I won't keep you. I just wanted to introduce myself in this area and find out what you do here.

Doreen knows it's a salesperson and greets him accordingly.

Doreen: We supply temporary support to companies in the region.

Earl: Must keep you pretty busy.

Doreen: We get our fair share of phone calls, especially first thing in the morning.

Earl: Well, the last thing you want to worry about is paper supplies. We've been able to help companies save time and money with our Easy Order Plan.

Doreen: What's that?

Earl: It's a way that you can judge your regular paper requirements so we can deliver them only when you need them. That way you don't have to store so much. How much paper do you use in a day?

Doreen: I don't really know, to be honest with you. Bob handles all that.

Earl: Can I talk to Bob . . . uh . . .

Doreen: Schmitz. Bob Schmitz. He's not here right now. Why don't I take your samples and make sure to give them to him.

Earl: Actually, we tailor our Easy Order Plan to each customer's needs, so I don't have a prepackaged sample to leave with you. When's the best time to talk to Bob so I can ask him a few questions?

Doreen gets a card.

Doreen: He's usually around in the late afternoon. Give him a call around 4 p.m. I'll let him know that we spoke.

> Builds conversation with receptionist.

> Pinpoints decision-maker for follow-up.

GETTING IN THE DOOR

Earl (looking at receptionist's sign): Thanks, Doreen. I look forward to seeing you again.

COMMENTARY:

Don't mistake cold calling for selling. Cold calling is very simply setting the stage to come back for a true sales call. To be effective you must build rapport and ask questions.

Keep in mind that cold calling should be an information-gathering session where you find out as much as possible about the prospect. You are qualifying them and positioning yourself as someone worth talking to. Come prepared with a good reason why they should see you, and make sure you establish next steps.

Look at cold calling as a great way to get connected and learn the pulse of a business community. From there, use the information and follow-up with the best prospects.

IDENTIFYING THE BUYER.

Tom Clements sells for Green-up Landscaping Services. He has been pitching McKinley Healthcare for several years without success. Now the contract is up for renewal again. The timing is good because the current contractor has been overextended and some of the work has been shoddy. Tom must find the real buyer and submit his proposal, being careful not to present it to a nonbuyer. Several people are involved, including the head of maintenance, the general manager, and the medical director. He calls on the supervisor of maintenance at McKinley.

THE INEFFECTIVE APPROACH

Tom: Hey, Maurice! How's it going?

Maurice is in charge of maintenance. He's an older man who has been around for years.

Maurice: Tommy. Haven't seen you in while. What you been doing? Playing too much golf, I bet.

Tom: Don't I wish. I haven't been out for weeks. Are you still doing maintenance work out at Riverbend's course?

Maurice: No, I don't have time for that anymore. They keep me pretty busy around this place.

Tom: Too bad. You helped keep it in great shape. Say, Maurice. Isn't your landscaping contract coming up for renewal soon?

Maurice: I believe it is, as a matter of fact. How did you remember?

Tom: That's what they pay me for. I've put together a proposal for you based on what we've talked about before. I thought you could look it over and then I could stop by and go over it.

Maurice: Sure, Tommy. I'll be happy to pass it along. I'll put in a good word for you, too.

> Doesn't get to decision-maker.

THE EFFECTIVE APPROACH

Tom: Hey, Maurice! How's it going?

Maurice is in charge of maintenance. He's an older man who has been around for years.

Maurice: Tommy. Haven't seen you in while. What have you been doing? Playing too much golf, I bet.

Tom: Don't I wish. I haven't been out for weeks. Are you still doing maintenance work out at Riverbend's course?

Maurice: No, I don't have time for that anymore. They keep me pretty busy around this place.

Tom: Too bad. You helped keep it in great shape. Say, Maurice. Isn't your landscaping contract coming up for renewal soon? What kinds of changes do you hope to see?

Maurice: Well, let's see. [He thinks.] I guess I'd like to see more regular visits. There are some bushes around the side that I think might be dying. Some areas didn't get watered as regularly as they should have. Of course, then I'm the one who's gotta fix it.

GETTING IN THE DOOR

Tom: I hear you. Listen, Maurice. We've known each other for a while and you're familiar with our work at the Center States Office Complex.

Maurice: You guys have got that place looking great.

Tom: Thanks. I'd like to make a proposal on this job and get your input. Who else do you think I should be talking to?

Maurice: Well, you should really meet my boss, Shirley Knight . . . and Dr. Conroy. He gets the final say about everything around here.

Tom is writing on a small notepad.

Tom (talking as he writes): Shirley Knight . . . and Dr. Conroy. He's the medical director, right?

Maurice: Yeah. Why don't I take you upstairs to meet them right now. See if they're in, anyway.

Tom: Sounds great. Let's do it.

> Identifies both decision-makers and their roles.

COMMENTARY:

When trying to get to the real buyer you need to be careful about assumptions. Don't try to sell the first person you come in contact with. Get that person's perspective and find out who else is involved.

Don't step on toes; rather invest the time in building the relationships. You can get initial contacts to lead you to the real decision-maker. Be tactful, be a great listener, and only "sell" when it's appropriate . . . to the real buyer!

Going from Being a Good Salesperson to Being a Great Salesperson . . .

Once you've gotten good at sales, once you've got some solid business under your belt, don't let up on cold calling. That's a mistake lots of salespeople make. They think: "Great, now I'm in the flow. I've got a bunch of business here. I'm going to cut way back on prospecting." Don't do that! Really top producers, really experienced people are always prospecting!

Although virtually all my business now comes through referrals, I still devote energy and time to prospecting. I do it on airplanes. I do it through speaking. I do it through my newsletter. I do it everywhere. When you get really good at it you prospect everywhere almost naturally, without giving it any thought or effort.

And with a great number of leads you get good at streamlining who you follow-up with. You get very, very selective, but you never stop prospecting. That's critical. And again, the prospecting is to include all methods—calling, networking, speaking, mailings, if they make sense. And when you're really experienced, you learn which ones your customers respond to best. My clients do not respond well to telemarketing. They don't respond well to cold calling. But I know that for many, many other salespeople, this is one of the very best bets when they start out. Eventually, as you get successful, you get a steady stream of people to talk to who are good, qualified people for your services or products.

CHAPTER

7

PRE-CALL
PLANNING

You can't expect to have a great sales call if you don't give it some planning in advance. Even if your product or service is more or less a commodity—highly similar to other people's—every sales situation is different because every customer is different. Every customer will have somewhat different concerns and put different weight on the importance of different features or services. So plan each call—and plan to get the sale!

P recall planning means taking anywhere from two minutes to two days to assess a potential sale before you meet the prospective client. It's an investment of time that will position you for a successful sales call.

When you plan for a sales call, there are always two "worlds" to consider: yours and theirs. Another way to describe these "worlds" is "your agenda" and "their agenda." Their world is bigger because their agenda is more important to them. If you can satisfy their world first, you will always satisfy your world and make the sale!

The better prepared you are at understanding both worlds, the closer you are to making a sale, even before you begin. This is the core of understanding what you need in the precall planning stages of the sales process.

There are always two "worlds" to consider.

INTERACTIVE CHECKLISTS—A SUMMARY.

Prospective client:_____

App't. date:_____

SECTION ONE: THE PROSPECT'S BUSINESS CLIMATE

1. What's going on in the prospective client's industry?
2. What, if any, are the changes impacting the prospective client's business?
3. How competitive is the client's marketplace right now?
4. What are the biggest issues, challenges, or problems facing the prospective client's industry right now?
5. How can your product or service better position your prospective client in the marketplace?

SECTION TWO: THE PROSPECTIVE CLIENT

1. Where did this lead come from? How can that help you?

PRE-CALL PLANNING

2. What level of authority does this person have on the buying decision?
3. What does this prospective client see as their biggest issue, challenge, or problem today?
4. Why did they agree to see you?
5. What does the prospective client want to achieve by meeting with you?

What results does the customer get?

SECTION THREE: THE PRODUCT OR SERVICE

1. Describe the features of your product or service.
2. What results does the customer get from using your product or service?
3. What is unique about the product or service you are selling?
4. Why should they buy your product or service instead of your competitors' product or service?
5. What sales tools will you use for the sales presentation?

Why buy from you?

SECTION FOUR: THE SALESPERSON: YOU!

1. Why do you want this sale?
2. Based on your assumptions of the prospective client's situation, what business opportunities can your product or service create for this client?
3. Why are you offering the best solution?
4. What else do you need to know before your meeting?
5. What are your three objectives for this sales call?

INTERACTIVE CHECKLISTS—AN ANALYSIS

Prospective client:_____

App't. date:_____

SECTION ONE: THE PROSPECT'S BUSINESS CLIMATE

1. **What's going on in the prospective client's industry?**

Take the big-picture view and consider what you know about the industry. Is it a mature industry? A new industry? A changing industry? In what ways is the industry changing? Is the industry faced with new regulations or new technology? Do you hear about the industry in the news often or rarely? Why? Why not? By thinking about these questions, you'll identify your perception of the prospective client's industry and learn how to position yourself to serve the client and his or her company better.

2. What, if any, are the changes impacting the prospective client's business?

Looking at your assessment of the industry, how does all this impact your prospective client? Is it causing the client to reexamine areas of his or her business? Change the size of the workforce? Invest in specific areas of the business? Take larger risks? Reduce risks? Spend more? Spend less? This question will help you transition from the big picture to the prospective client's specific situation and assist you in understanding how the industry climate is impacting the client.

3. How competitive is the client's marketplace right now?

Think about what you know, what you've observed, and what you've read. How stiff is the client's competition? How has the client positioned his or her company in the marketplace with respect to pricing? Is the company the most expensive, the least expensive, or somewhere in the middle? What is the competition doing? What kind of added value are you seeing in the client's marketplace? Incentives? Promotions? What is driving the competitive nature of the company: the industry or the consumer? You are uniquely positioned to look at the competition and better understand how the client sees the competition. Is the client on the mark, or has he or she missed the boat? Start thinking about how you can help!

4. What are the biggest issues, challenges, or problems facing the prospective client's industry right now?

Think about why you've been granted the appointment. Most likely it's because the prospective client is experiencing some kind of business challenge. Consider what it might be. Are the issues profit-based, people-based, time-based, technology-based, equipment-based, or a combination? Look at all the possibilities, including low margins and company inefficiencies, and jot down what you see as the company's biggest industry issues, challenges, or problems.

> Evaluate the business world from your prospect's perspective.

PRE-CALL PLANNING

> The source of the lead should help determine the tone of your sales call.

5. How can your product or service better position your prospective client in the marketplace?

Now that you've got a good idea as to what the company faces in the marketplace, you need to ask yourself: How can I help? Think about how your product or service can help them directly within their business, and how it can help them indirectly in their marketplace. Think through helping them on both levels and you'll be prepared to separate yourself from the crowd and win the sale!

SECTION TWO: THE PROSPECTIVE CLIENT

1. Where did this lead come from? How can that help you?

Make sure that you write down how you found the company. Was it a cold call from the phone book, a newspaper, or some other listing? Was it a referral from a friend, an existing customer, or another vender or service provider? Or was it an internal referral from someone at the company? Whatever the source, think about how you can leverage the "in."

2. What level of authority does this person have on the buying decision?

Don't be fooled by titles. Titles vary from company to company, and there is often a disconnection between what the title says and what level of authority a person really has over a buying decision. Think about your perception of this person's authority. Does he or she have responsibility for a budget? Or does he or she have responsibility for results? The higher up you can reach, the better off you are! Make sure you determine what the person does, and look for clues for an authorized decision-maker. We'll qualify them further in the face-to-face interview.

3. What does this prospective client see as his or her biggest issue, challenge, or problem today?

Think about the prospective client's day-to-day responsibilities. Based on these, what is the client facing as issues, challenges, or problems? These may be similar to those in the industry or very dif-

ferent. Try to complete this sentence for them: "If only
_____ were solved, then I'd be all set." Of course, we're
never all set, but it will help you identify your prospective client's
issues, challenges, or problems. Put yourself in the client's shoes and
adopt the client's thought patterns. Start to think about how you
can solve the client's problems.

4. Why did they agree to see you?

People are very busy these days, and their time is precious.
Think about why you were granted an appointment. What do they
want from you? How do they perceive you? Where did they find you?
Or did you find them? How do you think that makes them feel about
you? Is it a help or a hindrance? What's their sense of urgency? Very
high or very low? Why are they seeing you now? Think about these
and other items that help you understand the prospective client's
point of view. Do they see you the way you want them to? If not, you
should check out our section on Anatomy of the Sale.

5. What does the prospective client want to achieve by meeting with you?

Write down at least one and hopefully three things that you
think this prospective client is hoping to achieve by meeting with
you. Think about all the possibilities: product information, service
standards, pricing information, process information, company information, shopping the marketplace, or striving to understand the marketplace. Once you've identified what they most likely want, you are
better prepared to give it to them. The better you are at meeting
their agenda, the quicker you'll meet your own!

SECTION THREE: THE PRODUCT OR SERVICE

1. Describe the features of your product or service.

Jot down as many features of your product or service as you
can think of. These are all the specifics and details about your product or service. If you have a product, you might describe the size, the
color, the weight, and any special attributes. If you sell a service, you
are more likely to describe the number of years in business, number

> Buyers don't usually agree to
> see you because they just
> want someone to talk to!

PRE-CALL PLANNING

Don't sell features,
sell results!

of clients served, the typical length of a project, the number of people involved in a project, and any other descriptive details that you can provide the client. You need to identify as many features as possible to discuss the uniqueness of your product or service.

2. What results does the customer get from using your product or service?

Here's where you really make your sales grow. Don't just sell features, sell results! For example, when a customer buys a security alarm system, they might "buy" the hardware, but what they really want is the result: peace of mind. When a customer buys a retirement investment plan, they might buy stocks, bonds, and insurance, but what they really want is a secure source of income at a later date. Look at your product or service: What are the results customers really want? If you are not sure, ask some of your existing customers.

3. What is unique about the product or service you are selling?

"Why should I buy your product?" That's the ultimate question in every buyer's mind, and you need to know the answer in advance! Is your product faster, bigger, smaller, or smarter? Do you offer a different approach to an old problem? Do you customize and tailor to meet the specific needs of your customers? Figure out the distinguishing factors and then use the information in the section on Anatomy of the Sale. By the way, the most unique factor may be YOU!

4. Why should they buy your product or service versus your competitors' product or service?

You need to know your fit in the marketplace! Do your homework. Know what is out there. Are you priced high, low, or right in the middle? Do you offer more, less, or the same? Do you look like your competition? Or very different? You need to be able to have a conversation about how and why you are positioned in the marketplace. Once you've identified who you are in relation to your competitors, everything can be turned into a positive. For example, if your company is small, this would give you the advantage of great flexibility; if your company is large, this could give you the advantage of a wealth of resources. Know your position before you go on a sales call!

5. **What sales tools will you use for the sales presentation?**

In deciding what sales tools will be most helpful to you in selling, make sure they fit with your product or service. If you have a very visual product or service, be prepared to show it! If you have a service business, be prepared to show case studies that demonstrate results. Most of all, realize that the most important visual is you! Are you consistent with your business? If you want to present a professional, polished, expensive product or service, do you look the part? Are you consistent with the image you want to portray? Be aware of sales tools, and make sure you start with yourself!

> Be sure the sales tools are appropriate.

SECTION FOUR: THE SALESPERSON: YOU!

1. **Why do you want this sale?**

Think about why you want this sale. Is it a great client? A big client? A prestigious client? A financially rewarding client? A great avenue to other clients? Or a combination of these? Consider why you're attracted to this client and determine why you really want them as a client, and you'll be prepared to approach them with confidence and determination.

> What result can you create for the customer?

2. **Based on your assumptions of the prospective client's situation, what business results can your product or service create for this client?**

There are two considerations in buying decisions: One is the actual product or service; the second is the result it can create. Most sales are made for the second reason. Think about the business results your products or service can create. Are you going to help your client's business be more efficient? Increase sales? Reduce costs? Present a better image? Or retain customers? Think about the actual product or service and think about the business result!

PRE-CALL PLANNING

3. Why are you offering the best solution?

There are a lot of options out there today, but there's only one you. Think about how and why you are uniquely qualified as the best solution for this prospective client. Why are you better? Jot down five to seven reasons, and look at them. Are you detail-oriented, customer-focused, honest, experienced, dedicated, committed, knowledgeable, ethical? Most likely you are a great combination of these, so you should take credit for what you do well. This is often the reason why buyers decide to work with you. Identify your strengths, and understand why these are the reasons why you're the best solution!

4. What else do you need to know before your meeting?

Take a look at the precall planning you've done so far. What's missing? Do you need more detailed information on the industry, the company, the individual? Do you need more big-picture information on the industry, the company, or the individual? Do you need to examine your own positioning a little more? Do you need to talk to some folks inside your own company before you proceed? Think about your agenda and your client's agenda, and don't stop until you feel confident that you've got a solid preliminary assessment.

5. What are your three objectives for this sales call?

Make sure that you write down three objectives for your sales call. Think about what you want to have accomplished when you're walking out the door at the end of the call. The objectives might be related to building the relationship, gathering information, advancing the sale, gaining interim commitments, establishing next steps, or a combination of these. By identifying your objectives at the precall planning stage, you'll force yourself to be focused and set yourself up for success.

> Why are you better?

> Three objectives.

SAMPLE INTERACTIVE CHECKLIST: SERVICE COMPANY

Service: Human resources consulting services (benefits plans, policy and procedure manuals, compensation)

Prospective client: Midsize Regional Alarm Company

App't. date: 3/10

SECTION ONE: THE PROSPECT'S BUSINESS CLIMATE

1. **What's going on in the prospective client's industry?**
   - Rapidly changing technology in the field
   - New regulations require licensing for installers
   - Great reputation and PR, recent articles in the regional newspaper

2. **What, if any, are the changes impacting the prospective client's business?**
   - Tighter profit margins
   - Need to do business differently, reduce operational costs, and continue to deliver superior service
   - Difficult to attract employees into a maturing industry

3. **How competitive is the client's marketplace right now?**
   - Two major competitors, three emerging growth companies with new technologies
   - Lots of competing promotions (free installations if you buy ongoing monitoring)
   - This company is positioned as high-end, great added value, and with a loyal customer base

4. **What are the biggest issues, challenges, or problems facing the prospective client's industry right now?**
   - High turnover
   - Low morale due to rapid changes in business environment
   - Aging business systems

> Particularly focus on changes in the customer's business.

PRE-CALL PLANNING

Lead source.

Level of authority.

Challenge.

Achievement.

5. **How can your product or service better position your prospective client in the marketplace?**
   - Have more organized workplace to manage change
   - Clear guidelines to eliminate employee confusion
   - Add no-cost or low-cost benefits for employees
   - Build employee morale
   - Create compelling work environment

SECTION TWO: THE PROSPECTIVE CLIENT

1. **Where did this lead come from? How can that help you?**
   - Referral from company's C.P.A., Mike, remember to mention the name because they really respect his opinion; name other companies based on Mike's referral

2. **What level of authority does this person have on the buying decision?**
   - High-level, both are major decision-makers; meeting the president and general manager; might need to include the office manager in the decision to set the tone of teamwork

3. **What does this prospective client see as their biggest issue, challenge, or problem today?**
   - Profitability
   - Attracting and retaining high-caliber work force
   - Providing incentives other than financial

4. **Why did they agree to see you?**
   - They respect Mike
   - They need to look at options now to find and keep good people

5. **What does the prospective client want to achieve by meeting with you?**
   - Probably looking to see what's available, gathering information, and possibly after free advice. Be careful!

PRE-CALL PLANNING

SECTION THREE: THE PRODUCT OR SERVICE

1. **Describe the features of your product or service.**
   - Eight years in my own business, fourteen years' experience as internal human resources director for midsize company, more than a hundred satisfied clients to date, small business, four business associates to call upon for larger projects

2. **What results does the customer get from using your product or service?**
   - Increased employee morale, clear directions, organized workplace, increased profitability

3. **What is unique about the product or service you are selling?**
   - Every consulting project is tailored to meet the client's specific needs
   - Access to business associates for specialized information
   - Big-picture view of business

4. **Why should they buy your product or service versus your competitors' product or service?**
   - I'm priced competitively, right in the middle, and use unique business processes to accomplish my client's objectives

5. **What sales tools will you use for the sales presentation?**
   - Bring a sales packet, list of references with phone numbers, and several letters of reference
   - Bring my enthusiasm and dedication to the business!

Focus on how your strengths will help the customer.

SECTION FOUR: THE SALESPERSON: YOU!

1. **Why do you want this sale?**
   - New industry for me
   - Lots of referral potential
   - Great project with long-term revenue potential as they grow

PRE-CALL PLANNING

> How can you, the salesperson, help the customer?

2. **Based on your assumptions of the prospective client's situation, what business opportunities can your product or service create for them?**
   - Increase morale and reduce turnover
   - Create business climate to facilitate profitable growth
   - Add no-cost benefits to make overall employment package attractive to current and future employees

3. **Why are you offering the best solution?**
   - I'm knowledgeable, understand their business challenges, and am cost-effective and flexible to meet their changing and ongoing needs as they grow; implemented cost-effective solutions for two companies similar in size to this company

4. **What else do you need to know before your meeting?**
   - Verify how many employees they have; get the name and direct line of the office manager; and call Mike to thank him for the lead

5. **What are your three objectives for this sales call?**
   - Uncover buying decision criteria
   - Position myself as the best option
   - Establish next steps to move the sale forward

PRE-CALL PLANNING

SAMPLE INTERACTIVE CHECKLIST: PRODUCT COMPANY

Type of product: Bottled water supply company
Prospective client: Midsize C.P.A. firm
App't. date: 6/12

SECTION ONE: THE PROSPECT'S BUSINESS CLIMATE

1. What's going on in the prospective client's industry?
   - Client's are scrutinizing the services they receive from the firm
   - The entire accounting world is trying to incorporate added value to retain clients

2. What, if any, are the changes impacting the prospective client's business?
   - Difficulty maintaining profit margins
   - Possible cutbacks and staff reductions

3. How competitive is the client's marketplace right now?
   - Extremely competitive; large firms are adding consulting services, while small firms are cutting prices
   - Midsize firms are stuck in the middle, with significant overhead and limited resources

4. What are the biggest issues, challenges, or problems facing the prospective client's industry right now?
   - How to reduce overhead and retain clients in an increasingly competitive marketplace

5. How can your product or service better position your prospective client in the marketplace?
   - Increase morale
   - Reinforce a commitment to what is best for the employees
   - Provide a healthy environment for the employees

PRE-CALL PLANNING

SECTION TWO: THE PROSPECTIVE CLIENT

1. **Where did the lead come from? How can that help you?**
   - Telephone directory in my new territory
   - I bring a new perspective and new ideas

2. **What level of authority does this person have on the buying decision?**
   - Office manager should be able to make the go, no-go decision; I might need the partner to sign off—try to meet him!

Understand the roles of multiple decision-makers.

3. **What does this prospective client see as their biggest issue, challenge, or problem today?**
   - Keep the C.P.A.s' level of billable hours increasing

4. **Why did they agree to see you?**
   - The office manager had a bottled water service in his prior job and would love to get it into this firm.

5. **What does the prospective client want to achieve by meeting with you?**
   - They want me to provide them with enough information and reasons why a bottled water service would be worth the expense so they can convince the senior partner and get him to say "yes"

SECTION THREE: THE PRODUCT OR SERVICE

1. **Describe the features of your product or service**
   - 100 percent natural spring water
   - Free delivery
   - No-cost installed machine with a one-year revolving contract
   - Discounts available for employees to purchase the service for home use

Clearly and simply articulate the result.

2. **What results does the customer get from using your product or service?**
   - Increases employee morale
   - Demonstrates a commitment to a quality work environment
   - Healthy alternative to sodas and coffee

3. **What is unique about the product or service you are selling?**
   - This water comes from one of the oldest springs in America; our water purification standards are second to none; we maintain the highest standards of quality

4. **Why should they buy your product or service versus your competitors' product or service?**
   - I personally guarantee satisfaction with both the product and the service

5. **What sales tools will you use for the sales presentation?**
   - Bring sample of water for taste and a demonstration kit with video
   - Bring my "can do" attitude!

SECTION FOUR: THE SALESPERSON: YOU!

1. **Why do you want this sale?**
   - Great new account with lots of potential
   - Excellent reference within my new territory

2. **Based on your assumptions of the prospective client's situation, what business results can your product or service create for this client?**
   - Increased health and morale of staff, which will equal more billable hours

3. **Why are you the best solution?**
   - Determination to make them happy, commitment to the business, ability to build relationships

4. **What else do you need to know before your meeting?**
   - Need to find out if this firm has had any previous contracts with bottled water firms, and if so, with whom. Why did it end?

5. **What are your three objectives for this sales call?**
   - Find out who can say "yes"
   - Where is the money coming from?
   - Find the health advocates in the company

WHAT ARE THE ELEMENTS OF A SALE?

Selling is a dynamic process with lots of elements that can make it confusing and at times like a big puzzle with missing pieces. Clarity comes from a deep understanding of the Anatomy of a Sale. Each area of the sales process is predictable and consistent, occurring with every sale. How any given sale occurs can vary dramatically. In one instance all areas of the sales process may occur in one hour with a resulting sale. In another case, all areas may occur over the course of two years with a final sale resulting way down the road. The velocity of the sale is determined both by the urgency of the prospective customer and your skills and abilities at managing the sales process. Take your responsibility for managing the process very seriously, this is what you get paid for!

SALES MODEL

Break the Ice

Build Rapport

Gain Trust

Ask Strategic Questions

Seek Solutions

Work through Objections

Gain Agreement

Follow-Up after the Sale

C H A P T E R

BREAKING
THE ICE:
SETTING
THE TONE

You can really stand out from the pack and improve your sales ability by perfecting your ability to break the ice with customers. A lot of sales people don't do it as well as they could! And yet the first few minutes are so important! Like building a house on a cracked foundation—it's a lot more difficult to build a positive sales relationship, it you don't start out on a very positive footing!

BREAKING THE ICE: SETTING THE TONE

The first few seconds and minutes, when you first meet the prospective customer are crucial. In the initial moments of the meeting, impressions will be formed quickly, a tone will develop, a chemistry will or won't develop, and the foundation for all of the rest of your interactions with the customer will be built.

Why is the tone of the relationship set so early?

We all form almost instant subjective judgments about people we meet, and once they are formed, they are hard to change. This is bad news if your first impression is weak. But this is great news if your first impression is strong.

Don't be late . . . but don't be too early!

Be exactly five minutes early. No more, no less. Being late is an easy way to tell buyers you don't respect them and don't value their time. Some buyers aren't going to be annoyed if you're a couple minutes late . . . but others will. Don't risk it.

So why shouldn't you be ten or even thirty minutes early? Yes, it is better than being late . . . but it still could cause you to lose the sale. Arriving too early may signal to the customer messages you don't want to deliver. It may tell the customer that you are nervous about the sale, in which case, even if you aren't nervous, the buyer will be less relaxed thinking that you might be nervous. And if the buyer is less relaxed, it will be more difficult to build rapport and gain trust.

Another problem with being more than five minutes early is that the customer may feel pressured to see you before the appointed time. You may be thinking that you are in no rush to see the buyer; maybe it is your only appointment of the day. But your physical presence sends another message: "I am here . . . I am doing nothing else . . . I am available to see you now." Some buyers won't

Impressions are formed.

A tone develops.

Chemistry happens.

A foundation is built.

BREAKING THE ICE: SETTING THE TONE

feel pressured by your being extra early, but some will. At the typical business office, the receptionist will almost always tell the prospect exactly when you arrive. If you are calling on someone in an office or a home where there is no receptionist, the customer may feel even more pressured and more put off balance by your unexpected early presence.

How can you be exactly five minutes early every time?

Allow enough time so that even if traffic is heavier than expected, you will still arrive on time. Then go to a coffee shop in the immediate neighborhood or wait in the parking lot in your car, to time your arrival for exactly five minutes before the scheduled time.

Another reason it is important to allow plenty of time to get to an appointment is so you won't have to rush. Rushing to a sales appointment is a sure way to arrive frazzled, something the buyer is likely to pick up on; thus it risks endangering the tone of the meeting.

Always have something with you to read, so you won't have to fidget and get edgy before your meeting. Being relaxed when you meet the customer is important, and it is not just a matter of luck.

> Just arriving on time is no trivial matter.

THE RIGHT DRESS AND GROOMING.

One of the first things the customer is going to notice is your dress and grooming. Make it immaculate, but don't dress so you stand out and bring unnecessary attention to yourself. Remember, this is Customer-Focused Selling! The focus should be on the customer, not on you. Refer to the section later in this book for more tips on dress.

> Dress and grooming say a lot to your customer.

WHAT ARE YOU CARRYING?

What you are carrying can send an important message, too. A professional-looking briefcase will help set a professional, trusting tone in almost any business situation—even when you have nothing to carry in the briefcase.

Be wary on an initial visit of carrying an inappropriately large size or number of sample boxes. Too many sample boxes may make a buyer feel uneasy because he might feel the salesperson has unrealistically high expectations for the first meeting. The buyer also may

BREAKING THE ICE: SETTING THE TONE

feel that he or she is being pressured into having a longer or more serious meeting than was planned.

WHY CAN'T MORE PEOPLE SHAKE HANDS RIGHT?

There is a right way and a wrong way to shake hands. You want to reach out with your right hand and give a very firm handshake—but don't apply a vise grip.

I am always amazed at how many salespeople and how many buyers don't have a proper handshake. On the other hand, virtually all of the senior executives I meet at larger corporations know how to shake hands.

Like it or not, a proper handshake says a lot about you, and what you think of the person you are meeting.

Probably one of the reasons that customers, especially those who buy products from vendors all day long, shake hands poorly is that it becomes a tiring routine. Don't let handshaking become a routine matter for you!

Extend your hand with confidence.

You need to project a positive, confident image. So one of the first things you can do to establish the right tone is to extend your hand in confidence. You don't need to wait for the buyer to extend his or hers. Take the initiative, if the customer doesn't. Extend your hand within a second or two of when the customer approaches you. This little gesture may separate you from the crowd, because if you are dealing with a buyer who has been hesitant to extend his or her hand all day long, chances are the three people before you walked in and sat down and the three people after you will walk in and sit down, thinking that's what the person wants. But what you've done is made the personal connection and broken the barrier in what's gone on in that person's day up until now. You can also feel good that you have done what is businesslike and respectful.

Look the customer in the eye momentarily as you shake hands. It's not a silly detail. It's part of shaking hands right. If you look away, you give a feeling of distance and untrustworthiness.

> Handshaking helps set the tone.

BREAKING THE ICE: SETTING THE TONE

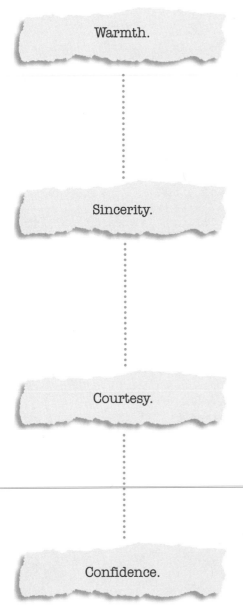

Warmth.

Sincerity.

Courtesy.

Confidence.

WARMLY AND CLEARLY ADDRESS THE CUSTOMER.

As soon as the customer is within reach and just as you are beginning to shake hands, you should introduce yourself. Again, you don't have to wait for the customer to take the initiative. Chances are the customer's mind is probably still focused on the past appointment or issue he or she was facing. Help bring the customer to focus on how you can help with a strong, confident address, such as:

"John Smith, I assume. I'm Nancy Stephens." (Simultaneous handshake.) It's a pleasure to meet you! (Genuine warmth in voice and good eye contact.)

At this point the customer might sit down and politely beckon you to do the same. If the customer sits and doesn't beckon, you should just take an available seat anyway—don't make the situation awkward by asking "May I have a seat?" But, be sure not to sit down until after the customer does. This may sound like a small detail, but sitting down even a few seconds before the customer is discourteous and will offend some people.

YOUR POSTURE MAKES A STRONG STATEMENT.

Even your posture in the first few seconds of meeting your prospect can make a difference. If you are slouching, or standing too casually, such as with your legs too far apart, you may come across as disrespectful, unenthusiastic, tired, or disinterested. On the other hand, if you are standing stiffly at attention, like a soldier being reviewed, you may come across as rigid, nervous, uncomfortable, unapproachable, or cold. How close to the customer are you standing? While standing, you should be about an arm's length away—close enough to shake hands at a good angle, but not close enough so the customer feels crowded. If the customer steps slightly forward or back, hold your ground: The customer is moving to the distance at which he or she feels most comfortable.

BREAKING THE ICE: SETTING THE TONE

YOUR SMILE TALKS FOR YOU.

Perhaps the most important body language is in your face. Most of
all, are you smiling? Are you showing a warm, natural, and genuine
smile? Suppose the customer isn't smiling at the first meeting.
Should you? Absolutely—we all like happy, cheerful people no matter
what mood we are in ourselves.

Make appropriate eye contact, focusing on the customer without nervously blinking or looking away.

Smiles sell.

SMALL TALK CAN BE A BIG DEAL.

After sharing introductions, you will almost always want to engage in
some small talk. Why is this so important? Small talk helps build a
rapport and a pleasant, nonconfrontational, conversational bond.
Good small talk can help set the tone for discussing substantive
issues; lack of small talk leaves you without a foundation for beginning your presentation. Building a strong bond early is particularly
important for Customer-Focused Selling, where you want to be able
to get the customer comfortably talking to you about his or her business issues as soon as possible, rather than just passively listening to
you make your sales pitch.

Small talk builds rapport.

BEGIN WITH SMALL TALK.

Ideally you want to roll smoothly right from the introductions into
small talk. Try to avoid awkward dead silences. Almost in the same
breath that you introduce yourself, start a two-way conversation.
Often you will want to begin simply with a "How are you today?" or
"How are you?" or "How is your day going?" This kind of question is
polite, it is nonobtrusive, and often it will get the customer talking. It
shows that you are customer-focused. And it also leaves the ball in
the customer's court—it gives the customer the chance to open up in
conversation, or to signal to you, with a curt answer, that he or she
wants to get to business quickly.

BREAKING THE ICE: SETTING THE TONE

> Common interests build trust.

CREATE ENGAGING CONVERSATION.

Common interests are often the best bet for quickly breaking the ice. Can you begin the conversation with a positive reference to a mutual acquaintance—perhaps the person who referred you to this customer? Do you belong to any of the same clubs or associations? Did you attend the same or similar schools? Don't fabricate or over-play a common interest, but if it's there, see if you can work it into the conversation.

BROADLY DEFINE COMMON INTERESTS.

You don't have to have been a fraternity brother or sorority sister to have common interests with a prospective customer. There are many other areas in which you may have common interests with your prospective customer. If you both work in the same industry, this is a common interest. You could ask, for example, "Are you ready for the trade show next week?" If the customer lives in the same town you could ask, "Did you see the big parade last weekend?"

SHOW AN INTEREST IN AND/OR ADMIRATION FOR THE CUSTOMER.

A positive comment about the customer helps set a good positive tone, but don't overdo it by being insincere. Ask a question or make a statement that may get the customer talking in a positive way, rather than simply saying, "Thank you."

> Sincere interests sets a positive tone.

"I'm really impressed with your product line. Are you adding many new items next year?"

"I've personally used your firm's services and I was very impressed by them. Do you serve the entire metro area now?"

"This is a beautiful home. Have you been here long?"

"I was just in your new format store last week, and I was sur-prised to see how much larger it seemed. Are you going to convert many existing stores to the new layout?"

"I just read about the big 17 percent sales increase over past year. Do you think you'll be able to keep up such fast growth this year?"

BREAKING THE ICE: SETTING THE TONE

PICK UP CUES FROM THE OFFICE.

Sure, it's a very traditional approach to start the conversation with a comment about something in the office, but it can be a good approach! Those items wouldn't be in the customer's office if he or she didn't want them displayed and talked about. The key is not to be phony. Don't say, "Oh, I love fishing!" if you've never gone fishing. Instead you could say, "Oh, you're a fisherman. I've never tried it. What's it like?" So again, you are coming from a foundation of honesty and truth. People will appreciate that. Make a comment or two, but keep it short unless the customer keeps the conversation going.

HOW MUCH SMALL TALK?

Generally you will want to keep your small talk or comments to a short sentence or two. If the buyer appears genuinely interested in developing the conversation further, go with the flow for a while. But remember how much time you have in the appointment, and be sure to save plenty of time for business. Once you feel the small talk is beginning to slow down at all (listen for fading voice tone and slower rate of speech), switch into business right away.

WHEN SMALL TALK IS NOT APPROPRIATE.

A big part of being a successful salesperson is listening. Listening to what the customer says. Listening to what the customer does not say. And "listening" to body language. Even while sharing greetings with the customer, you may very quickly get the message that this customer does not want to engage in any small talk. Maybe the customer will be curt with you. For example, when you ask, "How are you today?" they may answer with an abrupt, "Fine." Or maybe they will make it clear to you with body language that they are in a rush. Or maybe they will be verbally explicit by saying something like, "So, what have you got for me?"

Customer-Focused Selling means that you need to be responsive to the customer. If the customer is signaling to you that he or she doesn't want to engage in small talk, don't force it! Take the cue

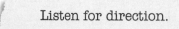

Listen for direction.

BREAKING THE ICE: SETTING THE TONE

and get right down to business. And keep your discussion as business-focused as possible. This will show customers that you appreciate their feelings, you are listening to them, and you understand that your job is to be responsive to their needs.

MAKE THE TRANSITION TO THE SALES DIALOGUE.

One of the best ways to switch to business and to start emphasizing the focus on the customer is to give a summary of what you hope to accomplish during the meeting—in other words, to outline an agenda for the meeting. You will want to have a transition such as thanking the client for getting together with you today. Importantly, you want to emphasize in a sincere way that you are here to help the customer achieve his or her goals—not just to sell your products or services. Right from the start, you want to make it clear that you are not here to waste the customer's time or just try to meet your sales quota; you are here to help the customer find solutions. For example, you might say:

"Well, Bob, I'm glad we had an opportunity to sit down today. What I would love to accomplish with you is to explore if we might be able to help you better serve the needs of your customers, or be able to help you lower costs or achieve other efficiencies."

or

"Linda, thanks for meeting with me. What I'd like to do is find out what your main concerns are in using services such as ours. Then I'd like to see if we can offer you any true advantages in these areas."

HOW TO MANAGE THE CONVERSATION WITHOUT BEING CONTROLLING.

By being the one to initiate small talk, you are also setting the stage to manage the meeting effectively. You want to try to walk the fine path of *controlling the meeting* without being a *controlling individual*. You can do this by carefully listening and reading the buyer and making transitions from greeting to small talk to talking business at the appropriate time—the time when the customer is ready to move to the next stage of conversation.

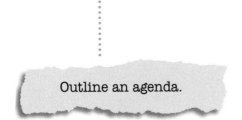

Outline an agenda.

BREAKING THE ICE: SETTING THE TONE

INTRODUCTORY APPROACHES SCENARIOS.

Janice Klesko sells for Direct Specialties, a firm that sells advertising items for companies to give to prospects and clients. She is calling on Jim Basset, the marketing director for Perpetual Technology, developer of accounting software for small businesses. Janice knows from her networking group that Perpetual is planning to attend a trade show soon and has set up the meeting through a cold call. Her objective is to set the tone of the first meeting and prepare the agenda for this call as well as future calls.

THE INEFFECTIVE APPROACH

Janice: Thanks for taking the time to see me today.

Jim: No problem, but as I told you on the phone, I only have thirty minutes, so we should get started.

Janice: Fine. I brought along some samples of our product line. Perhaps some of them can support your sales efforts at your trade show.

Jim: Could you be more specific?
Janice reaches into her sample case and pulls out a few items.

Janice: We helped another company like yours recently with these terrific coffee mugs. See how they have your company name on one side and your slogan on the other. And here, look inside. They have your logo on the bottom.

Jim: Nice, but we have several items with our logo imprinted on them already.

Janice: These keychains are very popular items, and we can get your logo and message printed inside the casing.

Jim (not very interested): These look okay.

THE EFFECTIVE APPROACH

Janice: Thanks for taking the time to see me today.

> Don't just dive into your approach!

BREAKING THE ICE: SETTING THE TONE

Jim: No problem, but as I told you on the phone, I only have thirty minutes, so we should get started.

Janice: Jim, in order to be helpful to you, I'd like to tell you about Direct Specialties and then hear a little bit about your business and your customers. Then we can talk about what the next steps might be. Is there anything else you'd like to cover?

Jim: Can you tell me about other companies like ours that you've worked with?

> **Shared information builds rapport.**

Janice: Sure. [*Pause.*] Since we haven't met before, we may not know much about Direct Specialties. We know that everybody's business is a little different, so we have specialized in custom work for the past fifteen years. We like to use this first meeting to understand more about what you do so we can tailor our recommendations to those needs. We've even set up our catalog into broad categories for different industries. (She shows catalog.) For instance, this section is designed for use by high-tech companies such as yours. What is your area of specialization?

Jim: We develop accounting software for small businesses, especially those in a client-server environment

Janice: Can you describe your primary prospects?

Jim: C.P.A.s and accounting managers for the most part. We are hoping that this trade show will expand our business to these customers.

COMMENTARY:

To effectively set the tone in the beginning of a sales call, you must acknowledge the other person, set an agenda, and give an overview of yourself and your company.

By covering these bases, you have answered all the initial questions the prospect has about you, such as: Who are you? What is this company all about? How long is this going to take? and, of course, What am I doing here?

BREAKING THE ICE: SETTING THE TONE

By setting the tone up front, you will reduce the prospect's concerns, appear organized and concise, and lay the groundwork for an effective sales call.

SALES METHODS ASSESSMENT.

This profile is designed to help you identify your strengths and weaknesses in selling and the methods you prefer to use when you sell to a client. When you finish taking the profile, calculate your score as indicated, then compare it to the explanations for the various totals. Good luck, and have fun with this segment.

TRUE FALSE

___ ___ 1. When I meet a prospective client I study his or her demeanor and dress.

___ ___ 2. To build rapport, I tell the customer about myself.

___ ___ 3. I feel comfortable proving my credibility in the first five minutes of the call.

___ ___ 4. I always make eye contact and give a warm smile when first meeting a prospective client.

___ ___ 5. To impress the client, right up front I describe how great my products and services are.

___ ___ 6. I understand the difference between open-ended and closed-ended questions, and when to use each kind.

___ ___ 7. When I need to understand a client's objectives, I ask why they are interested.

___ ___ 8. I'm familiar with and use investigative questions as much as possible.

BREAKING THE ICE: SETTING THE TONE

____ ____ 9. When it's time to give my presentation, I make sure to have numerous samples on hand.

____ ____ 10. I feel comfortable tailoring my product or service explanation to the specific buyer.

____ ____ 11. I feel comfortable controlling and managing my selling environment.

____ ____ 12. When I'm in the midst of giving my presentation, I'm aware of the physical cues from the buyer, and know how well I'm doing.

____ ____ 13. When it's time to "close the sale," doubt and fear creep in.

____ ____ 14. To get the customer to say "yes," I have many tactics memorized.

____ ____ 15. I have a good sense of what objections might arise as I sell my products or services.

____ ____ 16. When selling a new customer, I usually feel confident in managing next steps.

____ ____ 17. I never hesitate to ask for referrals.

____ ____ 18. Existing customers often lead me to new business.

____ ____ 19. I find it easy to book appointments over the phone.

____ ____ 20. I use a variety of methods to prospect for new clients.

BREAKING THE ICE: SETTING THE TONE

SCORING:

Give yourself 5 points for each true answer; 0 points for each false answer, then total your score.

IF YOU SCORED LESS THAN 40:

You are working hard for each and every sale you make. Now is the right time for you to study each area of this Anatomy of a Sale section and incorporate changes as they apply to your situation. You will see a dramatic improvement in your selling results by focusing on how to build trust and credibility and ask strategic questions. In the next chapters, take solid notes and start implementing the ideas.

IF YOU SCORED 40 THROUGH 80:

You are doing a good job of selling but are most likely feeling some up-and-down cycles. To build consistency into your sales, make sure you are exploring additional ways to fill the pipeline, look at building trust, and ask strategic questions. You may be having problems breaking the ice or finding it hard to close some particularly difficult sales. Read those parts in this Anatomy of a Sale section that cover these areas and see if you can identify strategies that will work for you. Leverage all of the hard work you have done so far and sharpen your skills.

IF YOU SCORED MORE THAN 80:

You are doing a great job! This program will serve you well as a reminder of the good things you're currently doing and as a catalyst to increase skills and add new ideas. As you are becoming more and more successful at sales, you are finding perhaps that your time is stretched. Study the chapter "Sales Coach" for ideas that can help you maximize your efforts. Build on the sales foundation you've got, and continue to go with your strengths.

CHAPTER

9

BUILDING TRUST

Trust is more than just convincing a buyer that you are honest–although this certainly is essential! You must also convince the buyer that they are not going to waste their time or money in dealing with you. Every buyer has been burned by salespeople in one way or another. You can easily lose the trust of the buyer in a second. You need to work very hard to win the trust of the buyer–and sometimes it might take a while for trust to develop. But trust is crucial for Customer-Focused Selling!

BUILDING TRUST

Trust is the foundation of every good sale. Trust means that the prospective customer believes in you. He or she must respect your product knowledge, your service standards, your sales abilities, and your approach to the business. In essence, they like you, they like how you operate, and they trust you. To build trust you must be genuine and work with the customer's interests in mind at all times.

First impressions are strong. Prospects take in all the cues, they listen to your tone, and they watch your body language. Stay calm, be centered, be fully present, and focus your energy on the prospect. Concentrate on finding common ground. Leave your ego at the door, and always begin your sales meeting focused on the prospective client. Be an observer and make connections. If you notice a picture on the wall, make an inquiry. If you've been referred, make a reference to the contact, and let the prospect respond. You build rapport by letting the prospect talk.

BUILDING TRUST IS MORE THAN DEMONSTRATING INTEGRITY.

This doesn't mean that integrity isn't important—quite the contrary! Absolute integrity is crucial! If the customer at any point has even the slightest suspicion (justified or not) that you are not being completely straightforward and honest with them, then any trust you have built will be gone! Furthermore, once trust is destroyed, it's extremely difficult if not impossible to re-create it.

The easiest way to appear to be of the highest integrity is to be of the highest integrity.

There are some salespeople who think they can effectively build trust without being 100 percent straightforward with the customer. But they are making a big mistake! Chances are, some of the people who are buying from them do so *despite them*, not because of them. Integrity is difficult to feign. Genuine sincerity is difficult

Product knowledge.

Service standards.

Sales abilities.

Approach to the business.

BUILDING TRUST

to fake. Sure, you can carefully control your words. But it's more difficult to control voice tone and body language. There is no better way to appear to be of the highest integrity than to be of the highest integrity—and to be that way for every customer, every day of the year!

You need a much broader trust than just a "I believe you are honest" trust.

It's not enough just to have the customer think you are as honest as the day is long. The customer needs to be able to trust that you are going to *do something* for him or her! And to have this trust the customer needs to be convinced of three things:

1. Trust that you *want* to help the customer
2. Trust that you *can* help the customer
3. Trust that you *will* help the customer

> Trust that you are going to *do something*.

VERY DIFFERENT TYPES OF TRUST.

At first glimpse the distinctions among these three types of trust might seem relatively trite—but they are not! They are very different. And you must win the customer's trust in all of these areas to effectively build trust with that customer. Not only that, you also must develop relatively *deep trust* in each of these areas to really get the customer to work with you. You must show that you can be trusted more than a competing salesperson.

> The trust . . . not that you are here just to push products or services.

TRUST THAT YOU *WANT* TO HELP THE CUSTOMER.

This goes beyond integrity. The trust you need to show is that you are here to help your customer find a solution first—not that you are here just to push products or services. This is the essence of Customer-Focused Selling and one of the most difficult trusts to develop. It is particularly difficult because the customer is predisposed to assume that you, like many other salespeople, want to sell as much product as fast as you can, at as high a price as you can, and rush along to the next account.

Throughout the entire sales process, from first phone call to agreement and follow-up, you need to remember that the customer may constantly be watching for any signs that you are just trying to dump products or services on them that don't meet their needs. Ways to retain this trust are discussed throughout the entire book, but among the most important are continually focusing on the customer's needs, and, when you do talk about how your products can deliver solutions, to make sure the focus remains more on the product benefits and how the products can provide solutions rather than dwelling on the product features themselves.

TRUST THAT YOU CAN HELP THE CUSTOMER.

Good intentions and good abilities are two very different things! Too many salespeople try to emphasize, right off the bat, a particular product feature or service feature to show that they can help the customer. This approach may show that the product or service may help the customer, but it doesn't show that the salesperson can help the customer. It also makes the customer "protective" about talking to or meeting with the salesperson. He or she may be thinking, "Do I really have to talk with or meet with this salesperson? I just know that they are going to rant and rave about how great their product is and waste my time."

This is why it is so important to develop rapport as fast as possible with a customer, both on the phone and in person. You need to show that you are going to provide useful information, not just trumped-up sales points. You need to show that it will be worthwhile to listen to you, not just because your product has a "hot" feature or a special price, but because you are going to help them by providing information the buyer wants. You need to show the buyer that you are not going to cloud the delivery of information with a lot of "noise" or sales puffery about how great your product is or how much better it is than a competing product.

Ideally you want to give customers the feeling right away that you are going to explore their needs and work with them to find a

> You need to show that you are going to provide useful information, not just trumped-up sales points.

BUILDING TRUST

solution. This may sound hokey and be a difficult claim for a customer to believe, especially when you are first talking over the phone or for the first couple of minutes in person. But at the very least, you can initially come across as someone who can provide the information the customer needs without the "sales baloney."

As you have more time with the customer, you can explain how you helped other customers and by analogy imply how you may be able to help this customer. As the relationship develops further, you can show your customers that you can help them by exploring their concerns and suggesting appropriate solutions.

> Building trust begins
> by being very
> customer-focused.

TRUST THAT YOU *WILL* HELP THE CUSTOMER.

Just because you want to help the customer and just because you can help the customer doesn't mean that you *will* help the customer. How often have you bought something from a salesperson and then found it difficult to get help from them afterward? It happens all too often. Usually the salesperson wants to help and can help but is too wrapped up in the next sale or just doesn't get around to it.

Building trust that you will help your customer begins by being very focused on the customer during the sales presentation. I was recently at a restaurant with a friend from out of town. The waitress appeared at our table and asked if we wanted to hear the dinner specials, paused, and then began to list them—not even hearing my friend ask, "Could we order drinks now?" She wanted to give good service. She could hear. But she was too focused on her own presentation of the specials to focus on her customers.

DON'T LET SELLING BLOCK YOUR VIEW OF THE CUSTOMER.

Especially in the early phases of customer contact, it's very easy to fall into the trap of giving a few "canned words." You may not think of them as "canned words," but we all tend to fall into habits, and after doing the same sales presentation again and again it is crucial to fight the tendency to focus on your presentation and instead focus on the customer. If you don't listen to your customers, you are not showing them that you are going to help them.

"HOMEWORK" IS A GREAT WAY TO BUILD THE TRUST THAT YOU WILL HELP THE CUSTOMER.

Work that you do for the customer outside of the sales presentation is a great way to build the trust that you will make the effort to help the customer. And real "effort" is what this third kind of trust is about. Just about all salespeople will make the effort while they are with the customer and interacting one-on-one. Most salespeople will respond to specific customer requests. But the way you can really separate yourself from the pack is to go a step or two farther—to suggest to the customer how you might be able to help outside of the sales meeting, or simply to provide the customer with information or help you found on your own initiative.

"HOMEWORK" BEGINS BEFORE THE FIRST SALES CALL.

Before the first sales call you need to find out at least the basic information about your customer. Why does this make a difference? Because the customer does not want to spend his or her time telling you the basic background of the company. And by coming to that first meeting with some knowledge of the customer's firm, you are already showing the customer that you are willing to put in the extra effort to help him or her.

KEEP THE "HOMEWORK" RELEVANT TO THE CUSTOMER.

The key is not showing the customer just how much effort you are putting into his or her account, but that you are focusing on the customer's needs. For example, rather than handing customers a boring statistical industry overview that you know they won't read, you'd be better to give them a clipping from a newspaper about the customer's hobby. At least you are showing that you understand the customer. But it's even better if you can provide the customer with information or services that will help his or her business.

"Homework" builds trust.

Relevant information is what matters.

BUILDING TRUST

> Building trust requires work.

Here's some of the "homework" you may be able to do to help the customer:

- Work with other departments at your company to provide information for the customer.
- Develop customized solutions for the customer.
- Work with relevant people at your firm to get the best pricing options for the customer.
- If your customer is a reseller, work with your marketing department to give the customer as much marketing support as possible.
- Work with your service department to be sure the customer gets excellent service.
- Create simple visual papers or slides or computer presentations that show how the product or service answers the customer's concerns.
- Provide the customer with industry information he or she may be interested in.
- Give the customer prompt notice of relevant new product information.
- Provide information and referrals for products and services that work in a complementary manner with your product or service.
- Develop customized references the customer may talk to whose situation is highly similar to the customer's.

While more complex products and services naturally lend themselves more easily to the opportunity to do homework, often with simpler products and services you can find ways to add value by extra homework. For example, once my uncle was selling shoes to a dealer who catered to low budget consumers. He was interested in a particular line of shoes, but he hesitated to buy them because they seemed too bland. So my uncle thought about it for a while and then proposed that the shoes be outfitted with multicolored shoelaces.

BUILDING TRUST

A HIGH LEVEL OF TRUST IS CRUCIAL FOR CUSTOMER-FOCUSED SELLING.

To get customers to the point where they work side by side with you and share their concerns and desired solutions and work toward a solution requires a very high level of trust. It requires a much higher level of trust than the trust required just to listen to a short sales pitch, for example. And today's customer is tired of listening to sales pitches.

Each product and each service has its sales points, and after a while the buyer has heard them all—and they seem to drone on like a broken record. This is one reason why, if you can get customers to give you their time and to give you their trust, you have a tremendous chance of success if you are able to work side by side with them in developing a solution to their problems. Few other salespeople are going to get to this position with the customer—they are too busy just trying to make the sale.

Instant trust.

HOW TO JUMP-START BUILDING TRUST.

It's impossible to develop *deep* trust instantly. Building trust takes time. But you can jump-start this process if you share common acquaintances. Particularly if it's a friend close to both of you, the trust each of you has with that friend can help accelerate building trust in the new relationship. Any common affiliations can help build trust. So can any common interests. These are reasons why selling by referrals or references can be so powerful—because you don't have to start building trust completely from ground zero.

YOU CAN BUILD TRUST WITH PEOPLE YOU HAVE ONLY MET BY COLD-CALLING.

You're not going to achieve a deep trust initially, but by following the right steps you can slowly and solidly build an increasingly meaningful trust. Even at the beginning of contact with the customer, you need to try to keep in mind the three kinds of trust you need to build: the trust that you *want* to help the customer; the trust that you *can* help the customer; and the trust that you *will* help the customer.

Three types of trust.

BUILDING TRUST

And right from the beginning, you should try to show a balance among the three trusts. If you scream at the customer about your latest price special or hottest feature, you are only showing that you can help the customer. But you are making the mistake of focusing on the product, not on the customer. If, on the other hand, you build some rapport with the customer and inquire about his or her needs, then you are showing that you want to help the customer. In an initial phone call it may be awkward or it may alienate the customer if you start to inquire about his or her needs. Instead you may need to focus on presenting yourself as willing to help the customer by sounding enthusiastic and pleasant and professional—without appearing overbearing or threatening.

Proving to customers very quickly that you will help them is important, too. One way to do this is by showing them that you've done some research about their company. Another way is by telling them about other, similar people or companies you have successfully delivered solutions for.

> Talking without words.

THE POWER OF THE UNSPOKEN WORD.

Building trust and credibility in face-to-face communications entails three elements: verbal, vocal, and visual. The verbal is the actual words you use in a sales presentation. The vocal is your voice, which is how you speak, your tone of voice, your pace. And then your visual is your body language. What are your facial expressions telling the customer? What are your hand gestures telling the customer? How do you look? Are you slouched? Are you standing up straight? So you have all three elements, and when you're face-to-face, an individual builds trust and credibility by taking in all three.

> Body language can
> build trust.

Let me give you numbers about the relative impact of these three elements. Most people guess absolutely way off, but the numbers are based on a study by Dr. Albert Morabian at UCLA. His study showed that trust is based 7 percent on the actual words you use; 38 percent on the tone and pace of speech; and an incredible 55 percent on nonspoken body language!

In the chapter "Breaking the Ice" in this book I explained the importance of each little step (such as shaking hands and saying "hello") to help start out with a strong, trusting impression. But it's important to remember that these steps can make a big difference for the first few subsequent meetings as well. Especially when you are dealing with busy corporate buyers who see many salespeople every day, you probably won't stand out as clearly in their mind as they might in your mind. This is why you must be careful to build the trust in each early meeting. Be careful your body language is right on the mark (shake hands firmly and don't get too comfortable or start slouching when sitting in their office), and be sure your voice tone is warm and genuine but not prematurely "too" familiar.

WHAT REALLY MATTERS ON THE INITIAL PHONE CALL.

Like it or not, what you say on the phone matters relatively little! Doesn't this sound crazy? Within reason you can say just about anything and it isn't going to make the big difference!

So what is going to make the big difference? Body language! Body language on the phone? Yes! The tone and other qualities of your voice are your body language when you are on the phone. Fully 85 percent of the trust you convey (or don't convey) on the phone comes from vocal (voice tone and rate of speech) and a mere 15 percent from the actual words you choose!

One of the fastest ways to build trust or to close out any possibility of building trust is with your voice!

If you have all the right words in your phone dialogue (such as a pleasant greeting and a good story of how you helped a similar customer) but your voice sounds insincere, you're not going to get very far.

On the other hand, if you have a relatively weak phone dialogue (such as immediately jumping into a product pitch) but your voice sounds sincere, and you sound like you really want to help the customer, you'll be a lot more likely to get the appointment and start making the sale.

The "secret" of phone selling.

BUILDING TRUST

And, of course, the right words, mixed in with great voice tone, are the most powerful combination.

How much practice should you give to voice tone and body language?

If you're like most salespeople, you spend a lot of time thinking about *what* you're going to say on the phone and when first meeting customers, but little thought as to how you're going to say it. Yet in building trust, what really matters is *how* you're going to say it.

It may seem foolish to you to practice voice tone or to practice body language. But think about how you react when you don't like someone's voice tone. Think about how when you first meet some people something seems to "click" and with other people at first greeting something doesn't seem to "click." This may very well be caused by effective versus ineffective body language. Simulate the first stages of your sales meeting with others, such as friends or coworkers. Ask what they think of your body language. Make practice phone calls. Tape them and listen: Is that how you would want someone to sound if that person were calling you?

MAKING THE "CHEMISTRY" HAPPEN.

With some customers you have that mutually warm feeling that the chemistry is there and with others you just know that even if you have a workable relationship, the chemistry is missing. Some people feel that chemistry is luck or happenstance, or that you have to be of the same sex or have gone to the same schools or have to be about the same age. I'm convinced that these are seldom true.

DEVELOPING "CHEMISTRY" IS NOT LUCK

I am convinced that you can develop good "chemistry" with just about any customer. It's not luck. It's not personality. It's a skill you can develop.

Developing "chemistry" is about timing.

The most crucial skill in developing chemistry is timing—know when to get closer to your customer and when to hold back; know when to make small talk and when to get to business; know how much distance you have to keep from your customer.

> Making relationships "click."

BUILDING TRUST

How one word can make or break the "chemistry"

Seventeen years ago, I was invited for a job interview at a prestigious management consulting firm. Upon entering the office of the first partner who was going to interview me, I saw a large painting of a sailboat behind his desk. I wanted to show this man right away that I was very much at ease in his presence and that we had a common interest in sailing. So I asked, "I bet you're a big sailor?" Although he didn't comment or really pause, the slightest twitch on his face told me that I had just lost any possible "chemistry" between us by being too familiar too quickly with my use of the word "big." We discussed his sailboat in a perfunctory way, but I know that I lost a wonderful chance to start this interview with some fun, enthusiastic discussion of sailing. If only I had said "I bet you're a sailor?" and left out the "big" word. My problem wasn't just in the word choice, it also was my mindset—I was assuming too much familiarity too quickly.

At the same time, however, you don't want to be too distant. In fact, you want to walk the fine line of being as "close" to the client as you can without risking alienating the customer by being too close, too quickly. One key is listening carefully to your customers' body language and voice tone, not just their words. When you are discussing a non-business topic and see their eyes begin to look away from you more, or hear their voice begin to lose enthusiasm, then get back to business quickly. When in doubt, it's better not to risk being too familiar.

As you get to know the customer better, you will find that even the most rigid person will eventually begin to open up with you some. But everyone has their own pace for "getting to know" other people, and often it is different from one situation to the next.

The more experience you have selling, the better you will become about reading people and determining how quickly you can act more relaxed and familiar around the customer, and you will know when it is, and isn't, appropriate to discuss non-business topics. However, the more you pay attention and explicitly notice the small steps that build "chemistry" between you and your customers, the

How familiar should you be?

BUILDING TRUST

more quickly you will be able to judge when you can act more familiar in new customer relationships.

TRY TO DEVELOP A RELATIONSHIP MORE AS A CONSULTANT THAN AS A SALESPERSON.

When seeking to build trust with a customer, try to envision yourself as a consultant who is trying to find solutions for the customer, rather than as a salesperson trying to sell a product. If you can get the customer to trust you as someone he or she can look to for help in tackling problems or finding solutions, you will be far ahead of your competition in getting the sale; in fact, it will be like having no competition at all!

A BUILDING-TRUST SALES SCENARIO.

In this scenario, Dan, a sales representative for Medco, a medical supplies company, is visiting Cynthia, a purchasing agent for Unicom, a manufacturer of medical devices. Dan sells a number of supplies such as latex gloves, face masks, and small tools to companies. The objective of this visit is to build rapport with the prospect, which will create an environment for an effective sales call. In the ineffective scenario, Dan's appearance is ruffled, he makes poor eye contact, he has trouble finding his materials, he does not smile enough, and hurries through the presentation. In the effective scenario, he takes the time to get to know Cynthia and establishes a solid rapport based on identifying what her needs are at Unicom.

THE INEFFECTIVE APPROACH

Dan: Uh, hi. I'm Dan Sandberg from Medco Products.

Cynthia: Oh, yes. Dan. I'm Cynthia Fenn. Welcome to Unicom.
Dan pulls out his binder and rummages around in it. He brings out a thick catalog and puts it on her desk.

Dan: I don't think you've ever done business with us. As you can see from our catalog, we carry just about everything a company like yours needs. [He starts flipping through the pages.] Here we have latex gloves, including the new 14-96ML models. And then we have a whole line of glass containers from seven different manufacturers.

Cynthia (looking bored): Uh-huh. Well, actually we're pretty well set on those types of items. We're really looking for more specialized products.

Dan doesn't pick up on her hint.

Dan: Well, Medco has been around for almost fifteen years and during that time we've picked up nearly every good line around. I'm sure that whatever you're looking for is in this catalog. Name a product.

Cynthia (a little annoyed): Okay. One thing we need is a small autoclave.

Dan: Autoclave, autoclave. [He flips through catalog.] Here we go. Now, this unit comes from United. I just had one of these installed in Freeman. It worked out great. I was able to get them a terrific deal on it, we installed the unit, and they were up and running in under a week. In fact, now they're looking to get another unit, the new Model 10/P, 504. Are you familiar with that model?

Cynthia (perturbed): Well, yes. But actually we need the small-size autoclave.

Dan: Hey, no problem. I'm sure we have them in stock.

THE EFFECTIVE APPROACH

Dan: Hi, Cynthia. Dan Sandberg from Medco. Thanks so much for taking the time to meet with me.

Cynthia: No problem. Have a seat.

Dan: That is an impressive timepiece. Worthington?

Cynthia (formal but friendly): No, it's a Gardington. What can I do for you?

Dan: Well, first I'd like to know a little bit about Unicom and you. How long have you been with the company?

Cynthia: I'm coming up on three years now.

> Jumping into a sales pitch too soon doesn't build trust.

> Small talk and common interests build trust.

BUILDING TRUST

Dan: Have you always been in the medical business?

Cynthia: Sort of. I worked for Bay Harbor labs in their testing division. Then I heard about this opportunity and came over to Unicom.

Dan: Did you work with Chuck Wendell at Bay Harbor? He's been a good customer of ours.

Cynthia: I didn't work for him directly but he's been there forever and is well respected.

Dan: He certainly is. I think Medco has been helping him with his supply needs for about thirteen years now, though I've only handled that account for the past four. [He makes the transition.] I'm interested in finding out how we might be able to help Unicom. Tell me a little bit about your current needs.

Cynthia: There are actually several areas in which we're looking for vendors. In particular, I'm looking for someone who carries small autoclaves.

COMMENTARY:

Be careful not to go headlong into a sales pitch for you products. Take the time to get to know the person on the other side of the desk. By asking questions about the other party and business, you're able to gather information that will be useful in positioning the right product or service. Dan is able to build trust and credibility here, as it is uncovered that he has been doing business with a third party whom Cynthia knows and respects.

10

UNDERSTANDING THE BUYER

Just as every buyer has different needs from services and products, every buyer has different style. They each have their own unique style of communicating, of listening, and of interacting with others. But as each buyer is different, buyers can generally be grouped into some broad categories for the purpose of trying to identify their styles and how best to sell to them. Some buyers may share characteristics from more than one category. The more you understand a buyer's style and communicate with them the way they want to be communicated with, the better your chance of getting the sale.

UNDERSTANDING THE BUYER

"Understanding the buyer" means being aware of the person at the other side of the desk. And being aware of that person can function on two different levels. In Customer-Focused Selling, the process dictates that you be aware of the customer's world.

A good part of understanding this "world" is explored throughout this book, most of it addressing how the salesperson should go about gaining insight into the business problems and pressures as seen through the customer's eyes.

However, this addresses only one part of the equation.

The second dimension to selling is understanding buyers through their personal style of social interaction.

This is equally important, for understanding buyers means understanding them on both a business and a personal plane. The message here is that to fully understand buyers, you must not only look at their business concerns but also at their social style. By understanding the color of the tinted glasses through which they view the world, you can gain valuable insights into how they will respond to your presentation.

Anticipating this, you can design your sales presentation to take their bias into account and thus greatly increase your chances for success.

The beauty of this approach is that you don't have to be a psychiatrist to utilize this concept. Ever since Carl Jung, research has been going on to gain an understanding of what drives the different personality styles. Understanding personality "types" has now become so common that TV is filled with sitcoms that continue to sensitize us to the different motivational nuances of people.

Adapt to the buyer.

UNDERSTANDING THE BUYER

Understanding people's styles means understanding their hot buttons.

With just a modest orientation on the various social types, you will find them quite recognizable.

And you will find that you can use this awareness to understand:

- How they define value
- Their "hot" buttons
- How they make decisions
- The best approach to use to gain agreement

No one sells in a vacuum. Each transaction, each interaction in the process of sales takes place between two different parties, really between two different people. In Customer-Focused Selling the salesperson's drive and focus should go beyond the obvious of understanding the sale in terms of what it does for the customer. Going farther, Customer-Focused Selling also means understanding the buyer's personality style, and then taking this into account when trying to work toward the close.

The study of various personalities and their characteristics generally falls under the umbrella of "social styles." And in selling, understanding the thought processes of people gives you a real edge against the competition if you use this knowledge to best position your product or service.

Understanding the implications of the various social styles enables you to anticipate the natural objections the potential buyer is predisposed to raise in the course of your presentation. You will also find yourself better armed in knowing what sort of things buyers will be looking for that will make them comfortable with proceeding, and even what approach to use when trying to get their commitment.

Understanding people's styles means understanding their hot buttons.

By knowing the normal thought patterns of different personalities, you are able to anticipate their reactions because you have inside information on how they like to be approached and what they're looking for. This additional dimension, outside of the customer's usual business parameters, really helps in giving you an understanding of what makes the buyer tick.

UNDERSTANDING THE BUYER

You can also use this process to analyze your own social style.
By understanding your predisposition and social style, you can develop
some insight and guidelines for adapting your approach to be most
effective in dealing with other social styles. And this will make you even
more successful in your sales presentations, as they can work at two
levels—addressing both the buyer's business and personal priorities.

Social styles are easily discernible through observable behaviors.

Fortunately, there are many telltale signs and obvious clues to
the various social styles, so that they are quite easily recognized. By
training yourself to look for these signs—something as obvious as the
pace of the buyer's speech—you can leverage this knowledge to
become much more effective in your sales presentations.

> There are many telltale signs
> and obvious clues to the
> various social styles.

SOCIAL STYLES

THERE ARE FOUR SOCIAL STYLES:
- Driver
- Analytical
- Amiable
- Expressive

THE DRIVER:

People who exhibit the driver social style are generally very
controlling in their approach to others. They are very bottom-line-
oriented and want to talk about results. They speak in bullets and
tend to be very forceful. They lean forward with their body and in
their language. They're extremely direct.

When you're looking from a sales perspective, this type of
buyer tends to be the most challenging because they don't monkey
around. They can also be the easiest buyer for the same reason.
Often their directness makes it easier to have your proposal judged
on its merits, with little distraction caused by extraneous relationship or political factors.

Driver personalities are, by far, the most difficult ones to build
rapport with, as they are usually all business.

> Driver personalities are,
> by far, the most difficult
> ones to build rapport
> with, as they are usually
> all business.

UNDERSTANDING THE BUYER

How to handle this style:
- Clearly define your purchase justification.
- Use facts and figures to document your case.
- Move briskly through your sales presentation.
- Let them be the boss.

THE ANALYTICAL:

The analytical personality is the typical thinker. They tend to be very facts- and figures-oriented. They tend to be more systematic and thorough in their decision-making. Usually they are quite reserved and not too outgoing.

During your sales presentation they will tend to avoid eye contact. The traditional approach of looking the customer in the eye will backfire here, as this direct approach will make them look away and withdraw their attention. So understand it isn't you, it's a style difference.

The key word here is "thinker." They're very process-oriented. They are much less talkative and much more thoughtful than others. They're going to try to analyze everything you tell them. When asked a question, the interim pause will be longer than usual as they take time to formulate their answer before speaking. Analytical people think with their mouth closed; other styles think with their mouth open.

How to handle this style:
- Be very accurate and precise in your supporting documentation.
- Support your case with facts.
- Move slowly through your presentation.
- Don't be aggressive.

THE AMIABLE:

"Relationship" is the key word for people with an amiable social style. They're very cooperative, friendly, easygoing, nice people. They don't like conflict and do not respond well to any pressure.

From the sales perspective, the interesting thing is that getting the buyer's attention is often the easiest thing. But getting them to

> Be accurate, precise and well-documented with analytical types.

> Slowly build a relationship with the amiable type.

UNDERSTANDING THE BUYER

make a decision is often the most difficult. They are very susceptible to "buyer's remorse," wherein their unease with making a decision will cause them to change their mind shortly after you've left the office. It is not uncommon with them to get a voice mail message two hours after getting their commitment, saying in a tiny voice, "Hello, I've decided that we're not going to go forward. Thank you very much and please don't call back." They say yes, yes, yes when you're in front of them, but find it too awkward to tell you what they really feel, "I'm not ready, and I haven't made the decision yet."

You should be more cautious selling to this style of individual. Always proceed slowly and cautiously through your sales presentation. You're going to want to take a few minutes and chat first, giving them attention and making them feel important, before proceeding.

How to handle this style:
- Give plenty of attention.
- Proceed slowly; give them time to talk.
- Make them feel comfortable with guarantees.
- Take the time to build a personal relationship first.

THE EXPRESSIVE:

Expressive people tend to be extremely outgoing. They tend to be very conceptual in how they think. They are big-picture operators with lots of body language and facial expressions. They like to tell stories and be onstage.

When presenting to them, sit back and become a very good listener. Let them pontificate about everything that's important to them. Be careful not to go into too much detail, as they will tend to get easily bored. Rather, appeal to them in terms of how you are addressing their concerns about the big picture, and how your product or service will have a tremendous impact on their business.

How to handle this style:
- React positively to their ideas.
- Be an interested audience.
- Provide them with testimonials.
- Give a fast-paced presentation.

Talk big-picture with the expressive types.

UNDERSTANDING THE BUYER

Change course to stay
with the buyer.

THE FOUR TYPES IN BRIEF

Generally speaking:

- Driver and analytical people tend to be task-oriented.
- Amiable and expressive people tend to be people-oriented.
- Analytical and amiable people tend to be slow-paced.
- Driver and expressive tend to be fast-paced.

By developing an ease with identifying these four unique types, and by remembering how the different styles approach buying decisions, you will be able to improve your sales successes dramatically.

READING THE BUYER'S BODY LANGUAGE.

Being aware of the buyer's body language throughout the presentation is a good means of assessing how your presentation is being received. Even with considerable preparation, and assuming you have tailored your presentation to incorporate the buyer's social style, you can be sure that your sales meeting will seldom stay on the charted course. Being aware of the feedback you're receiving from the customer in the form of body-language signals can be crucial in reading his or her concerns and in bringing the sale to the point of commitment.

If you pay appropriate attention to all the signs and signals that are continuously being sent as you progress through your sales presentation, you will be better able to do anything from addressing those "advertised" concerns, to picking up the pace if you begin losing the buyer through boredom. A good working knowledge of body language is crucial in staying tuned in to the buyer's interests.

Let's review some of the common signals we already know if we stop to consider them:

HEAD AND CHIN:

Positive:

- Nodding shows acceptance, agreement, positive response.
- Chin held level indicates confidence, equality.

Negative:

- Chin tilted down conveys shyness, lack of confidence.
- Chin tilted up conveys arrogant, "know it all" attitude.
- Scratching the head indicates confusion. puzzlement.

UNDERSTANDING THE BUYER

LEGS AND FEET:

Positive:

- Set comfortably apart, with little movement, shows confidence and being at ease

Negative:

- Tapping and shaking feet, lots of movement, indicate impatience, nervousness.

EYES:

Positive:

- Direct eye contact shows attention and respect.
- Eyes widening shows surprise.
- Sparkling eyes shows interest, excitement, happiness.

Negative:

- Darting eyes show nervousness, shyness, self-consciousness
- Staring at walls, ceiling, floor indicates apathy, disgust.

SMILE:

Positive:

- Smile shows friendliness, approval, warmth.

Negative:

- Nonsmiling conveys seriousness, reservation, hesitation.
- Yawning indicates boredom.
- Frown shows anger, disappointment, disbelief.

HANDS:

Positive:

- Open palms demonstrate honesty, sharing.
- "Steepling" of hands shows importance of message, honesty.

Negative:

- Clasped hands demonstrate withholding, dislike.
- Pointing fingers appears aggressive and threatening.
- Hands on hips seems aggressive.

As you can see from these listings, it is almost impossible for anyone engaged in conversation not to send body-language signals about how he or she is responding to the items being discussed.

By making a conscious effort to understand buyers through both their social style and body-language signals, it is very possible

> Control your eye contact.

> Watch what you do with your hands.

UNDERSTANDING THE BUYER

to dramatically increase your ability to "reach" the potential customer. This intangible quality results in your being perceived as more accessible and less distant, and it gives you a distinct advantage in building trusting relationships.

As you strive to build your working partnerships with potential accounts, it is key that you develop your image as positive, interested, and nonthreatening. Responding appropriately to buyers' social style, and using their body language to stay attuned to their thoughts, can be key ingredients in making this happen—and a major boost in helping you achieve higher sales.

11

SELLING
BY
ASKING
QUESTIONS

Y ou're going to get a lot further in selling by asking questions than by making statements. Asking questions builds a two-way dialogue. Dialogues build trust. Dialogues help you find out what the buyer wants. Dialogues help make the buyer more comfortable with you. Dialogues discourage you from making long-winded pitches about how great your product is.

SELLING BY ASKING QUESTIONS

Conventional selling essentially means the "dog and pony show": dazzle them with your brilliance . . . show them everything you've got . . . tell them why your stuff is the greatest in the universe! But Customer-Focused Selling means holding off on even discussing your products and services until later. First find out what the customer wants to accomplish.

STRATEGIC QUESTIONS ARE A CRUCIAL PART OF CUSTOMER-FOCUSED SELLING.

A critical part of every sale lies in your ability to ask strategic questions that will help you accurately assess the customer's situation. You'll need to ask at least several open-ended questions (i.e., questions that aren't answerable with a "yes" or a "no")—exploratory queries to gather the information you need. Use high-gain questions that start with words such as "describe," "explain," "tell," or "share" to elicit a useful response. Follow-up with closed-ended questions that begin with words such as "do," "does," "is," or "have" as you zero in on specific information or confirm with the customer a summary of your understanding of his or her needs.

GOOD QUESTIONS REQUIRE PREPARATION.

Asking good questions is not something that happens by chance. Your questions should be preplanned, stimulating, and thought-provoking. But listen to what the customer is telling you, and revise your preplanned questions accordingly. If your questions don't sound intelligent and stimulating or if the customer can't readily see that the questions might help find solutions, your sales call could be very short indeed. So make sure you give some good thought to what questions will not only sound good but also will help lead you to suggesting solutions for the customer. By asking strategic questions

Ask high-gain questions.

SELLING BY ASKING QUESTIONS

> Just keeping the customer focused on you is half the battle.

you'll truly understand the prospect's needs and know exactly how to position your product or service as the best solution.

QUESTIONS KEEP THE CUSTOMER INVOLVED IN THE SALES PROCESS.

Any time you are seeing a customer or calling a customer on the phone you want to start with a few easy questions, perhaps starting even with just "How are you?" and progressing into some small talk and then into more specific business questions. Even the small-talk questions and the "How are you?" questions are important because they get the customer involved in the conversation. So often in sales calls the customer never pays attention to the phone call, his or her mind wanders, and the salesperson doesn't have the slightest chance of getting the sale. And this is important to keep in mind throughout the sales process: Questions keep the customer involved. And questions focusing on the customer keep the focus where it should be.

Woody Allen made the famous comment that a lot of success in life is just showing up. Well, a lot of selling is just showing up *and* getting the customer to keep paying attention to you. Smart questions ensure that the customer is paying attention!

QUESTIONS GIVE YOU A REASON FOR BEING THERE.

In today's world information, product information is more plentiful than ever. There are product catalogs, product brochures, independent reviews, studies, and surveys. Customers have less and less need for general information about your product or service. They can usually get and refer to general information at their leisure. But by asking questions, you can work with them to develop a customized solution to their needs, or at the very least a customized explanation of how your product or service can suit their needs. But you can't deliver this solution or deliver this explanation until you find out what their needs are.

> Questions enable you to help the buyer more than a printed catalog could.

CUSTOMERS HAVE DIFFERENT NEEDS AND CONCERNS

It never ceases to amaze me how two very similar companies buying very similar products or services more often than not have

SELLING BY ASKING QUESTIONS

some significantly different concerns or issues. This doesn't mean there isn't any similarity in their concerns–sure there is! But there are almost always enough differences that a canned presentation is going to miss their primary concerns.

Too many salespeople lose sales because they assume that their customers have essentially the same concerns. But as today's buyers become increasingly sophisticated and as our world becomes increasingly complex, the needs of each buyer more and more demanding.

For example, I see too many salespeople, who when selling products to large retailers and wholesalers give too much focus to how well the product is going to sell. Today's retailers and wholesalers usually have many highly sellable products to choose from in each category, and hence their concerns might be much more complex. Their concerns might include: Will your co-op advertising allowance be applicable to my merchandising programs? Can I have an exclusive on any product? What's your return policy regarding defective merchandise? How fast can you restock us? And so on.

IF YOU DON'T ASK, YOU'LL NEVER KNOW.

If you don't start asking questions, you may never know what your customer–or lost prospect–was really interested in. For example, if you emphasize feature "A" in your presentation, your prospect is not going to say, "I would have bought your product if you gave emphasis to feature 'B.'" Instead, your prospect is going to buy from the salesperson who chooses to emphasize feature "B." But with Customer-Focused Selling and asking questions, you don't have to leave to chance that you will choose the right features or products to emphasize; instead, you will know which to emphasize because you will have asked. The independent publishers' rep sales scenarios in this chapter further exemplify the importance of asking questions first.

GOOD QUESTIONS CAN BUILD RAPPORT.

Good questions, asked properly, can help you build rapport with the customer. If you already have some rapport, intelligent questions can strengthen that rapport. But your questions need to sound intelli-

> Questions allow you to best focus your presentation.

SELLING BY ASKING QUESTIONS

gent and the customer needs to be able to feel that the salesperson is going to help find a solution.

ASKING QUESTIONS IS NOT WITHOUT RISK.

Asking the wrong questions can alienate the buyer or even end the sales meeting. This is why it is important to think out, in advance, the questions you want to ask—although you need to remain flexible in changing the questions if the feedback from the customer so dictates.

INVESTIGATIVE QUESTIONS.

To get the ball rolling, you need to ask investigative questions that get at the why, the motive, the reasons. You need to get at the goals or objectives your customer is trying to achieve. You need to find out what strategies or tactics he or she hopes to use to achieve those objectives. You need to find out what concerns or issues the customer has. You need to find out what are the "hot buttons" that are going to be of paramount concern is the customer's decision-making process.

To summarize, you are trying to get inside the customer's mind to truly understand what is driving that person's thinking process and to get the information that will enable you to help him or her.

But you've got to get inside the customer's mind unobtrusively! To do so, you must be careful how you ask questions and even how you phrase the questions.

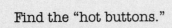

Find the "hot buttons."

AVOID USING "WHY" TO BEGIN A QUESTION

If you use the word "why" to ask a question people become very defensive. The tendency is to hear unspoken words such as "Why are you doing it this way?" or "Why don't you try other approaches?" Often there is a tendency to want to reply to a "why" question by saying "It's none of your business."

You still need to ask "why" kinds of questions, but you need to do so without using the dangerous "why" word.

SELLING BY ASKING QUESTIONS

HOW TO WORD INVESTIGATIVE QUESTIONS

To avoid a threatening word such as "why," you need to ask the same kind of question with less threatening wording. Instead, use words such as "explain," "describe," "share," or "explore." Also remember that there is probably a reason why the customer agreed to allow you to spend time with him or her. Maybe there is an issue with a current vendor; maybe there is some other kind of change under way.

EXAMPLES OF GOOD INVESTIGATIVE QUESTIONS

You really need to create questions that will best fit not only your product or service but also each selling situation. The extra effort spent developing good questions will go a long way in helping to find the best solution for your customer; in helping to explain it to them; and ultimately in helping to make the sale.

Here are some sample investigative questions to start the questioning process:

"Could you explain to me what some of your primary objectives are for this year?"

"Could you describe to me for a minute what you see the company looking like six months from now?"

"Could you share with me your main concerns in this product area?"

"Could you explain to me how the service you are seeking ideally would meet your needs?"

"Could you explore with me how you envision an outside service interacting with your department?"

"I remember you mentioned some problems that you were having in this area. Could you share with me any issues you are particularly concerned with?"

"Could you share for me what characteristics you would most want from your service provider?"

Good questions should not stump the customer, but they should make the customer think.

> Don't interrogate, but do investigate.

> Good questions to ask.

SELLING BY ASKING QUESTIONS

How to get useful answers.

A LAYERED QUESTIONING APPROACH.

Sometimes the first response you get from a customer may be too general or too standard, in which case you may need to dig deeper (into another layer) and ask another question to elaborate upon the answer to the previous question. Here's an example:

Sales rep (selling marketing consulting service): What is the vision for your marketing programs?

Decision-maker: "Oh, well, our vision is to be the best in the industry." (Standard nonthinking answer.)

Sales rep: "Could you describe to me what that looks like to you?"

Decision-maker: "I guess specifically we want our name to be widely perceived as at least one of the top brands in the field in terms of market share and also in terms of quality." (Now this answer begins to give the sales rep more specific information.)

USE CLOSED-ENDED QUESTIONS SPARINGLY.

A closed-ended question generally elicits a simple answer such as "yes" or "no." Examples are "What are your company's total yearly sales?" or "Do you have any plants overseas?" Use closed-ended questions sparingly—they tend to bring the conversational flow to a halt.

There are times when you need to get specific information and closed-ended questions are unavoidable, but since they are such con-versation stoppers, you should try to follow-up a close-ended ques-tion with an open-ended question.

AVOID CHOICE QUESTIONS.

Choice questions (such as "Do you use electric or oil heat?") are like closed-ended questions in that they elicit a short response and can stop the flow of the conversation. Use them sparingly as well.

START WITH BROADER QUESTIONS, NOT NARROWER QUESTIONS.

It's possible to ask a lot of questions and still not engage in Customer-Focused Selling. For example, you don't want to start out

SELLING BY ASKING QUESTIONS

with strictly product- or service-related questions such as "How many do you use?" or "What kind do you usually order?" or "Who are you buying from now?" These questions make it sound as if you are just interested in trying to figure out how much money you can make if you land the account!

Notice that these questions tend to be closed-ended and tend to have specific, short answers. This is the worst approach. This is what the "other" product-pushing salespeople do.

Instead, you want to be getting the broader perspective. If you're selling to a small department of a big corporation, that doesn't mean you need to get a fix on the overall corporate direction. But you want to start from the broader perspective that is relevant to the decision-maker you are meeting with.

THE KIND OF ANSWERS YOU WANT TO ELICIT.

Ideally with open-ended questions, customers will go on and on with their answer and tell you what's really on their mind. Often it won't be the specific answer to your question that gives the information that will help you solve a customer's need, but a follow-up comment the customer makes. Here's an example:

Salesperson: "Are there any paramount objectives or major challenges for your product group this year?"

Customer: "Well, we are supposed to achieve a 7 percent sales increase . . . but with the new competition we're facing from a much larger firm, any increase at all is going to be quite a challenge."

As soon as you hear information that may be useful, you need to be thinking, "How can my product or service help in this newly competitive environment? Do I need to ask more questions to try to find out how I might be able to help?"

HOW TO GET THE QUIET BUYER TO GIVE USEFUL ANSWERS.

There're two reasons why you get brief answers. One is because the person is extremely skeptical and very withholding and thinks "It's none of your darn business." In that case the setup of the question

Finding what's really on their mind.

SELLING BY ASKING QUESTIONS

may not have been appropriate, or maybe the question was too intrusive for that stage of the sales process.

In other words, the only reason why very reserved buyers are going to give you information is because they perceive it will benefit them in some way. So the setup may need to be an explanation. For example, "In order to best tell you how I may be able to help you, it would be helpful for me to know just a little more about what you do." Even most reserved buyers who are willing to meet with you will answer at least a few easy questions after a simple explanation like this one.

The other situation you need to be cautious about is that some buyers need to process information for a while. We salespeople probably tend to talk a little faster and respond a little more quickly than most people. Some people respond more slowly than others, especially to investigative questions that require some thought for a careful answer. So if you think this is the case, you may need to slow down and patiently wait for answers. Sometimes the customer will start with a very brief answer, but if you hesitate to jump in, and shut up for three pulses, that person may very well elaborate in a much more detailed response.

COMMUNICATION IS LIKE PING-PONG.

It's our cue to the other person that when I'm quiet, it's your cue to talk. If you don't start, then I still think it's my turn. So you've got to remind yourself, "Wait the extra pulse, let the customer keep talking."

HOW LONG SHOULD YOU SPEND ASKING QUESTIONS?

There is no cookie-cutter answer. But generally the more complicated and/or expensive the product or service, the more questions and information you are going to need to be able to determine and then explore with the customer how your products or services will suit their needs.

The size of the potential sale may also impact how much depth and how many issues to investigate with a customer. For example, if you are selling courier services to a small-business owner who

Why buyers answer questions.

How to keep them talking.

SELLING BY ASKING QUESTIONS

requires only a couple of deliveries a week, you may want to spend only a couple of minutes asking questions and exploring needs. On the other hand, you may want to spend a couple of hours exploring needs with the office manager of a large law firm that makes hundreds of courier shipments every day.

INDEPENDENT PUBLISHERS' REP SALES SCENARIO.

In this set of sales scenarios, George Johnson, an independent sales rep representing twenty small book publishers, is calling on Betty Newcomb, the manager of a new bookstore that opened just three months ago. In the ineffective presentation George basically starts with a standard, "one size fits all" presentation highlighting his best-selling book lines. In the effective presentation, George quickly gets a grasp on Betty's needs with just a few questions and then will tailor his presentation to suit her needs.

THE INEFFECTIVE APPROACH

George: You're really going to be impressed with some of the book lines I carry. General Humor Group, my top line, is a top-twenty publisher for many of my bookstores. Their low price points ensure very fast sell-through. And Smith House Books is, of course, one of the best-known value-based publishers in the business. I do real well with their remainder books. You're familiar with these lines . . . I assume?

Betty: Not really. In fact, I've only been in the book business for a few months. Before that I was managing a clothing store.

George: Oh . . . well, then . . . let me assure you that I'll help you out. Why don't we start with my top lines . . . you can't go wrong with them! Let's turn to General Publishing Group. Here [he offers her a catalog], why don't we go through the catalog together. The first book, A *New Look at*

> Jumps into presentation too soon.

SELLING BY ASKING QUESTIONS

> Good small talk leads to useful information.

> Questions help decide which products he should present.

American Politics [he motions to the first catalog page], I'm getting a great response on. I think it's really got the potential to break out. His last book sold more than fifty thousand copies. Many of my accounts are starting out with eight, ten, or even twelve copies. Store of your size . . . I'd suggest ten copies anyway . . . maybe more? What do you think?

Betty (feeling pressured): I don't know. You know, I appreciate your coming by, but I think I'll have to reflect for a while before I can place any orders.

THE EFFECTIVE APPROACH

George: This is an exceptionally attractive store! The rich woods and the wooden signs are really beautiful!

Betty: Thank you. Our whole concept here is to cater to the high end of the market.

George: Do you have a specific profile in mind of your typical customer?

Betty: We're specifically targeting the up-scale, female frequent-book buyer.

George: So you're going to emphasize some categories more than others?

Betty: We have a very strong emphasis on serious fiction and nonfiction, and how-to books that appeal to our target market such as cooking and art.

George: Any categories that you are skipping or deemphasizing?

Betty: Except for bestsellers, we want to avoid the books that you might see in department stores: You know, bargain books, remainders, low-priced humor books. (Good thing I didn't just lead off with my big humor and bargain-book lines, George thought!)

George: Any other guidelines that you are following in selecting books?

Betty: I might be interested in literary books that are getting good book-review attention, or elaborate four-color gift books. Another guideline is my budget—I've spent just

about all my opening budget with the big publishers, so I
need to be really selective at this point.

George: I have a few books that might be just what you're looking
for. I represent a beautiful small line of four-color cook-
books called *World Cookery* . . .

FINANCIAL SERVICES REP SALES SCENARIO.

In this set of scenarios, Gretchen Hibbing, a financial services representative with Keystone Financial, calls on Robert Bremen, the
owner of a local carpet company with twelve employees. Robert owns
80 percent of the business, while his parents own 20 percent.
Keystone provides small companies with profit-sharing, 401(k), and
pension plans. Gretchen's objective is to gain enough information to
know how to present her company's products and services so they
are tailored to the needs of Bremen Carpets. Robert has just turned
forty and he realizes that he has not adequately planned for his
future. In the ineffective scenario, Gretchen asks very basic questions
that do not get to the heart of Robert's business. In the effective scenario, she concentrates on Robert's financial objectives both personally and for the company.

> Weak introduction focuses
> on the seller's company.

THE INEFFECTIVE APPROACH

Gretchen: I'm glad that we have an opportunity to get together
because we have a terrific new plan that will be perfect
for Bremen Carpets. Keystone has this plan to offer
because we've been recognized by the National
Financial Planning Council as the number one company
in our region.
Robert listens and answers somewhat perfunctorily.

Robert: Oh, really.
*She shows him a form and then begins to fill out
the form.*

SELLING BY ASKING QUESTIONS

Gretchen: Yes. We have a staff of analysts so that we can design our own retirement plans. As a result, it's easy to set up. I just ask you a few questions and fill your answers in on this form. For example, how many employees do you have?

Robert: There are twelve of us.

Gretchen: Twelve employees. And how many are managers?

Robert: There are just three of us.

Gretchen: That's you, your wife, and . . .

Robert: Joe Burton. He's our operations manager.

Gretchen: Do you have any other retirement plan in effect now?

Robert: No, not at the moment.

Gretchen: Okay. We also need to look at what type of investments you'd like to make. We offer some with high risk, some with moderate risk, and others with low exposure. Which type would you prefer?

Robert: I'm not sure. I guess, low risk to start.

Gretchen (she writes that down): Low risk. Okay. Now let's talk about initial investment. What do you see as your short-term goals?

Robert looks uncomfortable and squirms in his chair.

THE EFFECTIVE APPROACH

Gretchen: Thanks so much for giving me this time today, Robert.

Robert: Delighted to do it. I'm interested in hearing about your company's financial products.

Gretchen: Great! First I'd like to ask you a few questions about your business and about your own plans for retirement. Then I'll give you some information about some of the pension alternatives available. Is there anything else you'd like to talk about while I'm here?

Robert: I don't think so, not at this time, anyway.

Gretchen starts to take notes.

Gretchen: So tell me a little bit about Bremen Carpets.

SELLING BY ASKING QUESTIONS

Robert: Well, as you may know, we're a family-owned business. My grandfather started it out of his own house right after the Depression. He was very successful and really established a niche here in the tricounty area. My parents took over about forty years ago, and now I'm running the business. We're the largest carpeting and flooring merchandiser in the area.

Gretchen: Are your parents still active in the business?

Robert: Dad likes to keep his hand in, but they go to Florida for the winter.

Gretchen: Anyone else in the family involved?

Robert: Yes. My wife helps out with the books three days a week.

Gretchen: It's great that your parents can spend their winters in the South. What are your plans for retirement?

Robert: At forty it's not easy to think about that. I guess I'd like to have a place down in the Keys, play some golf, make sure my family is comfortable. . .

Gretchen: In thinking about a retirement plan, were there any other objectives you had in mind?

Robert: My wife and I talked it over the other day and we want to be sure there are significant tax advantages for whatever we decide to do. For example, I understand that you can put money aside before you're taxed. Is that right?

Gretchen: There are ways to design what are called 401(k) plans so that you can save money before your taxable salary is computed. I'll give you an overview of some of your options in a few minutes. Are there other goals you would like to achieve?

Robert: Well . . . I guess that this plan—which, of course, will be for everyone in the company—should also be a smart move for the business.

Gretchen now reads back from her pad.

Gretchen: To review, then, you want to create an adequate nest egg for you and your family, lower your own personal taxes,

Questions elicit information to better serve the customer.

SELLING BY ASKING QUESTIONS

and make sure the plan is advantageous to Bremen Carpets. Do I have this right?

Robert looks satisfied.

Robert: Yes, that's right.

Gretchen gets some materials out of her briefcase.

Gretchen: Now let me give you an overview of some of the plans we have to offer. I think you'll find several here that will address your needs.

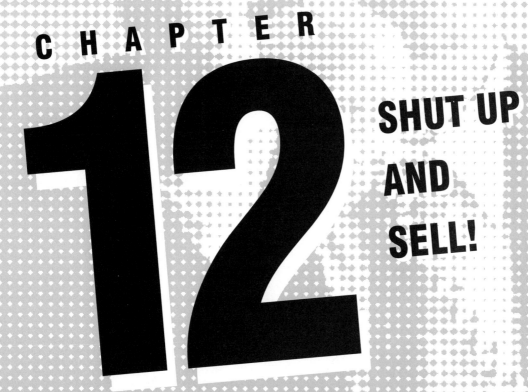

12

SHUT UP AND SELL!

There is a difference between not talking and listening. Too often in a sales situation the focus is on making your next point or quickly overcoming an objection. Instead, you need to really focus on and absorb what the customer is saying. Then you need to think about it. Then you need to think how you can help the customer find a solution to their need, now knowing what they have just told you.

SHUT UP AND SELL!

G ood selling requires more listening than talking. The farther away you get from making a canned sales presentation, the better. In fact, ideally the client should be doing more talking than you during much of the sales process.

When you first approach clients on the phone and when you first meet clients in person, you want to get them talking as soon as possible and as much as possible. The more they talk, the more of a rapport you will build. Sure, you need to get a few words in edgewise, and there needs to be a back-and-forth flow in conversation. But you need to make absolutely sure you are not doing most of the talking. And ideally you want clients to do more of the talking.

Of course, to have something to listen to, you need to get the customer talking, and to get him or her talking requires a little talk from you. Specifically, it requires a certain type of talk: questions. And a certain type of questions: open-ended questions. In the previous chapter we focused on how to ask the questions.

Now, in this chapter, I want to focus more specifically on listening. One of the keys to listening is not to be talking—I know it seems so obvious as to sound stupid—but I bring it up because it is so important.

Especially when you are filled with excitement and anticipatory energy on a sales call, it can be difficult to remain silent. When the customer pauses and the room is filled with silence, often the temptation is to jump in and fill the void with conversation. But often this is exactly when you need to be silent. Simply shut up and refrain from talking so the customer can talk.

When the customer talks, you are building rapport with the customer.

When the customer talks, you are focusing on the customer.

When the customer answers questions about his or her needs or desired solutions, you are moving toward a sale.

Questions lead to listening.

SHUT UP AND SELL!

> Good listening is a skill you can develop.

GOOD LISTENING REQUIRES IMMENSE CONCENTRATION.

To be able to ask good questions and to be able to show how your products or services meet the customer's needs, you need to listen with tremendous concentration. I don't know why, but by nature most of us are poor listeners. Who knows? Maybe it's a skill that salespeople are naturally weak in, but for whatever reason, it's a skill most of us need to develop.

Good listening requires a demonstration that we are listening.

If we can show our customers that we are really absorbing what they are saying, then we are showing the customers that they are really communicating with us. We are showing that we are really customer-focused. This is a big part of selling—continuing to build trust and demonstrating that we are focused on the customer.

In person we need to use body language to show we are listening—an occasional nod of the head, strong eye contact, alert head position, and erect posture. In person and especially on the phone, when the customer pauses, we may wish to say softly "yes" or "I see" or "I understand." Keep phrases like this brief and in a quiet voice so as not to stop the flow of conversation, but instead encourage the customer to continue.

Occasionally, especially when the customer has made a more complex or subtle point, you may wish to paraphrase it to be sure you have understood the point and to underscore that you are listening intently.

DON'T WRITE OFF THE CUSTOMER PREMATURELY.

> Never stop listening.

Sometimes customers may indicate at the beginning of the conversation that they have very little interest in your product, or perhaps they tell you that they are in love with a competitor's product. The tendency is to tune out or to mentally write off the customer and to start daydreaming perhaps about the next customer, who you may have a better chance of selling. Well, guess what? Don't write off that customer yet! As you long as you are in that office listening you still have a chance to sell that customer—who may be saying he or she loves the competitor's product, but maybe there is some problem in dealing with the other firm.

GOOD LISTENING REQUIRES LISTENING TO THE VERBAL, THE VOICE, AND THE BODY LANGUAGE.

Just as salespeople are judged more by their body language and voice tone than by the actual words they use, you need to listen very carefully to nonverbal communication.

This is particularly important when you suspect the customer may be saying one thing and meaning another.

For example, when customers say they have decided they are not interested in the product or service, what do the voice tone and the body language say? Do they say the customer really means this, or are they saying that the customer may very well be interested but is just tired of listening to any more sales pitches?

When customers raise an objection to buying the product or service, what do the body language and voice tone say? Is it a strong, legitimate reason not to buy the product? Have they decided not to buy the product for another reason? Or are they still considering buying the product but are just throwing out an objection because they feel the natural human hesitation to make a commitment?

"Listening" to body language, voice tone, and words at critical points like this in sales conversations can be critical. And while you want to concentrate as intently as possible, you may on occasion want to ask your prospects to "go over the objection again," just so you can try to hear any "hidden" messages.

LISTENING IS A SKILL THAT CAN BE DEVELOPED

You need to work at practicing listening to be good at it. And for this skill there is no better practice than listening during the real thing–actual sales presentations. Try to focus hard on each word. Try to put together the verbal, the vocal, and the body language in order to get the whole message. Good listening is a powerful skill, the successful development of which can really help set you off from the pack!

"Listen" to body language.

SHUT UP AND SELL!

Reasons Why People Forget to Use Customer-Focused Selling

Once you've used Customer-Focused Selling, you'll soon discover it is the most powerful sales method imaginable. It will make you feel good, you'll know that you're really helping your customers, and you'll succeed like never before.

But there are temptations that will pull you away from Customer-Focused Selling. You need to watch out for these temptations and be sure you don't allow them to compromise your Customer-Focused Selling approach or your integrity.

Watch out for these traps:

Trap 1. " My new product is so great that I can't wait to tell you about it."

Even a good Customer-Focused salesperson gets excited not just about helping customers but also about their products and services. And when you get the chance to sell a great new or upgraded service, there's a strong temptation to revert to selling the product, not the customer. Keep your excitement in stride. Even when the new item represents big potential sales for you, remember that the customer cares only about the benefit of the product for him or her. Keep your first focus on the customer and talk about the new product or product attributes only in the context of what it's going to mean for the customer's business. Don't get into how it's "a quantum leap for your company," don't get into how it's "a generation ahead of the competition," don't focus on how it's a great product or service. Focus on how it can help the individual needs of each customer.

Trap 2. "Buy our product because we have this great new bonus/discount/rebate, etc."

No one ever bought anything just because of the offer. Even when you are given a once-in-a-lifetime sales incentive program, your primary approach needs to be helping the customer with a solution to his or her needs. Once the customer is really interested, that's when you should mention the incentives to help cement the sale.

Trap 3. "Joe's sales have skyrocketed with his new trick close approach . . ."

Don't do it. Don't compromise your Customer-Focused Selling approach by adopting the latest sales gimmick. Don't ever compromise your integrity. Maybe Joe is getting a few more sales today. But are these sales that are going to lead to satisfied customers? Are these sales that are likely to lead to referrals? How are you going to feel about yourself if you start using any gimmicks in your sales presentation? How are you going to feel about your relationship with your customers? Over the long run, selling with integrity and Customer-Focused Selling are going to make you more successful and make you feel a lot better about yourself, too!

Trap 4. "Sorry to hear that our competitor's product failed for you and their company is flirting with bankruptcy . . ."

It's a natural human tendency to relish bad news about our competition. But fight the temptation. Never gloat, even to yourself, over bad news about a competitor. Instead, take the perspective that such knowledge is how you can help your customer, not take advantage of your competitor. And don't mention your competitor's product, service, or business problems to your customer. Chances are you customer is even more aware about them than you are. Even if your customer is not aware of your competitor's problems, if you bring up your competitor's problems, your own motives are going to be questioned. You are probably going to be seen less as somebody who wants to help the customer and more as somebody who's focused on outselling the competition.

13

SELLING SOLUTIONS, NOT PRODUCTS

Don't sell products! Sell solutions! Constantly think of what the customer needs now and how you can help them. Think of your product or service as not just having features . . . but as being a solution-delivery vehicle for your customer. Search in depth for the specifics of the customer's particular needs. Explore solutions with the customer. Then explain how your product will produce the desired solution. The customer doesn't want your product! They just want a solution to their needs!

SELLING SOLUTIONS, NOT PRODUCTS

The old school of selling is built around sales presentations, using canned pitches and often elaborate sales aids to dazzle the customer. Forget this approach! The customer does not want to be dazzled! The customer does not want to be sold your product! The customer does not care about your product! The customer cares about achieving his or her goals and creating his or her solutions!

The customer does not want to be "sold."

Also, the customer does not want to be "sold" by your persuasive sales talk about your product or by your fancy presentation. The customer does not want to feel that you "talked them into" committing to a product or service they were reluctant to consider in the first place.

But the customer does want to "buy"!

The customer wants not to "be sold" but to "buy." In other words, the customer wants to feel that he or she decided, without being "pushed," to buy the product. The customer wants to be involved in the process of deciding what to buy. He or she doesn't want to stand by the sidelines and watch you decide what is best for him or her! He or she wants to part of the process!

The customer wants to help you make the sale!

Customer-Focused Selling puts the energy of the customer on your side. Your customers want the best solutions for themselves or their business! If you can show your customers clearly how their problems can best be solved by your product or service, they will push you to sell them the product or service!

A SEAMLESS TRANSITION FROM ASKING QUESTIONS TO PROPOSING SOLUTIONS.

Customer-Focused Selling requires a seamless transition from breaking the ice to building rapport to asking questions to proposing solutions. It is particularly important that the "asking questions" part of selling is fully integrated with the "proposing solu-

> The customer wants not to "be sold" but to "buy."

SELLING SOLUTIONS, NOT PRODUCTS

tions" part of selling. In practice they should often overlap, as you may often continue to ask questions as you propose solutions to continue to best determine how you may be able to meet the customer's needs.

By asking relevant, "strategic" questions, as discussed in previous chapters, you should be building a picture of how your products or solutions may be able to help the customer.

IN RELATIVELY RARE CASES YOU MAY DETERMINE THAT YOU CANNOT HELP THE CUSTOMER.

In relatively rare cases you may decide that you can't really help the customer, in which case you should tell the customer this and walk away from the sale. The occasional lost sale is not worth compromising your integrity for! The occasional sale that you walk away from because you can't offer a good solution will strengthen your integrity and character, and make you even more effective in helping the customers you can deliver good solutions to.

By asking questions, you can determine exactly how your products meet the customer's needs.

By having asked strategic questions you will have determined how your products or services may meet the peculiar demands or solutions the customer is seeking.

> Paint a picture of how your products will provide a solution for the customer.

> Forget the "canned" presentation.

PRESENT YOUR PRODUCTS OR SERVICES ONLY AS SOLUTIONS TO THE CUSTOMER'S NEEDS.

By asking questions you will be able to present your products or services but not in a vacuum or in a "canned" presentation. Instead, you will be able to present them as solutions to the customer's problems.

For example, a basic canned presentation for a computer might be, "Again and again our XYZ computers get great product reviews and are a terrific value for the money."

SELLING SOLUTIONS, NOT PRODUCTS

However, you might start solution-selling (after having asked questions) by saying, "Since you are particularly increased in multimedia performance and reliability, I'd suggest we examine how our ABC computer may meet your expectations in these areas."

Focus, focus, focus on the one or two benefits that matter the most.

By asking questions, you should have learned what the "hot buttons" of your customers are. What are the benefits they are most concerned about getting from your product or service?

If you were simply to list ten product features or benefits, and the only one the customer really cared about was the tenth one, you could easily lose a potential sale. Customers don't want to listen to long presentations. They want to tell you what matters to them.

Furthermore, if the product benefit that really matters to them is at the end of a long list, customers may question how good a job your product does at providing that particular benefit. They would be more likely to buy an exactly similar product from another salesperson who happens to describe the benefit they are interested in first—because they are going to assume that the other product does a better job regarding what really matters to them.

THE INEFFECTIVE APPROACH

Sales rep: "You really can't beat our Super-Super industrial cleaning machine. It does everything; it's priced well; it's easy to use; it takes minimal storage space; it has a very strong engine; it's reliable; we offer on-site service; it cleans wet as well as dry work areas; and it can even work well cleaning office areas."

THE EFFECTIVE APPROACH

Sales rep: "With the problems you've had with industrial cleaning machines, I can certainly understand your primary concern with reliability. Our Super-Super machine has one of the best reliability records in the industry. We also offer guaranteed twenty-four-hour on-site service. And in the unlikely case we can't get you up and running in

> Focus your presentation.

> Addressing a buyer's unique needs is very powerful.

SELLING SOLUTIONS, NOT PRODUCTS

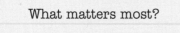

What matters most?

twenty-four hours, we even offer a free replacement loaner machine."

By asking questions, you can differentiate your products from competing products.

Often customers and buyers don't fully understand all the differences among machines. As a good salesperson you should have done your research and learned all the differences.

But remember, the customer does not care about all the differences. The customer cares about the differences that matter most to him or her. Don't assume what the customer cares about most. You need to ask.

Especially when competing products and services do not offer large substantive differences, the customer may be particularly interested in differences in a relatively small aspect of the product or what the product will do for him or her.

YOU NEED TO POSITION YOUR PRODUCT FOR THE CUSTOMER.

Even very bright human minds like to think in simple terms. Especially when we look at many similar or competing products or services, we like to be able to arrange them simply in our minds. Take cars, for example. People tend to associate one make of car with high performance, another make of car with luxury, another make of car with economy.

Similarly whatever product or service you are offering, your customers will tend to associate it with one particular benefit or feature. As sales rep intimately familiar with the product, you probably don't see the product or service in such simple terms. But most customers buy lots of different products and lots of different services, and hence their mind tends to "differentiate" similar products by one major attribute.

As the sales rep, you add tremendous value by positioning your product to fit the customers' needs exactly. Let's say, for example,

SELLING SOLUTIONS, NOT PRODUCTS

you are selling a machine that is strongly competitive in price, strongly competitive in performance and strongly competitive in safety. Let's say customer 1 is primarily interested in price. Fine. So for customer 1 you position your machine as being price-competitive. For customer 2 you position your machine first as being a strong performer. For customer 3 you first position your machine first as being strong in safety.

Of course, you need to be honest in this process. You don't want to say your machine is the lowest-priced alternative if it is not. On the other hand, by taking the benefit or feature that matters most to the customer and focusing on that first, you are helping the customer. You are helping the customer sort out the confusing array of product or service alternatives from which they have to choose. Remember, the customer wants to buy. The customer wants to achieve a solution. By making it easier for the customer to see how your product or service can help achieve this solution, you—the salesperson—are helping the customer.

> Make it easy for the customer to see how you will provide a solution.

HOW TO PREPARE FOR SELLING THE SOLUTION.

Should you develop a specific script? Should you just wing it? Neither. If you try to use a script, you're probably not going to be really listening to your customers, and you are not going to find out how best to serve their needs. And you are certainly not going to appear that you are really out to serve their needs, either. On the other hand, if you just "wing it," without any preparation at all, you are not going to be as effective in working with the customer as if you had prepared.

> How many questions?

Instead, you want to prepare an agenda.

Your agenda might look like this: brief introductions, brief overview, strategic questions, and then products or service solutions tailored to the customer. For simpler selling situations you might have little detail, such as three possible strategic questions. For more complex selling situations you might have a lot more detail. In fact, in some sophisticated sales situations you may want to give a copy of the agenda to the customer when you begin the sales call.

SELLING SOLUTIONS, NOT PRODUCTS

In your agenda you should include how you want to wrap up the meeting or what your goal for the meeting is. Are you ideally trying to complete a sale at this meeting? Or are you aiming to lay the groundwork for future meetings?

BUILDING FLEXIBILITY INTO YOUR AGENDA.

Of course, throughout your sales meeting you need to stay flexible; remember, this is Customer-Focused Selling. Change your course as you go if you see or hear (often through body language or voice tone) that another approach is needed.

Similarly, if you are summarizing your agenda at the beginning of the meeting (which is usually a good idea!), be sure to ask the cus-

Don't Get Seduced by Hi-Tech Presentation Gadgetry

Last fall one of my clients attended a software conference where they and many other software firms made twenty-minute presentations to buyers for computer stores. Each presentation involved some form of technology, most commonly computerized presentations or videos. Many firms spent a lot of money on their presentations. One firm spent hundreds of thousands of dollars putting on the largest fireworks display ever given in Southern California.

My client's firm, however, had previously asked the buyers what they looked for in presentations. And, just as importantly, they actually listened and acted on the response they got, not the response they expected to get. What the buyers uniformly said was, "Please! No more videos or computerized slide shows!" Yet amazingly this was exactly the kind of presentation almost every other company was offering.

Just before my client's firm was to begin its presentation, the sales manager was sharing a cig-arette break with a buyer on the small balcony adjoining the presentation room. The buyer complained how much he hated going to presentations and remarked, "Wouldn't it be great if we could have a presentation out in the nice, fresh air." The sales manager said, "Why not?" And he had all the chairs moved outside for the meeting.

Unlike the other firms, my client's company gave a very informal "chitchat" and passed around a few product box samples. They did not show a video. They did not do a computerized slide show. They did not even demonstrate how the software worked. Why should they? The buyers didn't care how the software *worked!* The buyers cared how the software *sold!* And they cared that they didn't have to sit through another boring presentation. At the end of the meeting the buyers broke into spontaneous applause for the fresh, low-tech approach to selling hi-tech products.

SELLING SOLUTIONS, NOT PRODUCTS

tomer: "While I'm here, is there anything else you'd like to accomplish?" Let them add to the agenda before you start. This gets the customer right on board with where you are going. It lets the customer know that your meeting will have direction and purpose. It underscores for the customer that there is a valuable reason why you are going to ask "all those questions."

Also, particularly by asking the customer if there is anything he or she would like to add to the agenda, it shares ownership of the agenda with the customer. Even if customers say, "Gee, I can't think of anything," at least they are going to feel that they had a chance for input in structuring the agenda.

SALES MATERIALS DON'T SELL ANYTHING!

Salespeople working closely with customers sell things. Sales materials can offer support.

Involving the customer in the sales process is going to be much more effective than any sales aids you can possibly muster. Even when you talk—live and in the flesh—you are going to get more attention than the same talk on a video or computer screen.

Make sure you are not competing with your sales tools! Don't pass out sales materials when you want people to focus on you! If you have a one-page complex diagram that you just have to show your customers, then pass it to the customers and let them focus on it. But if you really want them to focus on it, then don't talk while they are looking at it. Most of all, be cautious of handing your customers a big, glossy catalog with four-color pictures to look at while you want them to be focusing on you. Big, bright four-color pictures are interesting to flip through and look at even while someone is talking to you.

If you still feel compelled to include slides, videos, printed materials, or computer shows, don't let them overshadow you. And don't have them say the same thing the same way you are saying it.

One effective way to use sales aids might be to present testimonials from satisfied customers. But, effective as this might be, remember that buyers can quickly lose patience with sales aids. They made

> Don't compete with your sales tools.

SELLING SOLUTIONS, NOT PRODUCTS

an appointment with you, not with your sales aids. Their time is valuable, and they don't want to spend lots of time hearing about how great your product or service is. They want to know how it can help them address their individual needs.

MAKE THE LINK AND MAKE THE SALE!

Presenting your products and services means making a strong link between the customer's situation and your capabilities. Your job is to articulate that link for them, sharply and clearly. Don't just throw a lot of features at them. You need to have a highly focused presentation of how your product or service will definitively provide the solution they are looking for. Make sure they understand the link between their needs and your product's benefits.

Focus overwhelmingly on the product or service attributes that will bring about the solutions your customer is most interested in. Your job is to take away the guesswork and show them how your product or service solves their problem.

Your job is also to position your product or service in their mind as the product or service that delivers the solution they are looking for. Buyers are already overwhelmed with information. What they want to know is: Will your product or service clearly be suited to meeting their particular needs, or won't it? Too often salespeople lose the sale and waste the buyer's time by focusing on product features or benefits they think are important but that are not important to the buyer.

Make sure in presenting solutions that you use a nice balance of the three primary tools: verbal, vocal, and body language. Use descriptive language and balance it with concrete examples of results. Go carefully and meticulously through how your product or feature clearly meets the primary concerns of the buyer, rather than quickly touching the surface of all your product's features or benefits.

Involve your customers whenever possible. Check in with them with periodic questions to make sure they are with you every step of the way.

> Focus on how you will provide the solution.

SELLING SOLUTIONS, NOT PRODUCTS

THE "JEFF CRAIG SELLS SECURITY SYSTEMS" SCENARIO.

Jeff Craig sells security systems for small businesses. He's calling on the owner of a local restaurant, Kelly Ewing. The restaurant is undergoing renovations and, as a result, is an ideal prospect for Jeff. There is, however, a great deal of competition for the job, and Jeff is the third sales rep in today. Jeff's objective during this call is to tailor the products to the specific situation of the buyer and present himself as the best option.

In the ineffective approach, Jeff spends too much time showing off the features of his top-of-the-line model and does not address Kelly's concerns about price. In the effective approach, Jeff takes the time to demonstrate positive results, including security and fast response time, from the top-of-the-line model, thus reducing Kelly's concern about price. Jeff has just finished his questioning and is ready to deliver his pitch.

THE INEFFECTIVE APPROACH

Jeff: From what you say, I think I have the perfect security solution for you. These are the best detectors on the market, and they are unobtrusive. Our SL1400 is top-of-the-line. *He holds up a sample alarm.*

Jeff: Here, take a look. Now, these buttons are where you enter the code, and this one here dials the police automatically. This panel gives you a digital read-out indicating where the trouble is, and here is the indicator for the fire alarm. *Kelly is very unsure.*

Kelly: Uh-huh. What's that one there? [He gestures to another sample.] *Jeff picks up the second one.*

Jeff: Also a great model and state-of-the-art. This is the SL1250. It functions the same as the 1400 but doesn't have the

> Starts a feature demonstration too quickly.

SELLING SOLUTIONS, NOT PRODUCTS

digital read-out. Instead, these lights indicate the source of the trouble. We also have this one [picks it up]—the L750. Still a great alarm system but without some of the more sophisticated functions. So what do you think?

Kelly: Which one is the cheapest?

Jeff gets out brochures and writes prices on them.

Jeff: Now, the 1400, as I said, is the top-of-the-line but also well worth the money. It's got some great features. The 1250 is about $150 less, while the 750 is $300 lower than the 1250 model.

Kelly looks over a brochure for a few seconds before speaking.

Kelly: I see. Listen, why don't you leave this with me to look over and I'll give you a call in a week or so.

Jeff (crestfallen): Sure, no problem. [Sounding hopeful.] I can give you a little demo of each unit, if you'd like. We can even set up a real-life test.

Kelly: Sure. But today I'm a little short on time. Maybe we can set that up later.

Jeff: Okay. I'll leave you my card.

THE EFFECTIVE APPROACH

Jeff looks at his notes.

Jeff: From what you've said, it sounds like you'd like to accomplish three things: First, make sure your building is always secure; second, protect your property against fire; and third, feel more comfortable about who's going in and out. Does that sound about right?

Kelly (nodding in agreement): That's right. We are putting a lot of money into this building, and I want to protect the investment.

Jeff pulls his top-of-the-line model out of a leather case.

Jeff: Based on what you've told me I'd like to suggest this system for your restaurant. First of all, it has the capability to

> Emphasis here on selling solutions.

SELLING SOLUTIONS, NOT PRODUCTS

have eighteen separate access codes. That means that you can have a separate code for each of your ten employees, with a reserve for any part-timers you might hire. Using this system, you can tell who opens up and who locks the place at night.

Kelly: How would I know that?

Jeff shows Kelly the report.

Jeff: We generate a weekly report giving you the information. And, of course, you could get the report on any day, if you needed it. It's an ideal arrangement for any operation that has different people using the system every day.

Kelly: That would be a big help. I can't always keep track of who opens and who closes. It's a problem.

Jeff: Now, when employees leave you can change their code right here at the box. We don't need to come in and make the change. So if you ever fired someone you wouldn't have to worry about that employee coming back when you're not around.

Kelly: Yeah, I can think of someone right now who I am worried about.

Jeff shows Kelly the fire alarm on the panel.

Jeff: I know that fire is also another big worry for restaurants. This unit features an excellent fire detection system that we monitor twenty-four hours a day. If the detector goes off, we call the fire department right away.

Kelly: We have smoke detectors.

Jeff: That's great for when people are around. This unit, however, is heat-activated as well as smoke-activated and can detect a fire earlier than your current detectors. And, of course, it signals a problem to us right away so we can call for help. In addition, the twenty-four-hour monitoring will help with your insurance premiums.

Kelly: Anything that reduces premiums and saves me money is worth looking into.

By asking a lot of questions and really exploring a customer's needs, Customer-Focused Selling makes it a lot easier to get past a buyer's objections. Usually there will be some objections and how you handle them is very important. Be sure you are addressing the underlying concern of the buyer—not simply a knee-jerk response they are throwing out because they are uncomfortable buying for a reason they are not articulating. Ask questions, show empathy, find solutions, confirm interest, and get on with the sale!

GETTING PAST OBJECTIONS

Hearing objections is part of the sales process. Don't panic! With the process you're about to learn, you'll find that objections truly are buying signs. Objections show that the customer is considering using your product or service but isn't quite ready to go forward. Instead of simply leaving, or asking you to leave, the prospective customer is presenting objections or reasons for not buying. Once the customer voices his or her view, you are into a new area of the sales process known as "objection handling." Very simply, how you handle the objections will set the tone of how you work with the prospective customer on this particular sale and any future sales.

CONDITION VS. OBJECTION.

Before we get into the objection-handling process, let's take a minute to distinguish the difference between an objection and a "condition."

Objections are temporary reasons for not buying, often because the prospective customer is either skeptical or unclear about your product or service. In many cases objections are simply the natural human tendency to avoid making a commitment. Since we were young children we were always taught "Never sign anything." As a result, even as adults, we all tend to hesitate to make the final commitment to buy a product or service even when we rationally believe we should. The objection by nature is something that can change, either with input from you or by your helping the prospective customer change his or her perspective about the objection. Some of the ones you are used to hearing include "Your price is too high," "I want to think about it," or "I have to ask my partner [brother, uncle, sister, dog!]. All of these are objections you can work with!

A condition, on the other hand, is something that truly exists, and over which you have no control or influence. For exam-

> What is the real reason?

GETTING PAST OBJECTIONS

Acknowledge insurmountable conditions.

Then develop a new strategy.

ple, you present a fabulous proposal to a prospect; you've really taken the time to do it right. You covered all your bases, outlined exactly what they need based on your assessment questions, and designed the perfect solution . . . so you think. Surprise! After they thank you for your beautiful proposal, your excellent assessment of their needs, your professionalism, and most of all your great ideas, they mention that they'd love to do business with you, BUT their brother (father-in-law, sister's husband's nephew, etc.) handles all that for them! Ahhh! Yes, you can scream—partially at yourself, for not finding out such an important factor (condition) early on in the sales process when you were investigating, and partially at the prospective customer for using you for all your good ideas. Once you get over your little fit, calm down and assess the situation.

Whenever a condition exists, your best strategy is to position yourself for when the condition changes. Remember that one constant in business is that things always change. Position yourself as the very best option, the best bet for when things change, the outstanding number two. If the number one spot is held by a relative or simply a vendor or supplier who has done a great job, don't fight it; plan around it. Here are several ways to position you for the top spot:

- Keep an open door of communication with the key decision-makers
- Create internal friendships regardless of the current levels of business they're doing with you
- Network your way slowly around the company to expand your scope of influence
- Keep your visibility high enough to be seen, low enough not to feel like a threat
- Get time lines and time frames to keep on top of changes
- Impact their business in a positive way with delivery of information or resources
- Search for gaps between the levels of service or product they are currently receiving and what you could provide

GETTING PAST OBJECTIONS

Rest assured, when you handle conditions in a professional manner by positioning yourself as the best option available, once the condition changes—you're in! Test it out in the real world.

Objections are quite a different animal. Objections stem from a variety of sources, from skepticism to misunderstandings. They generally send out a warning signal that demonstrates a prospective customer's hesitancy or resistance to saying "yes" to your product or service. They're something you can work with, influence, and help the prospective customer to alter.

INTERPRETING OBJECTIONS AS REQUESTS.

The first key in managing objections is changing the way you "hear" them. Most buyers are conditioned to give out objections to salespeople when they aren't ready to buy. That's a buyer's right. However, too many salespeople take the objection at face value. Don't fall into that trap! Objections are very simply a REQUEST for something. Your real job is first and foremost to understand what the prospective customer needs from you, what he or she is requesting. This is a difficult mind shift on your part; it means listening and interpreting rather than responding. This skill will take a little patience, a lot of self-awareness, and an increased ability to see beyond the words.

The easiest way to identify the underlying request is to ask yourself what the prospective customer is requesting, what they really need to make this decision. For example, almost every sales rep at one time or another will hear that his or her "price is too high." Taken at face value, the sales rep will usually respond by lowering the price. The customer got just what he or she wanted! Or did the customer? What is more likely with the price objection the customer is really saying, "I don't feel that what you are asking me to pay is what I perceive your product or service to be worth." What the customer is really requesting is a conversation about the VALUE of your product or service and exactly how or why is it worth what you are asking the customer to pay. When you look at the objection as a request, there is plenty of opportunity to change the customer's perception.

What objections really mean.

Avoid lowering your price.

GETTING PAST OBJECTIONS

Here are some of the most common objections we hear and their interpretation as "requests":

Objection:	Customer Hesitation Around:	Request for:
Price too High	Perceived Cost vs. Benefit	Value Articulation
Think About	Afraid to Make Bad Decision	Create Comfort
Talk to My Partner	Justifying a Decision	Risk Reduction
Get Other Quotes	Unsure You Are Meeting Needs	Targeted Solutions
All Set with Current Supplier	Does Not Perceive You as Better	Differentiation
Bad History	Past Bad Experiences, Sees You as Them	Proof of Improvements

> Slow down and work the process.

THE OBJECTION-HANDLING PROCESS.

Once you have identified the "request," you are prepared to begin the objection-handling process. The premise of this process is that even during objections, selling is always collaborative. Selling through involvement will always serve you well, particularly in the area of objection handling. Key things for you to remember are to slow down and work the process rather than rush through to a quick close you're likely to lose.

Here's the model:

- Listen
- Acknowledge/Empathize
- Ask Questions
- Summarize
- Answer the Request
- Confirm Agreement

GETTING PAST OBJECTIONS

Listen. Step one in objection handling is to listen. Now, that might sound obvious, but now you know that what you are really listening for is the request. Take the time to hear the prospective customer out, even if you've heard that objection a thousand times before. Give positive body language of listening rather than body language that suggests you are preparing for a battle. Remember, this is a process, and together you and your prospective customer will be problem-solving the objection.

Acknowledge/Empathize. Let them know that you heard the objection by acknowledging or empathizing. A simple sentence such as "So what I'm hearing is that you have some concerns with our price, is that correct?" or "I can understand that..." Make sure that you don't jump on the bandwagon and confuse empathy with sympathy. Never make apologies or justify. At this point, keep it simple. If you tried to answer the objection at this point, the prospective customer wouldn't hear you; they are not ready to accept your ideas right now because they are still too attached to their objection.

Ask questions. The real power in handling objections is to uncover new information about the situation with good strategic questions. Those questions are very open-ended and investigative. Good starts include "Tell me about that..." or "Could you elaborate on that for me?" Your goal here is to ask at least two probing questions to get the prospective customer talking. You are searching for a deeper understanding of the objection, involving the prospective customer in the process, and buying yourself some time to think.

Summarize. Once you've asked your investigative questions and the buyer has disclosed additional information, summarize what he or she said. Put it into precise format, especially if the customer has been talking at length. For example, "Let me just recap what I've heard: 1. You're concerned with the pricing structure; 2. you have a limited budget for this project; and 3. you need to make sure that this product is superior in quality because this is a high-profile project. Does that sound accurate?" The prospective customer will either agree with you and be delighted that you actually listened, or will add additional facts to the list at this point. Once you have their

> Empathy sells.

GETTING PAST OBJECTIONS

agreement that you are on target with their concerns, they are ready to listen and you are prepared to talk!

Answer the Request. Now that you have new information and you understand the request, you can effectively answer and handle the objection. Different objections call for different interventions or answers. In the example above about price, a good start would be something like this: "You mentioned that this project is high-profile and that quality is essential. Let me share some additional information with you that might answer both of those concerns at once. . . " Now you can articulate value as it relates to your product or service and their objectives. Here are a few guidelines on how to answer various objections:

If	You Must
They're skeptical	Offer proof (testimonials, guarantees, case studies)
They misunderstood	Offer information (in writing, descriptive, or third party)
There are real drawbacks	Go to their original big-picture objectives (minimize the drawbacks)
There are real problems	Take action (describe what has or will change to eliminate it)

> Don't proceed without confirmation.

Confirm Agreement. You are never done with an objection until the prospective customer agrees that you're done. The only way to make sure that the objection has been thoroughly answered is to ask the prospect. This is a good time to be gentle and direct. Be straightforward and ask the prospect, "Does that satisfy those concerns?" Then be quiet; let the prospect think it over and answer you. If the answer is "yes," congratulate yourself; you did a terrific job of handling the objection with collaboration. If the answer is "no" or "yes, but I have some other concerns . . . " that's okay. Keep your

GETTING PAST OBJECTIONS

cool and go back to the beginning of the process and work the model again. This is where your professionalism will shine.

When objections arise, don't give up; hang in there for the long run and you will close many more sales. As you can see, this process is collaborative, includes the prospective customer as part of the solution, and solves the objection thoroughly. It's the smart way to handle objections!

OVERCOMING OBJECTIONS SCENARIO.

In this scenario, Sally Fitzpatrick represents Lacy Press, a midsize printer with many capabilities. She is selling to Gloria Crouch, the printing buyer for Mueller Advertising. The agency always beats up its vendor on price, even on rush jobs, when price is not as critical. The rush jobs are lucrative, and Lacy Press wants them, particularly because they run twenty-four hours a day. Lacy has completed a few jobs for Mueller and would like more work, especially large jobs or rush jobs. Sally's objective is to overcome any price objections and make sure she keeps Mueller's business flowing into Lacy Press. In the ineffective-approach scenario, we see Sally standing firm on price and basically ignoring Gloria's pleas for help. In the effective-approach scenario, Sally tries to work with Gloria to give her a break on price while ensuring more business for Lacy Press.

A typical price objection and weak response.

THE INEFFECTIVE APPROACH

Gloria: Sally, you've got to work with me on these prices.

Sally: Why? What's wrong?

Gloria: You're too high! I've checked around and your price is out of line. I really need you to work with me this time.

Sally (looking uncomfortable): I'd really love to help you out, Gloria, but I just can't. This is a rush order and our policy is strict on these types of jobs.

GETTING PAST OBJECTIONS

Gloria: Come on, Sally. Management is breathing down my neck. I've got to trim someplace, especially with our annual report coming out soon. That's our biggest printing job.

Sally: Well, let me see what I can do. I'll talk to my boss and call you back.

Gloria: Thanks, Sally. I know you'll come through for me. Will I hear from you by the end of the day?

Sally: (sounding discouraged): Yeah, sure. By the end of the day.

THE EFFECTIVE APPROACH

Gloria: Sally, you've got to work with me on these prices.

Sally: Why? What's wrong?

Gloria: You're too high! I've checked around and your price is out of line. I really need you to work with me this time.

Sally: Tell me a little bit more about what's happening.

Gloria: We just got behind on this job. We brought some new people in and they held the whole thing up. So even though we normally keep a reserve for rush orders, we weren't prepared on this one. It'll look bad for me if I have to pay more for something that's already over budget.

Sally: Maybe we can work together to solve this. So I gather that even though this is a rush job, you don't want to use up money you hold in reserve for emergencies?

Gloria: I'm in a tough spot.

Sally: Gloria, what if we go ahead with this job as it stands and then you and I can work out a way to preschedule jobs, even last-minute ones, so you don't get as many rush charges.

Better solution to a price objection.

GETTING PAST OBJECTIONS

Gloria: How would that work?

Sally writes some notes then hands them to Gloria.

Sally: Well, if you knew something was coming up we could schedule you for a particular press time. Since we'd know we were doing the work we could discount the price or at least avoid dipping into your rush reserve.

Gloria: Sounds workable.

Sally: Once this job is finished, why don't we sit down and see how we can work this out.

Gloria: Okay! I appreciate your working with me. The pressure here can be unbearable....

Sally: Oh, I'm sure. I'll give you a call in a couple of days to set up a meeting.

COMMENTARY:

When objections arise, especially where price is concerned, your gut reaction is either to defend your price or to lower your price. In both cases you lose! The effective approach to overcoming objections includes a four-step process:

1. *Show empathy, not sympathy.*
2. *Probe to uncover additional information.*
3. *Go back to big-picture objectives.*
4. *Introduce new ideas and solutions.*

This approach involves the buyer as part of the problem-solving process. Buyers are often conditioned to say that the price is high. Don't react to their concerns about price. Hang in there, follow the four steps, and watch your sales go up!

I n Customer-Focused Selling, gaining agreement should not be a traumatic experience for either buyer or salesperson. You're not using trick closes with all kinds of fancy names, you're not trying to get the buyer to buy something they don't want, and you're not exaggerating or misrepresenting your goods or services. Instead gaining agreement is just the next logical step in the process for you, the sales-person, and the buyer—all trying together to see how you can find a solution for the buyer's needs.

GAINING AGREEMENT

You don't need to learn fancy closing techniques. If you've had any experience selling, you've probably heard a lot about closing techniques. Traditional selling gives a lot of emphasis to mastering closing techniques that get the customer to agree to make the purchase even if they are not sure they want to. All kinds of different closing techniques exist with a variety of different names. But they are all more or less geared to pushing customers into purchases they are not sure they are ready to make.

With Customer-Focused Selling, I don't emphasize learning all kinds of fancy closing techniques. I don't even want you to learn how to pressure customers into buying products or services they are not sure they want.

Instead I am simply going to show you how to nudge a willing customer to that very last step in as candid and straightforward a manner as possible. You're not going to have to learn trick closes or fancy techniques, because you are going to sell the customer by showing how you can deliver the solution to the customer's needs. And you are going to make the sale—because the customer really wants to buy from you!

IF YOU ARE NOT CLOSE TO AGREEMENT, YOU NEED TO STEP BACK.

In Customer-Focused Selling, gaining agreement is much more tightly woven into the other parts of the sale process. By the time you are trying to finalize your agreement with the customer, you should have gotten the customer to the point where he or she wants to buy. If the customer is not at this point yet, you need to step back and figure out what is missing: Did you not show how the product's features will match the customer's needs? Did the customer raise a specific objection that you did not satisfactorily address? Is your timing

> Nudge a willing customer to that very last step.

GAINING AGREEMENT

off, and will you need to try to gain agreement during a subsequent sales visit?

In other words, in Customer-Focused Selling, you should have the customer very close to agreement by showing how your products match their solutions and in overcoming any remaining objections.

BE AS CANDID AND AS DIRECT AS POSSIBLE.

A lot of closing techniques try to avoid letting customers know you are closing the sale. For example, they might say, "So would you like the red car or the green car?"—skipping over the fact that you have not yet told them that you want any car at all. Or they might say, "Of that particular product you want, we only have one left and I know there is another party very interested in it. I'll tell you what I can do: If you put down some money right now, I can be sure to hold it for you"—pressuring the customer to make a decision they are not ready to make. You never want to use these crude, deceptive techniques.

Instead, you should be as candid and as direct as possible with your customers. Let them know exactly where you stand and what you are trying to do. And do it slowly.

> Let them know what you are trying to do.

MAKE SURE YOU DON'T SCARE THE CUSTOMER OFF.

Ever since we were young, we were all told, "Never sign anything." No wonder closing can be so difficult. It brings up subconscious negative feelings. To avoid triggering these irrational, emotional, negative feelings, avoid making a big deal out of the agreement process. Avoid using words that may be scary to people, such as "contract," "legal," "binding," "final," and "closing."

So you need to be both straightforward and nonthreatening.

Reaching agreement is an important time for positive voice tone and body language. Make sure the customer knows you are there to help them. Make sure they get the feeling you are not going to disappear after the sale. Reaching agreement is an emotional time, so the feeling of trust is particularly important; trust is largely generated by positive voice tone and body language.

> Avoid scary words.

GAINING AGREEMENT

Of course, choosing nonthreatening but straightforward words are important, too. Here's an example of some possible words to begin the process of gaining agreement:

"It sounds like we have answered everything."

"Am I pretty much on target with this?"

"Should we move forward from here?"

THE RIGHT MINDSET.

The sales rep's mindset on this should be, "We're going ahead with this....The process on this is..." These are some specific words that might work. The great thing about gaining agreement with Customer-Focused Selling is that you should be thinking the same words you are saying. You and the customer should be at the same place. And you are sharing your thoughts with the customer.

You are not playing the games that so many traditional closing approaches require, such as: "While I think this . . . I will say that . . . so they will think this other thing." That's no way to sell and it's no way to live! With Customer-Focused Selling you are right there with the customer.

If the customer hesitates . . .

Don't overlook a hesitation the customer has, either a hesitation that the customer verbally articulates or one that is expressed in body language. Identify any hesitation. Is there a particular objection that needs to be addressed? Is the customer still unclear how the product or service will really create a solution for them?

If the customer is on board . . .

Once you have made the agreement statement or question, you want to get some kind of positive indication from the customer before you proceed. Don't go on if you just have silence. You need something definite, such as a "Yes, I'm with you," or at least a positive nod of the head. If you continue to move ahead without getting a positive signal from the customer, the customer may feel manipulated. Wait a few seconds for a positive signal from the customer. If you don't get it, try to identify what is causing the hesitation.

Indentify any hesitation.

GAINING AGREEMENT

If the customer appears in agreement, then outline the next steps. "So, we'll move ahead. The next step in this process is . . ." or "Let's each check our calendars and schedule out the first planning meeting, maybe in about two weeks." Lead them through how you will do business together. Don't appear overeager to get them to "sign something"–it's better to outline the next steps first.

If you've just overcome an objection . . .

Once you think you've overcome an objection, you should double-check before you move along. For example, you might want to say, "Does that make sense to you at this point?" If the customer says "yes," then you could say, "Let's take a look at the next steps." At this point the customer may say "fine" or may say, "Before we do that, I do have another concern." And then you go back to the process of addressing that objection and trying to move forward again.

The sign to look for . . .

Ideally what should happen on at least some of your sales is that the customer will signal to you that they are ready to buy. An example of a ready-to-buy signal is when the customer asks, "What's your availability for this?" This is also a good sign that you are working collaboratively with your customer, not manipulatively.

Get to "yes" as a mutual decision.

GET TO "YES" THROUGH COLLABORATION RATHER THAN TACTICS.

Getting to agreement using Customer-Focused Selling requires working closely with the customer rather than fancy tactics. It requires you to listen to the cues, understand when the timing is right, and guide the prospect forward. It involves getting to "yes" as a mutual decision with the customer to advance the sale.

Gaining agreement is the natural step in a well-orchestrated sales process. You might simply guide the prospect with "Let's take a look at the next steps," or even more directly by asking, "Shall we move ahead with this?"

The key to gaining agreement is to remember that you and the prospect are a team, working together to solve their problem with your solution. If challenges come up, don't get defensive; jointly solve

GAINING AGREEMENT

the problem. Remember, the customer would like nothing better than to see how they can achieve their solutions using your products or services. So keep the customer involved and gain agreement.

GAINING AGREEMENT SCENARIO.

In this scenario, Bob Feltner, a recruitment advertising representative, is calling on Sandy Dillon, who purchases these services for McCormick Accounting. Bob's objective is to make the "close" collaborative rather than tactical and sell through involvement. McCormick Accounting has an ongoing need for recruitment advertising. They are working with one of Bob's competitors but are dissatisfied with the results and are considering a change. They liked Bob's presentation. He now has to close and gain agreement. In the ineffective-approach scenario, Bob assumes he has all the necessary information and presses Sandy into closing the sale without fully understanding her concerns. In the effective-approach scenario, Bob takes the time to understand and address Sandy's concerns and makes her feel more confident about going ahead with the sale.

THE INEFFECTIVE APPROACH

> *Bob has his briefcase on his lap. He's a little nervous as he prepares to try to close. He takes a sheet out of his case and hands it across to Sandy.*

Bob: That's about it, Sandy. So here's our agreement form. Just initial it where I marked an X and we'll start working for you right away.

> *Sandy leans back in her chair and doesn't pick up the sheet.*

Sandy: I'm not sure I'm ready to sign anything.

Bob: Really? Haven't you felt comfortable with everything I've shown you?

Sandy (hesitating): Yes. I just can't make a decision today. I need to think it over. It's a big step for us.

Premature aggressive close.

GAINING AGREEMENT

> Closing with the buyer
> on your side.

Bob leans forward

Bob: Yes, but you agreed that you liked our approach. Is it a money problem?

Sandy: The cost of something is always a consideration, but—

Bob (interrupts): Well, if I can show you that you can get all the services you want and pay no more—maybe even save money—will you do business with me today?

Sandy: Listen, Bob. I've appreciated hearing everything you have to say, but I'm going to have to think about this overnight.

THE EFFECTIVE APPROACH

Bob has just finished asking some questions and now reviews his notes.

Bob: Well, Sandy, it looks like we've covered just about everything. Do you have any other questions?

Sandy: No. I think you've answered all my questions.

Bob: Tell me how you want to proceed from here.

Sandy: I'll need you to put together a specific proposal for our review.

Bob: Who's involved in that review?

Sandy: Well, I take our proposal to a review board. We meet every Friday morning.

Bob: Can you tell me what the board looks for in a proposal?

Sandy: We're looking for people who want to understand our business inside and out. We also look for creativity, flexibility, and fresh ideas.

Bob: Is there anything I can do to make your process easier.

Sandy: If you could get me several references that I can check before the meeting, that would be helpful.
He writes this on a pad.

Bob: No problem. We've worked with several firms like yours. Anything else?

Sandy: No, this has been great.

Bob: I look forward to working together soon.

Sandy: So do I.

16

FOLLOWING-UP THE SALES CALL

Proper follow-up can increase you sales 20 or 30 percent! Don't let your enthusiasm level slip after the sales visit! Follow-up calls often take more energy than you might expect. Often the buyer, who may see salespeople constantly, may recollect your sales call more vaguely than you do. Don't be afraid to start selling all over again. Don't get frustrated! Don't give up! And keep on selling!

FOLLOWING-UP THE SALES CALL

W ithout exception, every sales presentation requires follow-up. This follow-up may take many forms, but in some way it must say, "Thank you, I appreciate your business (or the opportunity for your business)."

Thank-you's are still something that everyone knows they should do, and that very few people actually do. Your objective, consistent with building your business, is to separate yourself from the crowd. A timely thank-you note or thoughtful telephone call still stands out as proper business etiquette after any important meeting.

A prompt follow-up also maintains consistency with the Customer-Focused Selling approach, for it once again sends the message to the customer that he or she is important and not forgotten in all the activity. Let your follow-up contact be the first contact letting the customer know that you plan on staying in touch. Let it be the first step in building a long-term relationship with the buyer, a relationship that perhaps may even lead to future referrals.

So always add the personal touch and thank your customers. Make sure you do it because this is another step in keeping the customer satisfied and in building your reputation.

When should you send a follow-up thank-you?

Don't restrict your follow-up efforts to only just after successful sales presentations. They really are just as important, and have even more impact, when done after all significant activities.

Follow-up actions should occur after key meetings or events, such as:

> Think—what follow-up is appropriate?

- *Successful sales presentations and commitments.* There's nothing nicer than receiving an appropriate thank-you whenever you've made a sales commitment.

FOLLOWING-UP THE SALES CALL

- *Demonstrations*. Thanking the other party for the time they've given you to make the presentation is most appropriate. It lets them know that you respect the fact that their time is valuable, and that you will be respectful of this when asking for their attention.
- *Post-sale activities*. Any postsale activity should require follow-up and confirmation with the customer. This can be anything from a notice of a change in intended shipping dates, to clarification of questions that come up regarding any of the miscellaneous details.
- *Referrals*. Shame on anyone who receives a good referral and doesn't take the time to thank the other party for passing their name along. If you ever expect to get another from this party, and hopefully you expect to be in business a long time, then show them that you appreciate their efforts and send a personal thank-you.
- *Introduction of new products or services*. A great way to tell your past customers you're still thinking of them is by periodically sending them new literature or announcements about your new product or service offerings.
- *Account maintenance and relationship contacts*. Remember, "Out of sight, out of mind." Keep in touch with your important customer base through periodic phone calls, newsletters, articles—anything available to let the customer know that you are committed to a long-term partnership with them. And if they continue to feel you are, at least in spirit, still part of their team, then you'll reap the benefit of referrals that really makes this second effort pay off over the long run.
- *Product testimonials*. Whenever you've imposed on someone for their support in giving a "satisfied customer" testimonial, be sure to thank them. Save their support for important opportunities, and always take the time to let them know that you appreciate their support.
- *Sales refusal (more on this special case in a minute)*. If you didn't get the sale, it's still important to make a follow-up

> Think up reasons for following-up.

contact. Ask the customer if they would be open to talking again if things change in the future. If the answer is "yes," then ask them what an appropriate period would be for follow-up; "Perhaps in six months?" Immediately add the date to your time planner. You can also use this follow-up opportunity to explore what else you could have done that would have affected the outcome in a different way.

Include just about any other event or opportunity you can think of that provides a reason (or excuse) to demonstrate your good faith and commitment to staying in touch.

Even more than demonstrating your ability to stay in touch, the process of Customer-Focused Selling is based on the concept that your first priority is not the sale but rather building a partnership with the customer. By establishing an active system of following-up on major activities, you can enhance this posture by reinforcing the customer's perception that you're still there, even after the sale.

> Staying in touch builds relationships.

Actions speak louder than words. By maintaining a professional follow-through on important events, you'll be well on your way to cementing your relationship and showing that you mean what you say.

REVISITING SALES REJECTIONS.

If you didn't make the sale, the first thing you need to do is analyze what happened. In what areas was your approach inadequate? Sit back and ask yourself, "Where did I lose it? What did I do wrong, and what did somebody else do better?" It's not necessarily that you did it wrong, but perhaps that someone else covered some aspects of the customer's wants better than you did.

> Evaluate rejections.

In instances such as this, you should not jump to the easy conclusion that the customer just liked someone else's product or service better, because it's most often up to the salesperson to determine the sale, and much less likely to be determined by particular product or service features. Don't quickly discount your loss as, "Oh, they just had a better mousetrap." That's too easy. Use the experience as a learning opportunity, and look to see if you can find any opportunity for future sales.

FOLLOWING-UP THE SALES CALL

Can you have lost the business but have retained the relationship for the possibility of a future sale? And can you leave the door open? Is there a logical time period when you should be back in touch with this account?

The call back needs to be nonconfrontational.

Do not ask, "Why them, not me?" Your approach needs to be more along the lines of, "Is there anything else that we could have done that would have affected the outcome in a different way?" This is really asking, "Why did you pick them, not me?" but in a nonconfrontational way.

As we mentioned before, always ask, "If in the future things change, would you be open to talking again?" If they say, "no," then you really messed up and you might as well ask, "What is it we're not doing appropriately?" And then let them tell you. Most people will be honest in a situation like this, particularly if you are perceived as a professional. Oftentimes they will be apologetic about why they had to pick someone else, but hopefully you can probe to find out what ingredient you need for a successful presentation the next time. Many times they'll even say, "If anything happens, we'll use you in the future."

The key is that before you break off, make sure you're both clear on any next steps. Again, the best approach here might be to say, "You know, I'd like to keep in touch. What's comfortable for you?" Let the customer determine how frequently they'd like to hear from you. And then you may add, "Well, if there's anything new in the way of products or services, would you like me to update you on them?" If they say "yes," then you've still got a basis on which to rebuild your relationship and potential sales.

> Probe rejections.

WHAT FORMAT SHOULD YOU USE FOR CUSTOMER FOLLOW-UP?

There are any number of methods you can use in customer follow-up. Your choice of what method you choose is much less important than the fact that you do it in the first place. Remember, by making this

FOLLOWING-UP THE SALES CALL

slight extra effort, there's a good chance you'll stand out against the competition and be noticed. Make the effort to advertise that you're a professional and that that's how you do business.

Your follow-up can take many forms, as we've already mentioned:

- Telephone calls
- Letters
- Notes
- E-mail
- Faxes

No matter what the method, execute it in a high-level manner. Make the effort to purchase some quality business note cards and letterheads. When sending a fax, be sure to use a cover sheet and take the time to personalize your note. Whatever approach you choose, make sure it is a positive reflection on you and reinforces your professionalism. If in doubt how to best keep in touch with the customer, ask them how they would prefer future contact, and then make a note of it in your planner when entering the item.

CUSTOMER CONCERNS AFTER THE SALE.

The sale does not end with the signing of the agreement. Be aware that there always will be some concerns the customer has, even though they have felt confident enough to commit to the product or service. These questions will likely be along the lines of:

- Whom do I contact if I have problems?
- What is the status of my order?
- Who will handle delivery and installation?
- Who will be my customer service contact?

These concerns should be reason enough to maintain supportive customer contact. And when you add into this mix the opportunity for future sales and referrals, following-up with your customers becomes a very important part of your work activities.

How to follow-up.

The sale never ends.

FOLLOWING-UP THE SALES CALL

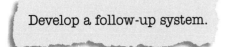

Develop a follow-up system.

PLANT REASONS FOR NEXT CONTACTS.

Because your approach in Customer-Focused Selling is to build a long-term relationship with your customers, it is important to seize every opportunity to interact with them. In your ongoing business activities, try to seed reasons in your conversation for getting back in touch with each other sometime in the near future. These interim contacts are a good method to keep your relationship alive and to show your ability to follow through on what you say.

For example, if the customer has expressed some concern about delivery dates, ask if they would like you to watch out for their shipment. Enter this commitment to check on the order's progress in the appropriate date in your time planner, and then make sure you call to reassure the customer that you're on top of it. While on the phone, you can use the contact to perhaps search for other opportunities with them.

STAY VISIBLE.

Developing an active system for following-up with customers is a key part of Customer-Focused Selling. It is a very powerful sales tool when used as a means for letting your customers know that you're part of their team and that you're committed to making their success your success.

In addition, staying active with accounts keeps your presence in front of them. Your contact doesn't always have to be in the form of addressing issues, as it can just as likely be signaling that you're there if they need you. Sending a copy of a trade article relevant to them or a thoughtful thank-you note may be just as meaningful, as your actions can speak more than words. So as important as it is to support the sales, use customer contact to distinguish you from your competitors, and demonstrate your commitment to and interest in being their provider of choice.

CHAPTER

17

GENERATING

REFERRALS

Referrals can be the bounty of Customer-Focused Selling. By using a sales approach that really trys to find the best solution for your customers—you are much more likely to get referrals. But you will also greatly increase the amount of referrals you get if you ask for them, and if you ask for them the right way!

GENERATING REFERRALS

To a salesperson, there's probably nothing better than receiving a great referral to a potential customer. Referrals are a sales rep's life line, but they seldom happen without some prior effort. So it makes sense to look at the referral process to see what can be done to maximize the number of positive referrals you receive.

One of the benefits of the Customer-Focused Selling approach is that you work from a position of strength. Your relationship with your customer is based on your approach of understanding their needs and problems, and then offering a best solution.

The credibility you build for yourself throughout this process is critical.

This process itself, is the first step in building a supporting referral system.

By the time you get to gaining agreement with the customer, they should have long before noticed your positive approach and positioning. They should have a strong sense that you are part of their team, as you have diligently tried to understand their needs. Further, you have restrained yourself from immediately jumping in to explain your wares or services, waiting until the time when you have heard the customer out, and only at the point when you feel you can make the best recommendation of your products or services.

This sales approach ends up giving you considerable credibility in the eyes of your customer. Your restraint, and your intention to help the customer address their needs, not your agenda, will not go unnoticed.

Having a Customer-Focused Selling approach will differentiate you from the competition because this sales process develops a trusting relationship with your customers.

This trusting relationship should lead to their feeling comfortable in recommending you to others.

Position of strength.

GENERATING REFERRALS

Good reputation.

Good referrals.

To understand how this positive relationship can help in referrals, it is important to understand that:

Referrals come from having a "good" reputation.

And as we've just discussed, the Customer-Focused Selling approach automatically builds a strong, positive image and reputation for you. The better your reputation, the more you will receive good referrals.

YOUR REPUTATION IS YOUR MOST SACRED POSSESSION!

The whole process of seeking referrals is based on the concept that customers will refer you to others only if they are pleased with the quality and service they've received.

After the sale has been made, it is important to follow-up with the account to make sure no issues or problems arise. A happy account is one who will refer you.

If you've been a good practitioner of the Customer-Focused Selling approach, you will eventually arrive at the point where you've completed the sale, and you're ready to go to the next step—capitalizing on all your hard work and seeking referrals.

ASK FOR REFERRALS

Referrals are the most potent form of new sales leads. Don't be afraid to ask for them.

After the sale has been made and while the customer is still feeling good about their smart choice in selecting you, that is the time to assert yourself and ask for referrals. With the goodwill and partnership image you've developed through the Customer-Focused Selling approach, customers will feel very comfortable referring you to others. Why not? You've been most helpful in trying to understand their problems and in supplying the most constructive solution.

They will perceive you not as a salesperson, but as a valued resource. And leveraging that worked-for respect is reasonable and easy to do if you've done your job well.

Asking for referrals doesn't mean begging. It means educating your client to what you're looking for in the way of potential

GENERATING REFERRALS

customers and sales opportunities. Take the time to explain to them that you're seeking contacts with people who have issues similar to those you've addressed with them.

Try to avoid asking too direct or too limited a question when looking for referrals. Rather than asking, "Is there anyone you know who wants my product or service?" it is best to phrase the question so it solicits their assistance. A better approach to the question would be to phrase it, "Is there anyone else in your company, or whom you know, who might have a need or problem similar to yours, which we just solved?"

It is always better to use an open-ended question, as it allows the person being questioned to add thoughts and issues that may not be covered in a more direct, and limited, question. Asking questions that can be answered with a simple remark, particularly with a "yes" or a "no," are self-limiting and usually not very productive.

This approach of asking open-ended questions is similarly described and used in the chapter "Networking" and elsewhere in this book, and is a key concept utilized again and again in Customer-Focused Selling. It is always better to ask questions that have words such as "explore," "explain," or "describe," in them, as they are much more likely to bring out the other person's thoughts and related issues, some of which may surprise you and be particularly valuable.

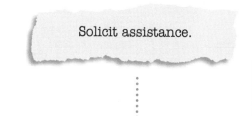

Solicit assistance.

GENERATING REFERRALS SCENARIO

Let's look at a real example of how this process works and how people sometimes go wrong with their referral requests.

In this scenario, Arlene Kutchell, a representative for Conlon Copiers, has just closed a sale with Maryann McClintock, the office manager for Huntington and Huntington, a midsize law firm in the downtown financial district. They have agreed on a delivery date, and now Arlene hopes to generate some referrals. In the ineffective approach, Arlene pushes to get referrals and ignores Maryann's attempt to squelch her request. In the effective approach, Arlene

GENERATING REFERRALS

asks Maryann for marketing materials, thereby extending an offer to help Maryann with her business and easing the way for a request for referrals.

THE INEFFECTIVE APPROACH

Arlene closes up her presentation materials and puts away a signed agreement.

Arlene: Thanks for the order, Maryann. We should be able to deliver your new copier the day after tomorrow. Will that be Okay?

Maryann: Sounds great, Arlene.

Arlene almost throws away the next part because she feels uncomfortable with it.

Arlene: Um, you know it's part of my job to get referrals after a sale. I was, uh, wondering if you knew anyone who needs a new copier.

Maryann: No. I can't say that I do.

Arlene has her notebook open.

Arlene: I just need five names. Isn't there anyone you can think of who's in the market for a new machine?

Maryann (turning cold): Sorry. I can't help you. We don't like to give out that kind of information.

Arlene: Okay. If you think of anyone I hope you'll give me a call.

Maryann: Sure.

THE EFFECTIVE APPROACH

Arlene closes up her presentation materials and puts away a signed agreement

Arlene: Thanks for the order, Maryann. We should be able to deliver your new copier the day after tomorrow. Will that be okay?

Maryann: Sounds great, Arlene.

Arlene: Maryann, before I leave, I wonder if you could give me some advice on a business matter.

Maryann (a little wary): Okay. What can I do for you?

> Crude, direct, and ineffective request for referrals.

GENERATING REFERRALS

Arlene: I've been expanding my business in this area of town and so far it's been working out really well. I know you've been in the area quite a while. If you were in my shoes, where would you look next?

Maryann: Well, let's see. I guess I'd call on that new accounting firm that just moved in upstairs. [Pauses to think.] Oh! I just remembered. Some good friends of mine just opened an architectural office a block from here. They're getting set up now, so they might need some additional equipment. Just tell them that I suggested you stop by.

Arlene: Thanks. I really appreciate your help.

Maryann: In fact, why don't we call them from here. That way you'll know if they're looking for something in your product line.

The first approach proved unsuccessful because Arlene asked Maryann a question to which the most likely answer was "no." The second approach was far more successful because Arlene used an open-ended question to solicit Maryann's help in figuring out where to look next for business.

> Polite, professional, effective request for leads and *indirect* referrals.

Remember, your work is not finished just because you've gotten the sale.

Don't fall back to rest on your laurels; use the positive image you've developed already in gaining the agreement. Continue to use the good will you've gained, and pursue those referrals.

Make sure you don't overlook seeking referrals within the client company.

While making the effort to seek out positive referrals, don't overlook the possibility of finding other opportunities within the same firm. Don't forget to find out if they have any other divisions out of state, or perhaps overseas, that could also use your services.

GENERATING REFERRALS

Stay in touch with your customer base.

As in any good sales effort, part of the job means periodic follow-up with the customer to see if any problems have arisen, and if they're still happy with your product or service. This is an excellent time to touch bases once again and to look for any newer potential referrals.

If your product or service has at the very least proven adequate, they should feel comfortable recommending you to their colleagues for your personal attention and focus on helping them; these should be the overriding factors that stand out in their recommendations of you.

With the referrals you do get, always remember to send a thank-you note, or give a follow-up phone call of acknowledgment.

Perhaps you can return the favor someday and bring someone or something important to their attention. Periodically sending a relevant article or trade publication is a great way of continuing to build buyer relationships and letting them know that you are still interested in helping them in their business.

CHAPTER

18 NETWORKING

Selling, networking is a pow

erful tool tha be used t

gain contacts

referr and cred

bility lays the

foun trusting

two-w ship. It i

an effective tool because i

gets you in the door base

on an existing relationshi

Networking offers a tremendous opportunity to jump-start your sales leads and to get into tough, important accounts through the back door. But like other aspects of selling, there is a right way and a wrong way to network. If you develop your networking skills, this venue of developing leads and referrals could become extremely powerful and rewarding for you!

NETWORKING

To understand networking and its role today, one must first look at the overall process of selling. The sales process no longer consists of tracking down potential buyers and then going in for the close. In this much more discriminating and competitive marketplace, a more professional approach of building trust and understanding is required. Before you can get the buyer to feel comfortable and commit to your service or product, you must have an in-depth knowledge of their business and have demonstrated your intent to partner with them in addressing their need. Then, to gain agreement, you must have educated them on how your product or service provides the best solution.

This whole process works best through personal relationships in an atmosphere of trust. This is where networking enters the picture, and why networking plays such an important role in today's sales successes.

Networking utilizes a system of relevant business contacts to give you personal introductions and leads for potential business. Almost everyone will take the time to talk or meet with someone who has been recommended by another trusted associate or respected business acquaintance. And this is where networking pays off, as it provides these personal, high-quality introductions.

Networking is building trusting, mutually beneficial relationships with people in similar or related businesses and professions, and using those relationships to give you meaningful introductions to potential customers.

Networking *is not* going out and directly trying to identify and approach potential customers.

> Building trusting, mutually beneficial relationships.

NETWORKING

Networking *is* finding, meeting, and developing relationships with people who are in the same or related business or service, and who can refer you to others who may be interested in purchasing your product or service, or can refer you to people who may know of others who might be potential buyers.

The important thing to remember is that you are not seeking to meet potential customers when networking. Rather, you are seeking to place yourself in an environment where you can meet others who may be able to refer you to possible buyers.

Networking is a process aimed at developing personal relationships with other businesspeople who can mutually benefit from a relationship with you. It is a process of placing yourself in environments where there is a high likelihood of meeting others with similar business and marketplace interests, actively seeking out and cultivating relationships with these people, building and supporting these relationships, and then using these relationships for the mutual benefit of both parties.

In Customer-Focused Selling, networking is a powerful tool that can be used to gain new business, contacts, referrals, visibility, and credibility. Networking lays the foundation for a trusting, two-way relationship. It is an effective tool because it gets you in the door based on an existing relationship the potential buyer has with the referring party.

This concept of networking does not focus on selling, but rather on understanding the work and challenges that associates face, and assisting them in ways in which you also hope to be supported. It gives you a basic, nonthreatening relationship from which to proceed when meeting referrals. And this can easily work to your advantage, as most sales (and long-term relationships) are built on trust.

To consistently gain business and referrals from networking, concentrate on developing long-term relationships that have a mutual benefit. Both sides need to profit in order for a networking relationship to be truly successful. Be selective. You don't have time to follow-up with everyone.

> Both sides need to profit in order for a networking relationship to be truly successful.

To make this process of networking easier to apply, it has been broken down into a five-step formula. If you conscientiously follow this process, you can be virtually guaranteed that your business will grow dramatically.

FIVE STEPS TO SUCCESSFUL NETWORKING.

1. CULTIVATE RELATIONSHIPS WITH PEOPLE WHO HAVE SIMILAR CLIENT BASES

Be selective; make sure you're cultivating relationships with people who have connections beneficial for your business.

2. AFTER THE FIRST MEETING, SEND A FOLLOW-UP NOTE

During your initial meeting, find a reason to reconnect. Then send a note to demonstrate how you operate as a business professional.

3. CALL FOR AN APPOINTMENT

Again, show you're as good as your word, and make that phone call for a follow-up meeting. The objective here is to set up a meeting to get together and share referrals.

4. HAVE THE NETWORKING MEETING

Make this a light meeting, perhaps over coffee, to educate each other about what would be a good referral, what types of business you do, and what would be the best sources of business for you.

5. SEND A SUMMARY NOTE

In your follow-up note, set the stage for an active relationship wherein you stay in touch.

When followed exactly, this process gives five sequential positive impressions of you to your networking partner, and this should make you almost indelible in their mind. The key to networking is then keeping in touch periodically to maintain and grow this new relationship. The old adage "Out of sight, out of mind" is especially true with networking. You need to keep people apprised of what you're up to, and educate them to the growth of and changes in your business. You may want this communication to take the form of a

> Networking requires an investment of time and energy.

> The key to networking is then keeping in touch periodically.

NETWORKING

> Networking takes a much broader approach, encompassing cultivating sources rather than looking for one sale.

newsletter, maybe monthly or quarterly, or perhaps an infrequent phone call. The key is to keep in touch, with a different frequency, depending on how much business they can send you.

WHY SHOULD YOU NETWORK?

Most salespeople are accustomed to prospecting for new business but may not be used to networking, which is a longer-term approach to the same ends. In prospecting, you're focused very directly on looking for new business. You meet someone, they're a prospective client, you follow-up, and you've got their business. In networking, your odds of finding a realdecision-maker at a meeting are very slim. Networking takes a much broader approach, encompassing cultivating sources rather than looking for one sale. Cultivating relationships, rather than seeking the next sale, can give you business year after year. So although it appears quicker, prospecting is good, but networking is better for the long term.

Anyone can use networking. Sometimes it may be used for internal communication or information, but by far the biggest use for networking is for new business development. This can include attorneys, accountants, consultants, and most typically, salespeople.

WHERE SHOULD YOU NETWORK?

There are literally hundreds of places where anyone can network. The key is to identify those places where the likelihood of finding others with potentially valuable connections is the highest. If you give some thought to networking event selection, it will be apparent which ones have the advantage of offering a richer environment of potential candidates.

One good place to start is with attendance at industry symposiums where relevant industry speakers or workshops can be found. What better place could there be for meeting others with similar business and market interests? Pick the top two or three seminar events in your specialty and make a point of attending them every year.

Another good place for finding likely candidates is at your one or two major industry trade shows held each year. Make it a must that you attend these; go early and stay late. Attend several of the key speaker programs, and always go to the trade dinners held the last night. This is not only a great way to meet prospects, but it also ensures that you're keeping current with your industry and your competitors.

Look around your daily business environment, and you will find there are numerous opportunities for networking. These can include meetings at your local chamber of commerce, Rotary Club, college alumni or alumnae groups, local health club, even local business networking meetings that are advertised. Pick up your local business journal or newspaper and you're very likely to find special networking events for women's organizations, workers over fifty, and many other special-interest groups.

Add another dimension to this and volunteer for committee membership, or even to become an officer, in any of the relevant trade organizations. Getting more involved and participating regularly in any of these will give you much more visibility and a greater chance of developing networking relationships over the long haul.

Better yet, write and present papers at these conferences. There is no better way to attract fellow networkers than by advertising just what you do through your talks and articles.

Be careful that you don't fall into the trap of attending anything that will get you out of the office, meeting new faces, for the day. Stay disciplined enough to look at the other attendees and make sure the event is a good environment in which to invest your time.

THREE THINGS TO KEEP IN MIND AT A NETWORKING EVENT

YOUR OBJECTIVE

When attending a possible networking event, the first things to ask yourself are, "Why am I going? What do I intend to walk away with at the end of the event?" Make sure you understand your objectives.

> There are endless opportunities for networking.

> Have clear objectives.

YOUR APPROACH

Do not go to the event to tell everyone there what you do. Spend most of your time listening rather than talking.

CREATING A REASON TO FOLLOW-UP

When you're having discussions with people, you need to be looking for logical reasons to follow-up. If you have a similar client base, you could send them an article that's informative, or you could call them with some information. In your conversations, find reasons to follow-up and do it.

Many people make the mistake of being too passive at networking meetings. They go to these meetings and look for familiar faces. Although it's fine to socialize and catch up with old friends, you need to realize that networking is an important part of your business. What's your objective? You need to make sure that's in the front of your mind at every meeting.

When attending networking events, it's important to stay in circulation, and not end up spending an unduly long time with any one person. Many times someone you know may try to latch on to you and say, "Gee, you're my best friend for the night." At the other end of the spectrum, you may find yourself wanting to talk to some new acquaintance for an extended time. This really isn't the time or the place for either of those. What you should really do is the same in both cases. Gently excuse yourself, remind the person why they're there, and then professionally exit. For example, you might say something like, "Gee, Michael, it's been really great talking with you tonight, and I realize I've taken up a lot of your time. You probably came here tonight to meet quite a few people, and I'll touch base with you at the next meeting." The key to this is never to promise something you don't intend doing. Don't say, "I'll give you a call, Michael" if you don't intend on calling.

ONE-ON-ONE NETWORKING

You will also find yourself in many one-on-one situations where this networking approach can work equally well. Again, you are looking for other businesspeople who have a similar client base, and

> Stay in circulation.

where you can mutually help each other. Just use the same five-step process. Cultivating good connections makes sense whenever and wherever you have the opportunity.

A NETWORKING SCENARIO

Let's look at how you might approach a typical networking conversation.

In this example, Evan Koren sells computer consulting services to small businesses. His company helps organizations set up small computer networks, consults with them on appropriate software, and helps them develop a presence on the World Wide Web. He's at a local chamber of commerce meeting to get to know new prospects. At this meeting he meets Cathy Walker, VP of a retail gift emporium. The objective here is to meet new prospects but not to try to sell them anything. In the ineffective approach, Evan spends too much time talking about his company and not enough time exploring what Cathy does for her company. In the effective approach, Evan gets Cathy to discuss her clients with him, which gives him an opportunity to explore the possibility of meeting with her to share information and referrals.

THE INEFFECTIVE APPROACH

Evan: Hi, I'm Evan Koren.
Cathy greets him with a smile
Cathy: Oh, hi. I'm Cathy Walker.
Evan: Cathy. Do you have a business card handy?
Evan (looking at card): Oh, you're at Gifts Galore.
Cathy: Yes. What do you do?
Evan: I'm with Pro Systems Group. We set up computer systems for small businesses. Do you have a system?
Cathy: We have some computers but that's about it. I don't know if I'd call it a system.
Evan: Well, Pro Group was the first company in the area to not only sell but also install networked systems for small businesses. The thing that's great about our services is that we

> Look for other business people with a similar client base.

> Don't focus too much on yourself.

NETWORKING

come into your business and work with all your people to get them up and running on the new network. We can work with any company in any industry.
She's not at all interested.

Cathy: Uh-huh.

THE EFFECTIVE APPROACH

Evan: Hi, I'm Evan Koren.
Cathy greets him with a smile

Cathy: Oh, hi. I'm Cathy Walker.

Evan: Cathy. Do you have a business card handy?

Evan (looking at card): Oh, you're at Gifts Galore.

Cathy: Yes. What do you do?

Evan: I'm with Pro Systems Group. We set up computer systems for small businesses.

Cathy: Oh, really?

Evan: Cathy, what do you do at Gifts Galore?

Cathy: I'm the vice president of sales.

Evan: How long have you been at the company?

Cathy: About six years. I used to be out selling, but I've been managing the department for about a year and a half.

Evan: What kinds of people are your customers?

Cathy: Well, the usual corporate accounts such as ad agencies, law firms, insurance companies.

Evan: It sounds as if we focus on the same client base. Who usually makes the buying decisions for advertising?

Cathy: Usually the owner. Sometimes we deal with a marketing person.

Evan: You know, some of my clients might need services such as yours. I'd like to get together for coffee so we can learn a little more about each other's business. We might be able to refer some work to each other.

Cathy: Well, I have a pretty tight schedule.

Evan: Why don't I give you a call next week to see if we can find time to meet?

Cathy: Sure, that would be fine.

> Find out about others' contact base.

THE KEY TO NETWORKING: EDUCATE, DON'T SELL

Networking is not selling! Save the pitch. The way to get business from networking is to educate yourself about what others do. First, find common ground, and then educate them about what you do. Educate through examples. Provide clear illustrations of the type of business results you provide for your clients. Ask for clear examples of the results they create for their clients. *Cultivate relationships with education.*

NETWORKING WITH YOUR CLIENT BASE

While certain occasions or meetings are obvious places for networking, many people overlook networking with their own client base. It is very easy to look at your clients with a stereotyping eye: "I am the service provider and you are my client." You need to leverage these relationships and gain the benefits of additional, strong referrals.

To do this, you need to separate your work from this new positioning and outlook on the relationship. Take a specific amount of time, perhaps suggest meeting over coffee or lunch, and get them out of their environment if possible. Sit down with your key buyer and talk about how you could help each other in business beyond the obvious service or product you provide. Say, "It's been wonderful working with you. In what other ways can I be helpful to you?" When you try that approach first, it comes back to you. The client starts to say, "And in what other ways can I be helpful to you?"

Offer to help.

ANYONE CAN BE TRAINED TO NETWORK

It is a common misconception that only some people make great networkers. Many people believe that to be the ideal salesperson, and ideal networker, you must be very outgoing, very social, and very comfortable in numerous settings. In fact, some of the people thought to be not as effective may be quieter, may be a little more reserved, but are oftentimes the best networkers because they're

NETWORKING

more focused on listening. The key to building your networking skills is first to identify your strengths, and then transfer them into the networking arena. Don't try to be somebody else. Cultivate and grow your own style.

GETTING FRUSTRATED WITH NETWORKING

There are really two major reasons why people get frustrated with networking.

The process is too slow.

Most people go to networking meetings, meet interesting people, and the process just drags along. It may take six months or a year before you get any referrals, and you're discouraged. The solution is to look again at how you are handling the process. Look at your approach to networking. Are you cultivating these sources, or are you just sort of letting it happen very passively? Go back to the five-step methodology and put it into use.

Where are my results?

You don't want to be investing time if you're not seeing results. The problem is that although you may be investing time in networking, you may not be *educating* people on how to give you referrals. What's interesting is that most of these other people would often like to help, but don't know for sure what kind of a referral you're looking for. It's your responsibility to educate people on exactly what business you're seeking and how to refer people to you.

There's no such thing as being done with networking. If you're maintaining too many contacts, lessen your focus on the less productive ones. If you are comfortable with the contacts of six good people, maybe it's time to expand and get out there again. Always continue to look at the quantity, and quality, of the relationships you are grooming.

How Much Time Should You Devote to Networking?

There is no magic answer, but this should not be a big drain on your time. More important is keeping a networking attitude. Throughout the day, in situations with clients, individual contacts, and in meetings, networking should come naturally to you. If you're constantly putting networking as part of your personal marketing agenda, you'll continue to see the results grow. Don't overdo your

Evaluate your results.

efforts on weekends and evenings. Keep in mind that friendships come first. You should not be at parties handing out business cards, but natural curiosity about people is fine. Part of developing good friendships and relationships is asking good questions. Keep a proper perspective on networking, but be open for new opportunities all the time.

THE THREE MOST COMMON MISTAKES PEOPLE MAKE WHEN NETWORKING.

FOCUSING ON YOURSELF

Rather than focusing on "Whom do you know?" or "What should I do next?," shift your focus to the people in the room around you. Better to ask, "Who are these people?" and "What do they do?" You'll find that with this mindset your listening skills go way up.

Have a networking attitude.

BROADCASTING YOUR BUSINESS

Broadcasting is showing up at a meeting and believing your job is to tell the world what you do. Typically, this person shows up with a pocketful of cards, which he or she is intent to distribute before the night is over. In fact, the real power in networking is to spend the night investigating. Don't tell; ask. Find those few right connections and you'll have even more opportunity out of the group.

LACK OF FOLLOW-UP

Lack of follow-up is one of the biggest problems in networking. When you say, "I'll give you a call, we should meet for lunch," mean it. We've all got busy lives, so without a system for follow-up, nothing happens. All that time you've invested up-front in networking is really going to be just a waste of time. The solution, as described in the chapter "Time Management," is to put some kind of system in place, and use it.

Asking yourself, "Are you getting business client referrals?" is the best way of determining if your networking is going well. If it's not working, it's typically in one of two areas.

One usual problem is that you're probably not networking in the right places. Being in the right place doesn't necessarily mean

Follow-up is key.

NETWORKING

meeting the right decision-makers for your product or service; it may very well mean developing access to decision-makers through the people you are meeting.

The second key area to look at is making sure you are educating the right people. You'll find, almost universally, that people like to help other people, but if they don't know what you need, it's difficult. Take the responsibility of educating people on how to give you referrals.

SEPARATE YOURSELF FROM THE CROWD

If you happen to be in a profession or service where you risk being lumped in with a much larger group, make the effort to differentiate yourself. For example, if you're a lawyer, differentiate yourself by saying, "I'm a lawyer who helps people with real-estate purchases." The key here is to focus on the "I help people" or "I help companies" statement. You aren't a provider of a commodity, you're a provider of results. That's what you need to articulate when you're out networking.

Also, when you're educating people in this process, make sure you also let them know what level of management you would prefer access to. Remember, it's always easier to start at the top and work your way down than it is to start at the bottom and work your way up.

Networking is an important part of your job. Traditionally, good business has always been done through relationships. That's what networking is: building good business relationships, over time. Today the new emphasis on networking really comes from the fact that many of the competitive differences between and among companies and services are shrinking. You can see the differences shrinking in technology, in pricing, and in the delivery of goods and services. So more and more, the salesperson is the deciding, and differentiating, factor in landing new business. The customer is no longer king; the relationship is king. More than ever before, to be successful in sales today you need to cultivate key relationships through networking.

> Be specific, but brief, about what you do.

If you want to take your selling to a higher level and get customers coming to you, you should think about increasing your visibility. There are all kinds of different ways of going about this, some will probably be more appropriate for your situation than others. But almost no matter what you are selling, there is probably an effective avenue to increase your visibility and build a pipeline of customers coming to you!

GETTING NOTICED

V isibility is the issue. If no one knows that you exist, who will buy from you? The answer is no one, except those you contact directly. Beyond your efforts to approach potential customers, your visibility as a salesperson determines if potential buyers can find you and purchase from you.

It is essential that you learn how to "get your message out" and build awareness for your particular product or service. Potential customers must know where to come when looking to purchase.

In businesses where you are selling a very specific product to a very broad market, it is virtually impossible to identify potential customers. In such cases, promoting awareness of your services is the only practical means of finding and attracting new business.

"Getting noticed" is really a very important part of the sales cycle. No matter how hard you work trying to develop leads through your direct-contact methods, nothing beats the lead generation of a program that builds a general awareness in your marketplace for yourself and for your product or services.

If you are not spending a significant part of your lead-generating efforts developing visibility in the business community, then you are overlooking a significant piece of your sales program.

Don't fall prey to the mistake of focusing solely on identifying and approaching potential new accounts as your only means of bringing in new business.

How can potential customers purchase from you if they simply are not aware that you and your business exist?

To be successful at sales you have to do more than make solid presentations. A good part of your sales efforts should focus on promoting yourself and your message to potential customers.

> Get your message out!

GETTING NOTICED

GET YOUR NAME OUT FRONT THROUGH:

- Speaking engagements.

- Articles.

- White papers.

- Newsletters.

- Advertising.

- Yellow pages.

- Trade shows.

- Industry symposiums.

- Professional societies.

- Memberships.

- Publicity.

- Networking events.

There are any number of things you can do to get yourself noticed. The secret is to be not just noticed, but also *remembered*, for the service or products you provide.

How you tell people what you do plays a big part in their remembering and recounting of your abilities.

DEVELOPING A PRESENCE.

COMMON METHODS FOR GETTING YOURSELF NOTICED

Knowing what to do when you meet someone is only half of the answer; getting remembered by them is the other half. As we've noted in the chapters "Generating Referrals" and "Networking," there are literally hundreds of places you can go to make business contacts.

What we want to talk about here is how you get the most visibility for yourself and your business when at these events. The following is a list of ways to get noticed through actions I have found most effective.

SPEAKING ENGAGEMENTS

Speaking engagements work well in eliciting new business because they create a nonthreatening environment for someone to check you out. The audience gets to watch how you operate and can evaluate your message and style with no pressure on themselves. They can decide from their chair if what you say is relevant to them, and then respond accordingly.

To be most effective, your speech should be engaging, with entertaining anecdotes, and full of thought-provoking examples. Audience members will begin to "buy" when they feel a personal relevance to your message.

Your job is to capitalize on their enthusiasm for your message while they're interested and before it wears off!

Pull the audience into your world by involvement and relevance.

For example, an effective introduction could go along these lines:

"Good afternoon. [Pause and make eye contact with audience.] Negotiation is a vital business skill. You use it every day in your business life and your personal life. Today we'll cover three ways in which you can increase your negotiation skills immediately.

"Before I begin, let me ask for a show of hands of how many people engage in business negotiations on a daily basis. And how many of you feel that both parties can "win" in a negotiation? Great!

"Most of us have heard that negotiations should be win/win, that we should strive for solutions that are mutually beneficial, but we often wonder how that is possible. Let's take a look at creating effective outcomes for both parties involved . . . "

Use your speaking opportunities to inform people about relevant issues or solutions to problems they encounter every day in their business.

Always educate, never sell, when speaking in public

Selling from any platform is a big mistake. It works in reverse: The more you sell, the quicker they write you off. When you are onstage you should be educating, not selling. But before and after your talk you should talk with as many people as you can on a one-to-one basis to develop sales leads.

Create a positive image by helping them first

If you bring added value to your speaking engagements through constructive business commentary, attendees will want to come back for more. By demonstrating your value and creating a positive image, you will be more inviting to them. Don't worry about selling; let them judge your value for themselves. Focus on keeping the message clear, concise, and filled with business-building value.

Speaking Tips

Ask for referrals

When you are done with your speech, it's time to ask for referrals, but not from the platform. Supply your attendees with a simple card to fill out that lets them request more information. Provide them with several options, such as "Get added to the mailing list" or "Please mail me information" or better yet, "Please contact me about your products or services." In most speaking engagements, about 40 to 50 percent of the participants will respond to your request. These individuals have prequalified themselves for you and want more information.

> Speaking is one of the most popular and effective ways to gain visibility.

> When to ask for leads.

GETTING NOTICED

> Give them something to
> take with them.

Come early, stay late

Don't be a prima donna: Get to your speaking engagements early and plan on staying late. Especially, stay late. Audience members want to feel connected to you and in some cases may approach you after your speech to ask you private questions. All of these are buying signs, so stay, and listen to and cultivate the potential contacts who come up to see you afterward. Build interest one-on-one, develop leads, but don't try to close the sale in this environment. Instead, follow-up later.

Always give a handout

When the audience leaves, they should take a piece of you with them...in this case, in the form of a handout. Why? You want to make sure that your points are driven home in a clear and concise manner, and you want them to be able to reference these points back at their office. The handout should provide some real value (information) and include your name, address, and phone number if they are to be able to find you again.

Use memorable examples

When you are speaking, don't give a laundry list of capabilities. People get bored and entertain themselves with daydreaming. The best way to leverage your speaking engagement is to use interesting examples to illustrate your points. Make a point, attach a story; make a point, attach a story. When you finish, they remember the example, the point, and you!

ARTICLES

Writing is a powerful tool with which to attract new clients. It can position you as an expert in a particular field, and it forces you to articulate your thoughts on a specific area of your business. Writing and publishing articles works as a business tool by increasing your credibility and your exposure.

To gain writing opportunities, start locally and work your way up. Everything and anything in print works well—newspapers, trade journals and publications, national and international magazines.

Publishing Tips

Always include a photo

Every time you uncover an opportunity to write, ask if you can supply the publisher with a photo. People always look at pictures first. Your visibility increases tenfold when someone can read an article and then attach your name and face to it. Keep several 5x7 black-and-white glossy head shots on hand for newspapers, trade publications, and newsletters. Also keep a few color shots available for the national and international magazines (most will only print color). Have the photos ready because they won't wait for you.

Photos get noticed.

1-800-Business

At the end of most articles you should supply the publisher with a short biography of yourself. *Make sure it includes an 800 number*. If the object of the article is to generate business, it doesn't work if readers can't find you quickly and easily. Take the work out of it and give your readers an easy way to find you; 800 numbers are inexpensive and can easily ring into your regular line or voice mail. You'll be surprised at how many calls you get!

The gold is in the reprints

If writing is the investment, then reprints are the dividends. How does it work? Very simply. Whenever you are in print, order 250 to 500 copies. Don't be cheap; order them directly from the publisher and get the nice, glossy finish. Then use them all the time! Use them as part of your introduction in telemarketing, as an added value in proposals, to reconnect with a client or prospect, or as part of a press kit for other writing assignments. You will find numerous opportunities to use them for building your professional image and reputation.

Revise and adapt articles

Once you've developed a successful position on an area in your business, take that same message and revise and adapt it to other markets. Take the foundation article and change the language, examples, and jargon to reflect a different industry. This is a painless way to gain credibility in new markets. You don't need to reinvent the wheel; just revise and adapt it to suit your needs.

Reprints work.

GETTING NOTICED

Combine articles with your speaking

Whenever you have an opportunity to speak, view it as another opportunity to write. Ask the people who are coordinating the speaking engagement if you can also supply them with an article of interest for their newsletter. If it's printed before your speaking engagement, you'll have better attendance and a wider degree of recognition. If it's printed afterward, you'll get more inquiries as a result of their "seeing" you again. Combine writing with speaking for double impact.

WHITE PAPERS

White papers are self-published works that reflect your position on a particular issue. They are a great way to start generating recognition for your business. Write and edit the article professionally, then have copies made.

Use them as a way to introduce or educate prospects on your view of the business. Include the paper in precall letters, in proposals, or as part of a follow-up packet. The goal is to gain credibility as an expert. White papers can also be submitted for publication to newspapers and magazines. Make the commitment to this type of communication and start reaping the benefits!

NEWSLETTERS

Newsletters are always a great option because the audience is so focused. Consider contributing an article to your company's newsletter, a client's newsletter, an associate's newsletter, or better yet, start your own newsletter.

Starting your own newsletter is a great way to get yourself noticed, and stay noticed. Periodic mailings keep you alive in customers' minds as they continue to reinforce your first impression and message.

Refer to the Appendices in this book for sample newsletters and a template with helpful comments.

Whatever approach you choose, incorporate writing as a key business development tool, and stick with it .

GETTING NOTICED

ADVERTISING

With paid advertising you don't just have to advertise your business. Be creative and promote information seminars at your office. Perhaps you can publicize a free "question and answer" hot line that positions you as a resource to potential customers.

Think of unique ways to draw people to you where you can first offer something of value to them. When you can begin any interaction with potential customers in such a way that you first build your credibility, you are well on your way to establishing a relationship that can then be leveraged into a sale.

With paid advertising, direct mail is the best bet for most business. Your message reaches every recipient in a personalized way and at a moment when they have chosen to consider your message.

Magazine and newspaper ads are less costly and usually less effective. Carefully consider the subscription demographics before selecting the best option. Radio and TV ads can be more effective with captive audiences but also are considerably more costly.

Whichever medium you may choose, be sure to monitor the results to determine which option is the most cost-effective in the long run.

YELLOW PAGES

For the right business, nothing beats advertising in the yellow pages.

For the wrong business, however, the yellow pages may be a complete waste of money. Try to gauge how well your competitors are doing with their yellow pages ads. Are many of the phones listed in your category of the yellow pages disconnected? Not a good sign! Get the previous year's yellow pages directory. Did most businesses repeat their ads? Did the businesses with larger ads go with the same large ads two years in a row?

> Start small with paid ads and watch the results carefully.

GETTING NOTICED

Join-up!

TRADE SHOWS

Trade shows are a great place be noticed. Working in the booth or circulating through the aisles, make an effort *not* to sell.

Be consistent with the Customer-Focused Selling approach and use new introductions to send the message that you are there to assist others in addressing their problems and needs.

INDUSTRY SYMPOSIUMS

Pick the right topics and you'll have an audience full of prospects. Buy the attendees list and get noticed by everyone through follow-up mailings.

But remember, selling turns people off, so concentrate on getting to know others and their needs when at these events.

PROFESSIONAL SOCIETIES

Becoming widely known in professional societies is a good way of attracting new business leads. Many times you will find two groups in attendance, generally breaking down to a provider or services group, and interested users group. So it's very likely you'll find yourself meeting both your competitors and potential customers.

Beyond the normal networking you should do at such events, publishing articles or lecturing is a great way to call attention to your capabilities and services without appearing to be overly aggressive.

MEMBERSHIPS

It used to be that joining the right golf course was the best way to make business connections on your own time. Today, people feel much freer in promoting their business throughout their busy schedules, both business and private. This can be almost anywhere, including health and fitness clubs, town committees, volunteer organizations, or even the local PTA.

Be discreet, but when asked, remember to tell others, "I help people to . . . " or "I help businesses to . . . "

GETTING NOTICED

PUBLICITY

Publicity is often overlooked as a primary marketing tool to gain attention and interest in a product, service, or company. Using publicity as a sales tool can be a more cost-effective method for generating sales than buying advertising.

No matter what business you are in, you can be your own publicist. If you want to act as your own PR firm, you can readily produce a simple press kit. This kit should include a "pitch" letter and a press release regarding your company, a new product, or a unique service. You will become the center of attention as you create an awareness of your business that will turn into sales leads.

Whether it's local radio or TV, business panel discussions, chamber of commerce gatherings, or whatever, the creative publicist can find thousands of publicity opportunities that allow for increasing image or product awareness.

However, the best part of publicity is that, for the most part, it is free!

NETWORKING EVENTS

Networking is one of the best ways to be brought to someone else's attention, for nothing beats a word-of-mouth introduction.

It gives you instant credibility where it could otherwise take weeks, or even months, to earn the same status. Everyone can recall a time when they were first introduced to a potential account as "someone who does a good job" or as "someone who really saved my tail." And if the person doing the introduction has any credibility, then you're off to a great start.

Customer-Focused Selling should get you a great start with every referral. Even if you weren't able to sell the account, you will have earned a reputation for being constructive in your involvement. Similarly, in your networking efforts, your professional and constructive image will serve you well as others remember it when recommending you.

Tell the press!

GETTING NOTICED

Educate.

Be focused.

GUIDELINES FOR INDELIBLE IMPRESSIONS.

1. First meeting? . . . educate, don't sell

Nothing can put a potential customer off more than a salesperson who immediately goes into a prepared sales pitch.

Alternatively, taking the time to understand and relate to the customer can pay big dividends. Being seen as an interested and supportive problem-solver will distinguish you from the competition. Understanding their needs will allow you to then educate the customer on how your product or service addresses those problems.

As the customers' confidence in you and your approach grows, they will increasingly seek to enlist your aid in their business efforts. And it is this building partnership that will ultimately bring the sales successes you seek.

2. Be brief and succinct in your introductions

First impressions are lasting impressions.

If you ramble or go on at any length describing yourself and your services, then you can be sure the other party is tuning out and you've lost them. No matter what the occasion, don't ever focus on yourself during an introduction. To be consistent with the Customer-Focused Selling approach, focus on understanding what they do and on learning the challenges and problems they face.

Use introductions as an opportunity to learn more about their business, not to sell your business.

Being brief and focused sends a simple message that is most easily remembered

The more you say about yourself and your business, the greater the chance the other party will say to themselves, "I'd never use a service or product like yours." Don't give the person a chance to tune you out with limited knowledge about what you do. By keeping the conversation focused on them and their business, you learn what you need to evaluate the potential contact. And you leave them with a favorable impression, for you have valued them enough to inquire and listen about their business.

3. First impressions are lasting impressions

Unless you're Bill Gates of Microsoft, there's little chance people are going to remember you based solely on your name and title. What gives a lasting impression is your attitude and constructive interest in their business. Whenever you find yourself in a situation where you're being introduced or meeting someone for the first time, make sure you give a brief, focused description of what you do; then follow-up with a question about them.

When introducing yourself, a good way to tell people what you do is by responding with a statement such as "I help people to . . . " or "I help businesses to . . . " Develop your own tag line and use it repeatedly to consistently get out the message of what you do.

4. Don't confuse getting attention with getting noticed

Getting noticed does not mean getting attention. It means leaving people with a clear and simple understanding of what you do. You want to have made a favorable, professional impression so that they remember you should the need for your services or products arise.

If you've made a good first impression, then you can reinforce this by using the five-step method highlighted in the chapter "Networking." Getting noticed is being remembered for the right reasons.

You get noticed when you send the right messages:

- **A brief first response**
- **Avoiding the spotlight for yourself or your business**
- **Interest in understanding their business problems and needs**
- **Educating, not selling**
- **Following-up to reinforce the message that "they're important."**
- **Professionalism in all your dealings**

> The right message.

GETTING NOTICED

CUSTOMER-FOCUSED SELLING GETS YOU NOTICED

Using the Customer-Focused Selling approach in your sales efforts means you're always building the positive message that really makes you stand out. No need to impress everybody how smart you are, or how great all of your products or services are. You're in it for the long haul, so slow down and take the time to build the right relationships. That's how you stay noticed over the long run.

Make the effort to build visibility for this approach through your speaking, your writing, and your day-to-day business, and you'll amplify this message and your sales successes!

Look long-term.

CHAPTER

20

GETTING
AND
STAYING
ENTHUSIASTIC

Enthusiasm isn't automatic, especially when you're starting to sell. Sometimes it doesn't come easily. Sometimes it doesn't come at all. But you can work at enthusiasm. You can build it and sustain it. But developing strong, consistent enthusiasm takes a plan, a program, and effort. But when you've got it—enthusiam pulls everyone right through the sales process!

GETTING AND STAYING ENTHUSIASTIC

I f there is one sacred concept that everyone in sales acknowledges, it's that enthusiasm sells! Thinking back on your own personal experiences, almost everyone can easily recall a time when they were caught up in a zealous sales presentation by someone trying to sell them something. Like the contagiousness of someone else's laughter, enthusiasm has an attraction that is hard to beat. We all know from personal experience that it is almost impossible to get excited about something we don't believe in or don't respect. When you see that special quality of enthusiasm in someone else's sales delivery, it's hard not to accept that the person giving the sales presentation really believes in the quality, performance, etc., of the product or service being offered. And, as with the laughter example, it's even harder not to get enthused yourself.

It is hard to go wrong, for within limits, the more enthusiasm you show, the better. And so the real question in sales is not "Should you be enthusiastic?" but rather, "How do you become enthusiastic about your product or service?" and "How do you do this in a genuine and credible way?"

HOW YOU DO WHAT YOU DO IS AS IMPORTANT AS WHAT YOU DO!

It's not just what you sell, it's how you sell, that makes the dramatic difference in sales results. You're missing the other half of the sales presentation if you are just trying to reason with your customers.

It is hard to describe the true value that enthusiasm plays in the sales process because it is hard to quantify this intangible quality. There is no denying that enthusiasm builds sales, yet many people remain stoical when it comes to using this powerful asset.

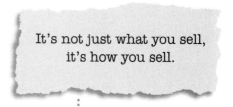

It's not just what you sell, it's how you sell.

GETTING AND STAYING ENTHUSIASTIC

There is nothing you can do throughout your sales effort that will give you the same results as developing an enthusiastic style.

Each day you should make the effort to show your enthusiasm for what you do. You don't have to bridle your enthusiasm just because you don't have the best product on the market. Instead, think about its positives, that it's a good product and will make money for the customer. And then start each day, or each meeting, on a positive note. Don't hold back. Have some fun with your work and broadcast it through your enthusiastic delivery.

HELPING THE CUSTOMER HELPS YOU STAY ENTHUSED.

With Customer-Focused Selling, you can't help but develop good feelings about the work you do. Knowing that the focus of your sales efforts is helping your customers solve their problems is a great way to start each day. And you can feel good about what you do. Building partnerships, avoiding high-pressure tactics, seeking to bring real value with your product or service—these are all positive activities that build your general sense of well-being and serve to keep you happy and enthusiastic about what you do. Customer-Focused Selling makes you feel great about your work.

ENTHUSIASM GETS THE RIGHT MESSAGE ACROSS.

If you're still wondering about the value of an enthusiastic approach, there is very credible scientific evidence in its support. Studies have shown that:

The data supports it.

- In face-to-face meetings, 93 percent of the message gets communicated through tone of voice and body language, and only 7 percent through words.
- In phone conversations, 85 percent of communications is through tone of voice, and 15 percent through words.

Pity the salesperson who's not using enthusiasm in their sales delivery; their message could be six to twelve times stronger!

GETTING AND STAYING ENTHUSIASTIC

If you're not using the persuasive powers of enthusiasm, now is a good time to get with the program.

BE APPROPRIATE WITH YOUR LEVEL OF ENTHUSIASM.

As great as it is to show your enthusiasm, it is important to make sure it is not overdone. Match the degree to which it is used to the occasion, to the phase of the selling cycle, and even to the various customers or marketplaces.

For instance, a strong, enthusiastic introduction of your firm's capabilities might be followed by a calmer period of serious questioning and listening while getting input on the nature and scope of the sales opportunity. Interjecting an enthusiastic "That's great, we have just the solution for your problem" is poor timing if it's in the middle of your customer's commentary. Later in the presentation, when you're summing up the customer's problems and explaining what your recommendations are, is the time to be more exuberant and send the message that you're very confident your product or service will fit the bill.

You also may find that you have various customers or occasions where different levels of enthusiasm are appropriate. Presenting to one person, or to a smaller, start-up business might dictate a different delivery than to a large *Fortune* 500 firm with a room full of attendees. When cold-calling on the phone, you might want to put a little extra emphasis in your introduction versus your calls to stay current with someone you're working with on an ongoing project. As your circumstances and audiences vary throughout the day, stay conscious of the need to adjust your delivery.

Using enthusiasm as an extra edge in your sales efforts should become second nature to you. Remember, your enthusiasm will loose its credible edge if it seems too high or forced. It is best to let it ebb out in your normal conversation. Say things with a conviction that portrays your confidence. Your customer is smart enough to read the signs of your enthusiasm, and you will find that you don't have to raise your voice to get your message across. A modulated delivery

> Be appropriate.

> Don't force it.

GETTING AND STAYING ENTHUSIASTIC

can be even more convincing, as it is more subtle, and tends to build your credibility without putting anyone off.

MODERATE YOUR HIGHS AND LOWS.

Because having a positive attitude plays such an important role in sales, it is important to develop an ability to deal with the highs and lows you normally encounter in your sales efforts. You must learn to understand that dealing with the good and bad days is just another aspect of your job.

When you've had a particularly good run of sales and everything seems to be going great, don't expect it to go on forever. Enjoy your successes, but be prepared for things to get back to normal (as they surely will).

Conversely, when you hit a slow stretch and nothing seems to be going right, remember that we've all been there before. It's part of sales learning to keep your confidence and belief in your consistent and quality approach.

Customer-Focused Selling delivers real value to your accounts. Over time you will learn that it is the inherent value of this approach that ensures your ultimate success. Keep your focus on what matters. If you consistently provide assistance and support to your customers, you will build a winning business reputation that will bring you the sales success you seek.

FIRST AID FOR THE BLAHS.

Always be conscious of your level of energy. If you're feeling off your game, pay attention to getting yourself back on track. Try one of the following tips to get back the right, enthusiastic frame of mind:

TAKE A COFFEE BREAK

When you find yourself not at peak performance, get up and stretch. Get a cup of coffee and relax for a few minutes. Perhaps make a personal call to rest your mind. When the smile comes back, then you are ready to get back to business. On a larger scale, this concept holds true for vacations as well. Don't skip them. They are the best method of recharging your batteries, and you've earned them.

> Everyone has had low stretches.

> The little things can make a big difference.

GETTING AND STAYING ENTHUSIASTIC

EXERCISE REGULARLY

Make sure you exercise three to four times a week at least twenty minutes at a time. Regular exercise releases a euphoria chemical into the bloodstream that gives you a sense of well-being.

DEVELOP A WORK ROUTINE

People are generally happier when they have some routine in their work. Use your time management planning to reward yourself with work you like to do after you've finished some of your less desirable tasks.

DON'T BE AFRAID TO LOOSEN UP

Have some fun with what you do well. Let your personality emerge in areas that are your strong suits. Rather than try to meet someone else's expectations, feel comfortable being yourself, and have fun with what you do.

TALK TO SOMEONE ELSE

When feeling a little overwhelmed, it's always helpful to find a trusted peer and discuss your situation. Almost certainly they have experienced these same low points and have some suggestions on what you might do to perk up your mood and your business.

PUT THINGS IN PERSPECTIVE

Is it really the end of the world? Not likely. Try putting things in perspective, and think about all the things you are doing right. Remember those times when everything went right, and realize that you are still using that winning approach. It's only a matter of time before the odds are in your favor if you keep up your spirits and don't let it get to you.

BUILD ENTHUSIASM BY BUILDING CONFIDENCE

You build enthusiasm for your sales presentations by building your level of confidence in your presentation. When you are comfortable and confident with your sales material and presentation, it is much easier to relax and enjoy the process of Customer-Focused Selling. And this enjoyment is easily translated into enthusiasm. There are no

Talk breeds enthusiasm.

Develop confidence.

GETTING AND STAYING ENTHUSIASTIC

tricks or games you're playing with the customer. You are there to better understand their problems and to present your solutions. If you've done your homework in prospect selection, then it should be very appropriate for you to be before them. By considering yourself their partner in this process, you should not really feel any intense stress. Hopefully, your comments and suggestions can be directed more with a sense of support, rather than with a focus on closing the sale.

And if you are following this prescribed approach, you should see yourself as a manager of the process. Imagine yourself as a solutions specialist, arriving on the scene with the skills and ability to assist the customer in solving their needs or problems. Envisioning this approach, who wouldn't be enthusiastic to be the white knight coming to the customer's rescue? It's when you lose this focus on the customer, and fall back to simply showing your products, that your presentations will go flat.

Real enthusiasm can't be manufactured. Enjoy the role you can play in this partnership, and project that enjoyment in your work.

Build confidence through:

- Product knowledge
- Competitor knowledge
- Industry knowledge
- Mastering the sales process
- Your sales successes

Knowledge breeds confidence.

Confidence breeds enthusiasm.

Confidence comes from product and customer knowledge. If you want to build your level of enthusiasm, a great place to start is by building your knowledge level. In the chapter "Knowledge Is Power!" we highlighted the importance of product and customer knowledge from the viewpoint of the role and credibility this knowledge will build for you with your customer base. Use this knowledge to position yourself as a resource to them. You will find that the questions you've asked trying to understand your customers' needs, and the homework you've done in getting up to speed on their products and industry, will have a bolstering effect to your image and to

GETTING AND STAYING ENTHUSIASTIC

your spirits. And the more you see yourself in this role, the more fun and enthusiasm you can show in your work.

This building enthusiasm leads to ever more confidence as it steadily increases your sales successes. Eventually you will arrive at the point where the sum total of your positive selling experiences, coupled with your wealth of knowledge, give you a bubbling confidence that is recognized by all. This unbridled enthusiasm will become your greatest asset, attracting customers to your product or service solutions that they confidently purchase.

HANDLING REJECTION.

No matter how good a salesperson you are, there will be times when the loss of a sale will hit you particularly hard. From time to time there are bound to be tough sales periods when several sales you thought you should have had, got away from you. At times like this it is important that you not take it personally, but rather see this low period as part of the whole process.

Putting lost sales in context with all the other positive sales activities you are doing is the best way to deal with rejection. Handling rejection well has most to do with how you perceive that rejection.

If you are really following the sales process described here, you should have a broad and varied sales effort under way at all times. You should simultaneously be working on any number of prospects at various stages of the sales cycle, from new leads, to developing accounts, to maintaining contact with old customers. Rejections, seen in the light of all this other ongoing activity, don't seem nearly as critical. What you've just lost on the one hand, you are very likely to replace with successes on other fronts.

Whatever you do, don't get hysterical or lose your self-confidence. Whenever one of these "slow periods" occurs, it is a good time to take a moment to review your activities to see if you are adhering to all the steps in the Customer-Focused Selling process. Perhaps, as we've mentioned elsewhere, you are skipping one of the bases you should be covering, and giving undue attention to others.

Put rejection in perspecive.

GETTING AND STAYING ENTHUSIASTIC

Are you spending too little time qualifying leads, and too much time trying to close those opportunities where your products or services aren't a best fit? Are you more focused on the older accounts and not spending enough time prospecting or networking for new leads? Are you still planning and managing your time well? This is a good time to double-check that you are following the prescribed process. If you can say you are, with no qualms, then get right back into your sales routine. Have confidence that this process, which creates real value for your customers, will bring you, over time, the sales successes you seek.

DEVELOP A SELF-IDENTITY SEPARATE FROM YOUR SALES RESULTS.

"Don't get too wrapped up in your work." You've all heard this expression, and nowhere is it more true than in sales. Be careful that you do not become so absorbed in your sales activities that you lose perspective on the rest of the world. As the pace of work around you continues to build, it is not uncommon for people to find themselves working harder and harder, but getting farther and farther behind. This is a very dangerous syndrome, for it can become self-defeating as you focus harder and harder on the individual stages of each sale, but lose the context of the overall process. See yourself as being in charge of this sales process. Don't put everything on the line emotionally with one or two opportunities. Rather, keep your perspective and balance by managing the whole process. Making sure that you allocate time to all activities is the best way to ensure that no one activity becomes overly important.

Be yourself, not your work.

CUSTOMER-FOCUSED SELLING WORKS ON YOUR INTEGRITY.

One of the real advantages to the Customer-Focused Selling approach is that it focuses on the honesty and integrity of the salesperson. By approaching each sale as an opportunity to find the right product or service solution for your customer's needs, you will not find yourself in the position of having to misrepresent yourself or

Integrity fuels enthusiasm.

GETTING AND STAYING ENTHUSIASTIC

your wares. This is one of the main reasons why you should feel comfortable and enthusiastic about your work.

Being comfortable with what you do, and don't do, can have surprising benefits. For instance, let's say you're in the graphics arts business. You get an inquiry from a potential customer for the printing of a new catalog, but this is not the kind of work you do. Although you know others you could subcontract the work out to, this is a big project, and with your markup, this customer would be paying a "long" price for the work. You decide that rather than bid on the project, you'll call the customer back and tell them that this sort of work is really not what you do, and that you would recommend they call firm XYZ, whom you know does a great job with this kind of project. You then go on to explain what different services you do provide and that you would like them to keep you in mind next time they have a need for them. Hopefully they will find your candor refreshing and realize that you have just saved them your markup on the job had it been placed through you. Chances are this purchaser will take notice and call you next time your business is the appropriate fit. And certainly you're on firm XYZ's preferred graphics artist referral list next time someone asks them for a recommended source.

It is through the integrity and honesty of your day-to-day business dealings that you set the mental climate of your business. If you build your reputation positively and constructively, you will find it very easy to maintain a happy, spirited image. And this enthusiasm is your best business spokesperson.

Remember, you sell solutions, and this is a big advantage over the older systems. Each sale is not a result of some closing technique where the customer has been manipulated into submissive agreement. You are a positive force for your customers, working to understand their problems and supply the right solutions for these needs. Of course, not every sale can be positioned such that your product or service is an overwhelming favorite. But you should at least be competitive and offer a reasonable choice to the potential customer. See your efforts as part of the support you give to your customers,

> Integrity and honesty are pivotal for a positive mental attitude.

> Solution-based selling builds enthusiasm

GETTING AND STAYING ENTHUSIASTIC

helping them in their work, and providing work for your firm with the sales success you do accomplish.

Customer-Focused Selling is a positive process. It should allow you to feel good about the assistance you offer, and your intent to build "win-win" relationships where both parties gain because of the appropriateness of the transaction. Customer-Focused Selling builds enthusiasm, and enthusiasm builds sales success.

21

GOAL SETTING

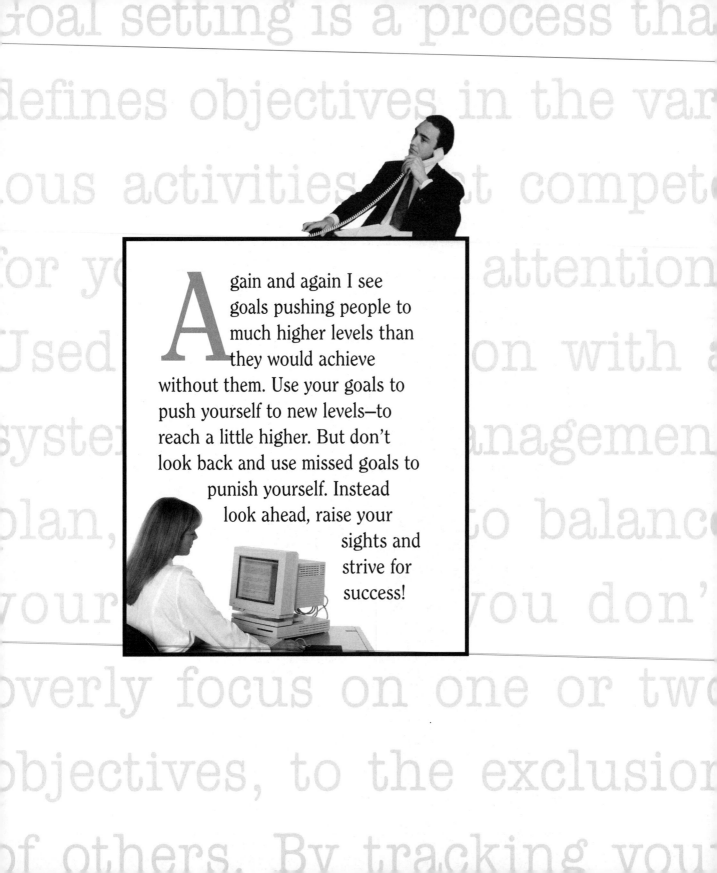

Again and again I see goals pushing people to much higher levels than they would achieve without them. Use your goals to push yourself to new levels—to reach a little higher. But don't look back and use missed goals to punish yourself. Instead look ahead, raise your sights and strive for success!

W

hy set goals? Sales success is not an accident. Those salespeople who achieve the most in their careers generally have one thing in common: They know where they are going and exactly how they are going to get there.

Goal setting is the process you use to accomplish this. Why do you need to set goals? The answer is really very simple. Setting goals is the most efficient way to accomplish your objectives. It works in a number of ways to accomplish this.

Goal setting achieves the following:

- It directs and coordinates your activities.
- It increases efficiency through prioritizing.
- It keeps you motivated.
- Most importantly, it is the way you steer your ship.

What good is making efficient use of your time without ensuring that you're headed in the right direction? When properly used, goal setting should be the rudder that directs and coordinates your business activities. It keeps you focused on what's important, and on what's necessary to grow to the next level of success.

> Goal setting should be the rudder that directs and coordinates your business activities.

GOAL SETTING INCREASES EFFICIENCY THROUGH PRIORITIZING.

Goal setting focuses and prioritizes your activities so the bulk of your energy goes into accomplishing those objectives that are key to achieving your major goals. It avoids the trap of keeping too many balls in the air, and it emphasizes those two or three key activities that are really critical to bigger successes. Rather than wasting your time trying to accomplish everything in your workday, it helps you sort through those "must do" activities from those "like to do" ones that can eat up your precious time and dramatically slow you down.

GOAL SETTING

GOAL SETTING KEEPS YOU MOTIVATED.

Establishing goals that are meaningful and personally challenging is a good way to keep yourself motivated and interested in the progress of your business activities. Imagine your work without any goals. Can you just see yourself toiling away endlessly to do better and better, with no real sense of progress? Goal setting turns this around by defining significant steps you focus on in your quest for larger, broader goals. It gives you a sense of accomplishment as interim objectives are achieved, and it provides a way for you to take pride in the recognition of your progress.

PLAN FOR SUCCESS.

One of the most important aspects of goal setting is that it helps you visualize exactly what success means to you.

The process of establishing goals demands that you review all the business and personal options open to you. From these options, you must then select the goals that are most important—by your definition, and by your analysis of your business objectives. These goals, when achieved over long periods of time, will give you a sense of excitement and enthusiasm as they are planned for, methodically worked toward, and hopefully achieved after significant hard work.

Goal setting is a way for you to define success on your own terms. It gives you a framework from which to look at the various aspects of your work and life, and then it allows you to assign priorities and objectives to these so you can develop a sense of control over your future.

DEFINE YOUR BUSINESS BY DEFINING YOUR GOALS.

The process of defining your business goals really defines the actual business you're in. After you've set down those goals that are key to your success and growth, what you've really done is define those guidelines that are going to regulate your day-to-day activities and control how, and on what, you spend your workday.

That's why setting goals is so key, for how well you define your goals determines how well your time will be spent in your daily

> Visualize success.

> Goals increase excitement and enthusiam.

activities. You can easily spend your days caught in the frenzied pace of uncoordinated, hectic activities that lead nowhere, or you can grab the bull by the horns and establish a disciplined effort to build your sales and your career.

SETTING GOALS AVOIDS SALES PLATEAUING.

As your sales successes grow over time, you can approach the point where you keep tremendously busy but make no more headway in increasing your sales productivity. Whatever objectives you have set for yourself, you can reach a point of comfortable sales activity at which it appears you can continue indefinitely. You're making a good living, and without any unforeseen problems arising, why change things?

Sounds good, but this kind of thinking is dangerous.

It's hard to stay motivated and at the peak of your game if each day feels like a repeat of the last. By keeping aggressive plans and objectives, you are able to keep that "carrot" of sales growth in front of you. By having an eye on the future, you are better able to fight through the morass of those hectic daily activities that can easily swamp you. And it's far easier to stay enthused if you perceive your activities as means to an end rather than ongoing tasks with no objectives.

If you find your attitude or your sales slumping, perhaps it's a good time to review your goals to make sure you're still imposing a sense of urgency about your business. Being successful in sales has a lot to do with keeping aggressive goals for yourself, and enjoying the accomplishment of those goals by having a good attitude and a realistic plan for accomplishing them.

For similar reasons, goal setting avoids stagnation in your business. It's important to cultivate a healthy attitude toward continually improving your sales and business targets. By placing pressure on yourself to do better each successive period, you automatically are forced to review your past activities to look for more productive approaches. Also, you develop the orientation of continuously looking for personal and business efficiency improvements, which means

The "carrot" of sales growth.

GOAL SETTING

that you never end up resting on your past accomplishments. This constant focus on business growth and improvement avoids much of the stagnation that can follow when one becomes too complacent with past performance. Active goal setting breaks down the lulling effect of "business as usual."

Goal setting is also an excellent technique to promote business growth. Beyond providing personal motivation and avoiding a sense of stagnation, the process of defining your goals yields the means through which you actually grow, and direct, your business. For example, seeking to get sales from some new market segment may not only bring you those additional sales, it also may position your business in a particularly attractive growth market, which may be critical to its long-term survival.

> Goals help prevent stagnation.

GOAL SETTING KEEPS ACTIVITIES IN BALANCE.

Goal setting is a process that defines objectives in the various activities that compete for your time and attention. Used in conjunction with a systematic time management plan, it is a way to balance your efforts so you don't focus on one or two objectives to the exclusion of others. By tracking your progress toward these goals, you ensure that objectives of equal importance receive similar attention and efforts. When you don't take the time to manage your time and goals, you lose your perspective of what's important to your business, and focus more on what you like to do. Be aware of how much you gain in efficiency and control by utilizing a strong goal-setting approach in your daily, monthly, and yearly planning.

WHERE SHOULD YOU SET GOALS?

Goal setting should not be restricted to your business efforts only. Of course, it makes sense to plan your sales activities with major accounts or for key industry objectives. Certainly you can apply this same discipline more broadly to your business as you build, from a focus on individual accounts, to include major programs that address significant business activities.

GOAL SETTING

Expand the application of goal setting and planning further to include your personal life, family and friends. Many people overlook the importance of planning for their personal life as well as for their business activities. Don't write this area off. It's equally important to your overall mental health, and if you're not making the effort to enjoy and reward yourself, then maybe you've forgotten the whole point of working so hard in the first place.

If it's a goal that's important to you, plan for its success by focusing on the individual steps that will eventually lead to even more accomplishments and satisfaction. Follow the old adage, "Work hard, play hard." Perhaps rewrite it, "Plan your work, plan your play," and you'll find time for both and enjoy success with both.

THE PROCESS OF GOAL SETTING.

- Put your goals in writing.
- Make your goals personally challenging.
- Actively pursue your goals.
- Reward yourself when you succeed.
- Update your goals periodically.

PUT YOUR GOALS IN WRITING

If it's important enough to spend this amount of time and effort figuring out what you want to accomplish, then its important enough to put it in writing. Take out three pieces of paper. Label the first, "Account Goals"; label the second, "Business Goals"; and label the third, "Personal–Self, Family, and Friends." Then take the time to *define what's both important and critical for you* in each of these areas.

Be specific in your goals. Quantify them to the best extent possible. Rather than saying, "I want to greatly increase my sales next year," state specifically, "I want to achieve sales growth of $300,000 next year." Instead of planning on spending more quality time with your family, define the number and length of vacations you are going to take with them over the next year, and even the number of hours you are planning to spend in play activities with your kids each weekend.

Put 'em in writing.

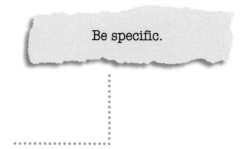

Be specific.

GOAL SETTING

Commit yourself in writing to your goals. Put them on the bulletin board over your desk so you can continually remind yourself what you should be focused on.

MAKE YOUR GOALS PERSONALLY CHALLENGING

Don't define mediocrity with your goals. Make them significant and worthy of your best efforts. How can anyone be expected to get excited and motivated over goals that require no straining or heavy lifting? Remember, these goals are for yourself. Make them a stretch. Make them difficult and large enough so you get excited just at the thought of accomplishing them.

Alternatively, as challenging as they should be, they should not be unattainable. If they're almost out of the question, how can you ever be expected to commit to them wholeheartedly?

Then get a second opinion wherever possible. Test these goals on your peers, your accountant, your family, on whomever it may be appropriate. If they say, "So what?," crank them up a notch. If they give a little smile or a low whistle, you know they're just right.

> Challenging, but not unattainable.

ACTIVELY PURSUE YOUR GOALS

If you've taken the time to establish meaningful and challenging goals for yourself and your business activities, then fully committing to them should be your endorsement that they are truly important to you. If you just give lip service to this activity, don't expect too much. Maybe you'll knock off a couple of the easier items, but what the heck, who has time for all this stuff anyway?

Take the time, make the effort, or stop kidding yourself. Life—and your workday—are too short to waste giving token attention to an activity as important as this. Commitment to your goals should be your highest priority. Work like a demon, believe you're going to succeed, and you will. You'll find yourself fully absorbed and having fun in the process. Remember, you can achieve only what you believe you can achieve. Set your goals high, be tenacious, and expect to win. You will!

> Give it your full commitment.

GOAL SETTING

REWARD YOURSELF WHEN YOU SUCCEED

What's the fun of working so hard if you don't take the time to enjoy your accomplishments? Feeling good about yourself is half the battle, anyway. And as important, since these are valid and challenging goals, realize these really are significant accomplishments and that you deserve credit for them.

Acknowledge your successful efforts, and help keep your spirits up by rewarding yourself whenever you have a chance to cross off one of the items on your goal lists. It's not that often that you'll get the chance to acknowledge your successes. Take the time to pat yourself on the back and spoil yourself a little.

Again, the whole point of your work is to enjoy your successes on both business and personal fronts. Do something special to celebrate. Perhaps a long-promised fishing trip, perhaps even trading in the car for an upgrade. Take the time to recognize and celebrate your successes and you'll stay motivated toward even greater achievements.

UPDATE YOUR GOALS PERIODICALLY

As you find yourself making periodic progress toward your goals, make sure you modify or add others to reflect this. Although the goals should be personally challenging and significant, you will find that by breaking them down into smaller time frames, monthly or weekly, they become more manageable.

You will also find that your short-term goals will have to be amended more often than your longer-range goals. Although the long-term objectives for yourself and your business tend to change slowly, the methods and opportunities to implement many of the building-block activities will change in response to numerous factors. You will find it vital to review your goals quite regularly in response to competition, other opportunities, or even a family illness.

PLANNERS WIN!

People who plan their daily activities have a competitive advantage over those who don't. Defining your goals and developing a time

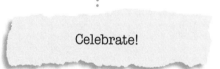
Celebrate!

GOAL SETTING

management system to accomplish them is the best way to succeed in your business.

For you, and for your business success, attainment of these goals is recognition of your commitment to the quality and high performance of your personal business efforts. Sales can be a very lone effort, and likely you receive little attention for your daily routine. Of course, everyone likes to look at their sales tally at the end of the month or quarter, but that speaks little about all of the other activities you must address throughout the same period. Don't let all the other sales development and support efforts slip from your attention. Recognize, through your goal achievement, that they are also important parts of your work.

Besides giving you a sense of progress, the setting of goals and their periodic attainment is a good mechanism to keep you feeling positive about your work. If you limit all your positive feedback simply to your bottom-line sales, then you are measuring only one dimension of your progress and performance.

Additionally, such a singular measure may keep you overly focused on the sales numbers not focused enough on the balance of your business activities. Over the long term, your sales success will come from having a system that defines and controls your efforts over the broad range of your total business activities.

Goal setting should be the foundation of your business.

By setting goals that are meaningful, being fully committed to their attainment, and tracking your progress against them, you can develop a powerful formula for sales success.

Set non-sales goals, too.

CHAPTER

22

TIME
MANAGEMENT

Time is money, especially in sales! If you're going to make it big in sales, you've got to really aggressively budget your time. You've got to be constantly weighing how effectively you are spending your time. You need to plan it out as carefully as you can. And you've got to be ruthless in re-assigning the use of your time to be used more effectively.

TIME MANAGEMENT

Effective time management is critical if you are to be highly successful in sales. Anyone who follows the Customer-Focused Selling approach outlined here is on the right path, but this path can become a superhighway when you harness the power of time management.

As we've all heard a million times, time is money. This is never truer than when applied to selling, for the more time you put directly into the sales effort, the more sales you will likely close. Hopefully, you've seen from the earlier chapters that this time should be used in the most meaningful way, and that working hard does not mean working smart. But if you are working smart, how do you get the most out of each day? The answer is through implementing a rigorous approach to time management, and then sticking with this system until it becomes an ingrained way of doing business.

Remember, how you invest your time is directly related to the results you will create.

Starting with this in mind, the most important advice you can learn here is to develop an approach to planning all your activities. This simply means that you should plan your monthly activities; your weekly activities; your daily activities; and, of course, each meeting's agenda. Anyone who is accustomed to planning their work will attest to the fact that they have become more efficient through better time management and utilization. If not easily apparent to you now, it should become so when you consider many of the positive aspects covered in the next pages.

To begin, it is highly recommended that everyone use a time planner system of some sort. There are many fine ones on the market to choose from. One that allows you to plan each day in detail is much preferred over one that covers a whole week, or even month, on one page. You will need this level of detail to best organize each day.

> How you invest your time is directly related to the results you will create.

TIME MANAGEMENT

Plan each week.

Plan each day.

You might also want to look at one of the new contact management software packages now on the market, as these are great planning companions. However, for most people, the everyday use of a good time planner system should suffice.

Now that you're in agreement to start planning your time, or perhaps to make even better use of the time you are already trying to plan, let's look at how you should go about the process of time management.

To start, it is good to pick a set time every week to sit down and organize your thoughts and efforts. Friday afternoon might be a good time to use, as it is often a slow period when customers can't be reached, and it allows you to come in Monday mornings knowing just what to target for the coming week. There's nothing better than starting each week with a good understanding and plan of just what you would like to accomplish in the coming days.

Similarly, planning each day is just as important. The last thing you do each day before shutting off the office lights should be to take the few moments required to see what progress you made against your daily task sheet, and then plan tomorrow's work. It is much easier to leave your work at the office when you know just what needs addressing first thing tomorrow. And if you enter this plan into your daily planner schedule, when the random thought strikes you of something you've overlooked, it's easy to pick up your planner and add the item. With a system like this you will find that very little gets missed and that you will become even more effective with your time.

As important as it is to plan your time, it is *equally* important to plan your time well. This simply means that rather that simply listing out each day's, week's, or month's scheduled activities, you should stand back and look to optimize the whole.

MAJOR CONSIDERATIONS TO KEEP IN MIND WHEN PLANNING YOUR SCHEDULE:

- Group like activities.
- Define blocks of time.

TIME MANAGEMENT

- Plan for each of your goals—account, business, and personal.
- Prioritize your tasks.
- Delegate whenever possible.
- Use the 80/20 rule.
- Update your plans frequently.

Each of these items brings an important benefit to the overall time management effort and should be considered in its own right. Taken together, they provide a real boost to your time management planning, for they will lift both your personal efficiency, and the level of sales proficiency you present to potential customers.

GROUP LIKE ACTIVITIES

Grouping like activities is the first key element of this system. This is an excellent place to start, for it makes for a much more efficient use of time. There's no denying that making several outside meetings in one day is more efficient than several half-day trips, or that an extended road trip hitting several cities is more efficient, and cheaper, than many shorter day or overnight flights.

At the outset, this may appear to be an obvious point. But given the hectic schedules most people have, the constant ringing of the phone, and the firefighting of problems that are constantly coming out of the blue, it requires superhuman powers to keep your concentration and not end up jumping from one task to another all day long. Setting aside a set time every day, or throughout the week, is the best way to prevent the inefficiency of jumping from one type of task to another, losing your prior train of thought or task focus and never going back to fully completing what you've already started. Unless you develop the discipline and ability to organize your day, you stand the risk of constantly being on the verge of being out of control.

DEFINE BLOCKS OF TIME

Going hand in hand with this ability to group similar activities is the ability to set aside a preferred block of time in which to carry out these similar activities. With almost all business activities, there is a best time to work on several of your key activities, and by

> You can develop the discipline to use time more efficiently.

TIME MANAGEMENT

Synchronize your time
management with your
customers.

manipulating your schedule, you can become much more effective by optimizing and managing your time.

For example, let's consider the basic activity of phone use. In Customer-Focused Selling we are constantly talking about being aware of both "your" world and the "client's" world. Keeping this in mind, let's think about the important considerations to be addressed when trying to handle your phone activities for the day and the week.

Looking at your customer's business, you are likely to find that their Monday mornings are primarily occupied with beginning-of-the-week meetings as people generally use this time to organize and direct their staff's work for the week. Or perhaps they have been mulling over some problem all weekend that they just want to jump on Monday morning when they're back in the office. Friday afternoons might also be inappropriate for phone calling, as people generally leave earlier on Fridays, particularly in the summer when some companies even go to the routine of four long days, then one-half day on Friday. Alternatively, some sales people may find Fridays the most productive time. Perhaps you're in the building trade industry and this is the day when most people are commonly back in the home office reporting on field progress made that week.

Other factors you may want to take into consideration when planning for phone activities are:

- Various time zones of customers
- National and international business
- Holidays and vacation periods (particularly international, as they are so varied)
- Competitors' activities
- Follow-up required for typing and faxing
- Need and timing of customer responses
- Staffing availability
- Least expensive phone time
- Seasonality of their, and your, business
- Client availability

TIME MANAGEMENT

Now you should consider your own best time for telephone activities. Are you a morning person or an afternoon person? Is this a task you look forward to or one you put off because it wears you down? Are you going to be cold calling, or are you following with information that is very positive and that will likely please the potential account?

Looking over all your personal factors, and taking into account your customer's factors, decide what would comprise a good time period for you to handle these phone activities. You might, for example, even end up with two periods, one in the morning for cold calling, and one, when you're more tired in the late afternoon, for follow-up with old accounts with which you just need to touch base. Perhaps you may want to intersperse these calls, as you could make several of the harder cold calls (if this might apply to you), and then reward yourself with one to a comfortable, good account with whom you have an excellent relationship.

All of your basic business activities should be similarly approached and planned. The important thing here is to realize the increased efficiency to be gained by not having a helter-skelter schedule throughout your day and week.

PLAN FOR EACH OF YOUR GOALS

Accepting the basis of grouping and managing like tasks, the next logical question to ask is, "What tasks require this in-depth planning?" The answer is virtually everything you'll encounter in your workday.

In fact, the concept of adequate time management and planning is so powerful that it should be expanded to cover all aspects of your business and personal life. In a prior chapter, "Precall Planning," the importance of an organized and focused sales call was developed. What works so well for a single task, works equally well for the numerous other tasks that envelop you throughout your workday. And expanding this concept broadly to include your personal and business goals puts you on track to accomplish even more than you might believe possible.

Group related types of calls.

Longer-term planning.

TIME MANAGEMENT

For this reason, it is suggested that once a year, or even better, every six months, you sit down and spend the time to define your business, personal, and family goals. The actual identification and setting of these goals is covered in another chapter, but the significant issue to recognize here is the importance of having these goals and plans.

The chapter "Goal Setting" covers, in detail, the understanding and setting of goals, which should be integrated with your time planning.

Remember, it is almost impossible to accomplish something of real significance, over any period of time, that does not require a well-organized, planned effort!

PRIORITIZE YOUR TASKS

Keeping in mind that you now should have developed sizable lists covering the time you will be investing in accomplishing your account, business, personal and family goals, you will likely be overwhelmed by the size of the task facing you. The key to remember is that this project becomes manageable when you begin prioritizing your lists.

Prioritizing should be done at two levels—within each list, and among the lists. That is to say, you should review each list to bring the more urgent activities to the top. Having done this, you must then look at all your lists to assign relative values among them.

Make your prioritizing self-serving and logical. For instance, you might have made a great list of potential new accounts with whom you would like to land first orders over the next three months. But you have a second list of things you would like to do to increase you professional capabilities (such as attending professional seminars, trade shows, etc.). Knowing that the landing of new accounts is more important and urgent to you than long-term professional development, you first tackle trying to define how much time you can allocate to each area. Treating this simplistically, and assuming these were the only two tasks to divide your time between, you might assign 90 percent of your time to new account prospecting and only 10 percent of your week to professional development. With thirty-six

Prioritizing brings order to chaos.

TIME MANAGEMENT

hours a week to pursue new accounts, you can likely make a big dent in your new-account targets. Unfortunately, this leaves only four hours a week for professional development, and you can hardly tackle your list here. But having prioritized it, there are probably one or two top items you might be able to undertake. Perhaps this might be a one-day seminar the next month, and one or two local trade shows.

Use this same logic to review and integrate your full schedule for the planning period.

The bottom line here is that when you are done with this process, you will have a well-defined plan for managing and prioritizing your time. Doing this process well will also have the added benefit of giving you peace of mind that things are under control and leave you freer to enjoy going about the other tasks of your business.

DELEGATE WHENEVER POSSIBLE

Delegate tasks whenever possible! Trying to do everything yourself is something that old-timers, as well as beginners, are often guilty of doing. They forget that there are others available to help and that many of the more mundane or less critical tasks can often be delegated. Or they like doing something that is routine and easy, for it gives them a sense of comfort being busy, or maybe avoids other, more difficult tasks.

This can be the case even in a one-person office. If you've taken the time to group all your travel plans in one megatrip, fax the itinerary to your travel agent and let them plan the trip. Don't spend your valuable time browsing the Internet looking for the best airline options. That's the travel agent's job, which they likely can do better than you anyway.

USE THE 80/20 RULE

You can get 80 percent of the job done with the first 20 percent of effort It has long been an understood phenomenon that the first efforts on any task accomplish the most. Or said another way, it takes a lot more effort to dot the last "i" and cross the last "t." When undertaking any task, it is a good thing to keep in mind the point of diminishing returns. Your time is a very limited commodity, and you

> Prioritizing gives you the feeling of being in control.

TIME MANAGEMENT

should develop a sense of when you are bogging down trying to complete any one project. Perhaps it is better to move along and finish 80 percent of the next task than not get to it at all.

UPDATE YOUR PLANS FREQUENTLY

No good system of time management would be complete without a periodic point for review and evaluation. Each month, just before you plan for the coming period, take the time to reflect on the progress you've made against your objectives. More likely than not, you're in the same boat as everyone else, and you didn't quite get to everything you intended. If you find you're falling farther behind, take the time to review all the tasks to make sure they're all critical tasks that must be done. When you're too busy, it's a sure sign that you should go back through the planning process again and that maybe you're trying to do the work of more than one person. Remember, an onerous workload may prove you're a super salesperson, but in the long term it's demoralizing and ultimately works against your personal productivity. As a result of too heavy a workload, you'll find yourself unhappy, and this weariness will carry over into your presentation, dampening both your enthusiasm and your delivery.

Many people who are too busy also fall into the trap of increasingly working on pending business only. Before long, they're doing no prospecting and things begin slowing up. And they don't know what's happening, as they have been busier than ever. At times like this it is wise to do a good review of your planned time and drop 10 to 15 percent of the least productive tasks. It is usually quite easy to identify those few items that are associated with a low chance of success, and simply reduce your efforts on those fronts, or drop them completely for greener pastures.

Follow these simple guidelines, and you are sure to give your customers ever better, timelier attention, and see these efforts rewarded with increased sales.

By the way, if you don't have or use a time planner, stop right now and make a note to yourself to pick up one ASAP!

Re-evaluate your time plan.

THE SALES/EFFORT CYCLE.

It is important to note that the sales effort you will have to expend will not only vary by account and project, but also by the timing of the sales cycle. As illustrated in the following model, efforts to initiate an account will be generally light when looking for potential sales. When genuine leads are developed, the efforts rise dramatically as the sales person is required to cultivate a better understanding of the account and potential sale. This increased effort should extend into the first sales, as the salesperson must nurture this account to maximize the sales, and make themselves available to answer those new account type of questions.

But as this diagram indicates, the good news is that if you've done your job well, this effort drops off to a maintenance effort where you strive to maintain, or increase, the sales volume. At this point the salesperson usually begins a "business as usual" relationship and can often seek to develop new sales opportunities within the existing account.

> Because the effort required is different at different points in the sales cycle, you should always be soliciting new accounts.

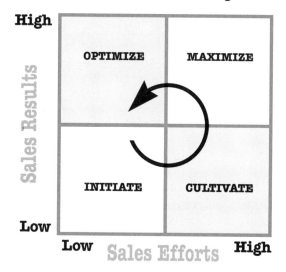

Sales/Effort Cycle

TIME MANAGEMENT

PLAN YOUR SALES CALL AND BE IN CONTROL!

FIVE MINUTES OF PLANNING = THE WINNING MARGIN

One to Two Weeks in Advance

- Review company sales literature, annual reports, publications, etc.
- Identify competitors and review their products and literature.
- Review trade magazines, visit relevant trade shows.
- Talk to someone within organization to find out current business issues.
- Read recent press releases, newspaper articles, quotes of senior management, etc.
- Visit their Web site.
- Use their product or service.
- Prepare and send introductory letter or fax (see the section "Start Selling with Letters").

One to Two Days in Advance

- List key issues and problems of client.
- Identify need or problem(s) you will address and advantages of your product or service.
- Prepare a customer-specific presentation (see the section: "Delivering Presentations").
- Call to confirm your appointment.

In the Parking Lot

- Review the names of all the people you will meet with.
- Review your presentation and refresh your memory with the main advantages of your product or service to which the customer will most likely respond.
- Take a deep breath, smile, go in, and give your great presentation.

A little planning for each sales call goes a long way towards success.

TIME MANAGEMENT

Immediately Afterward
- Mentally review the high and low points of the meeting.
- Fill out the postmeeting summary and action list items.

Back at the Office
- Send a follow-up letter detailing activities or a thank-you note.
- Transcribe action list items and date for follow-up phone call into your time planner.

CHAPTER

23

THE TWELVE
BIG KEYS
TO
SALES SUCCESS

W hether you're just starting or have some sales experience, here's a few important keys to sales success to remember and practice day in and day out. This list seems short, easy and relatively self-evident—yet it is *consistently using* these keys to success that really separates top sales performers from average ones.

THE TWELVE BIG KEYS TO SALES SUCCESS

1. KNOW YOUR "STUFF" AND BELIEVE IN IT.

You can't sell it if you don't believe in it! Taking this concept even farther, you can't sell it if you don't feel it! To best represent a product or service (with sales results that prove it), you need to have experienced the benefits of that product or service. For example, if you sell life insurance, you had better own life insurance so you can have experienced, firsthand, the benefits of it—peace of mind, protecting your family, planning for retirement, etc. Rather than just talking about the benefits theoretically, you can now speak from your heart when a prospective customer asks your opinion about your product or service. *Customers know the difference between a learned sales presentation and a heartfelt one.*

2. STOP SELLING AND START LISTENING.

The best approach to Customer-Focused Selling is asking good questions, then *listening intently* to the answers. Selling is not about talking well; it's the ability to gather information, consolidate the information, and provide a helpful intervention (your product or service). Customers want to talk! They want to tell you about their "world," about their "unique" problems, about themselves! Even if you've heard it a million times before and you know what they are going to say before they say it . . . let them talk. *Customers buy from you based more on how well you listen than on how well you talk.* Stop selling and start listening.

3. LEAVE YOUR EGO AT THE DOOR AND LEARN FLEXIBILITY.

Can you remember a time when you got in your own way, just by being you? Most experienced sales reps can. The point is, add a healthy dose of flexibility whenever your personal agenda enters into the situation. Let's say you scheduled a one-hour appointment for a sales presentation on human resources consulting services to the president of a midsize company. You've spent hours preparing a beautiful electronic presentation that you feel does a great job of explaining your capabilities. When you walk into the meeting, you

Believe in your product!

THE TWELVE BIG KEYS TO SALES SUCCESS

find out that there will be three additional people attending; that you have only twenty minutes, not sixty; and that you are one of six consultants they are interviewing that morning. What do you do? You could rush through your presentation because *YOU want to do it the way YOU'VE prepared.* Or you could put it aside and probably be better off investing your time in establishing trust, credibility, and in making a deeper business connection to each member of the team. Going with your ego could kill that sale; going with flexibility and good judgment could lead to that sale. Keep an open mind and always address the *current* circumstances.

4. RESPECT HOW YOUR CUSTOMER PREFERS TO COMMUNICATE.

You might be fast-paced and outgoing, or maybe you're more reserved and slower-paced. How you like to interact with others should be secondary to how your customer naturally interacts. Be aware of your customer's style of communication and respond accordingly. This is not to say don't be yourself, but rather, honor your customer's preference for style. Remember, nonverbal language is a powerful tool in building a bridge for communication. It's the chemistry side of the sale, the hard-to-put-your-finger-on-it part that says, "I'm not quite sure why but I really like (or don't like) this salesperson." It's your responsibility in selling to be the one who adapts and therefore makes the communication more comfortable and more effective. *The end result is that customers who feel that you communicate on their wavelength will open up to you more readily, be more forthcoming with information, and trust you more rapidly.* Your sales results will tell you how well you're doing in respecting your customers' communication preference.

5. PLANT TRIGGERS AND LEAVE FOOTPRINTS.

Make it easy for your prospective customers to work with you. Planting triggers means that every time you interact with an existing customer or a prospective customer, you provide them with

Make it easy for your customer to communicate with you.

THE TWELVE BIG KEYS TO SALES SUCCESS

"triggers," or reasons why they might need to work with you or buy from you. For example, if you are selling advertising specialties and the prospect doesn't seem to be particularly interested in doing business now, provide them with triggers by saying, "Some of the clients we work with use mugs at trade shows, water bottles on the Fourth of July, and hats for the first day of summer." The trigger you're giving the prospect is that of dates and events. You want them to think of you if a date or event triggers a need for your product. Next, make sure you leave "footprints," which are the ways a customer can find you again if they need you. Some of these you probably use now—a business card or a company brochure. But what are some of the other ways in which you can help them "find" you should a need arise between your regular contacts with them? How about a newsletter, written articles, advertising in a local paper, an easy-to-remember 800 number, a memorable company name, sending them a postcard from your office location, or maybe a calendar to hang on their wall all year? The objective of planting triggers and leaving footprints is to make it easy for your customers to remember and find you when thinking of your product or service. Exactly what you want!

"Triggers" and "foot prints" make sure your customers remember you.

6. MANAGE YOURSELF LIKE A BUSINESS.

You know the saying "Time is money." On the money side, businesses focus on both revenue and profitability. In sales, the tendency is toward focusing only on revenue. Look at how you operate, and include the principles of good business with a review of time, money, and profit. Segment your accounts and determine the gems. Look for the ones that are most profitable, the ones that have the most potential, and those that can keep a stream of revenue with the least amount of handholding. You might find that Pareto's Rule of 20/80 is true, that 80 percent of your sales come from 20 percent of your accounts. As any business should, simply ask yourself how you can do more business with those kinds of accounts and manage the other accounts differently. *Your time is your money.* Invest your time in the places that generate the most profit.

Manage your time with a vengeance!

THE TWELVE BIG KEYS TO SALES SUCCESS

7. PLANT SEEDS EVERY DAY.

Prospecting is a big key to your success. In your early days of selling you will have all day, every day, to prospect. As you become more experienced, you will tend to spend more time with your customer base, but this leaves less time for prospecting. That's the root of the problem. If you look at your success today, it is a direct result of the good prospecting you did six months ago. The question now is: What are you doing today to make sure that business is great six months from now? The answer: Plant seeds every day. No matter how busy or great business is today, *to attain consistently high sales results you must engage in prospecting activities daily.* Your efforts may shift over time, but regardless, you must do something every day toward new business development. Use the methods most effective for you—cold calls, warm calls, networking, speaking, writing. Get out there, be proactive, and set up your future by planting seeds today.

8. LET GO OF TACTICS AND DEVELOP PERSONAL JUDGMENT SKILLS.

Using personal judgment skills means trusting yourself to say the right thing, at the right time, in the right way. Personal judgment skills come from knowing your products or services inside out, doing an accurate assessment of your potential client, and then answering directly how your product or service can link the two. With Customer-Focused Selling you have to let go of the need for manipulation, and trust the process of working with your customer. Step one is to let go of the crutches and believe in yourself. Step two is understanding that the customer wants that degree of true connection. And step three is to practice, practice, practice. *Sharp personal judgment skills come from the day-to-day experiences of letting go of tactics and replacing them with outstanding customer focus.*

9. MANAGE THE SALES PROCESS WITH NEXT STEPS.

You know it's your job to manage the sales process, but how often do you really feel like you're in the driver's seat? The desired answer

THE TWELVE BIG KEYS TO SALES SUCCESS

should be that you feel you're always in control. Managing the Customer-Focused Selling process means knowing exactly where you stand at all times and what it will take to advance the sale. *The best way to stay in control is to make sure you establish "next steps" at the close of every interaction.* Whether it's a phone call, a face-to-face meeting, E-mail, or a letter . . . ALWAYS clearly state or determine next steps. Focus on defining a summary of the sales status, and a statement of what each party will do next. By managing the sales process you eliminate misconceptions, misunderstandings, and stalled sales. In effect you are collaboratively agreeing to move the process ahead by agreeing on next steps!

| Establish "next steps" at the end of each sales call. |

10. LET YOUR ENTHUSIASM SHOW.

Letting your enthusiasm show doesn't mean jumping up and down with a big toothy grin in your customer's office. It does mean letting them see how much you care. Do you love what you do? Would you do it for free? Is it fun? Do you get excited when you uncover your customer's problems and solve them with your product or service? Enthusiasm comes from passion about what you do, what you represent, and how you impact your customers. Customer-Focused Selling lets you show your customers that you "hear them," understand them, can help them, and like doing it! Enjoy, and let them see the enthusiasm in your work.

| Enthusiasm sells! |

11. BE A STUDENT OF THE WORLD.

In sales you should strive to be a good communicator and to develop the ability to connect with others. The more you are aware of the world around you, the better you will reach your customers on diverse levels. When was the last time you took a field trip to your local library and walked from aisle to aisle with no specific book in mind? Take the time to wander into the world of books, to journey into unknown areas, to explore new hobbies. Whatever your interests, be they in science, psychology, travel, business, self-development, or spirituality, you are best served by expanding your outlook. You may be in sales, but *you don't sell to companies, you sell to people in companies*. People relate to people. Be a student of the

THE TWELVE BIG KEYS TO SALES SUCCESS

world and you will grow in your ability to relate to others on different planes, in different ways, and in different worlds.

12. ALWAYS BE POSITIVE.

Being in sales, you are likely a "people person" and out in the business world all day long. This provides a great opportunity to touch many people in positive ways. Take this part of your job very seriously because your words can have great impact. Positive words can build an opportunity; negative words can leave harmful debris. Most importantly, the way you operate day-to-day speaks volumes about your character and who you really are. You can't be a louse one minute and a charmer the next and expect to be successful. Commit yourself to living with the highest integrity every day. Respect your profession, respect others, and always be positive.

Everyone likes positive people!

CHAPTER

24

THE TWELVE BIG SALES MISTAKES

I t's probably around the time of your first sales call that you start to fall into habits—some good and some not so good. This section focuses on some of the bad habits that salespeople tend to fall into, habits that often take a lot of effort, energy, and concentration to break out of. For example it's always "easier" just to run through your sales pitch as opposed to really interacting with your customer, asking probing questions, listening intently and helping find and explain to the customer solutions to their particular needs. But it's by doing the harder work of getting closely involved with your customer that will often make the difference between getting the sale and losing the sale.

THE TWELVE BIG SALES MISTAKES

1. TALKING TOO MUCH.

The most common mistake salespeople make is talking too much! The problem can easily arise because you know your stuff really well. You're talking to someone for a couple of minutes, they'll say something you see as a buying sign, and you immediately jump in, "I can do that!" Meanwhile, they had ten other things they wanted to ask you about. If you talk too much you can easily make a huge mistake and miss a lot of important information.

2. TOO FAST A PACE IN YOUR SALES PITCH.

Proceed at a leisurely pace when explaining yourself and your product. One of the common pitfalls of the inexperienced salesperson is a tendency to proceed too fast through the prepared presentation. Obviously you know the material very well, but this may be the first time your potential customer has been exposed to it. Take the time to explain all aspects of your presentation, and pause periodically to give an opportunity for questions. Remember, this is their first time, even if it's your four-millionth time. So pace yourself; don't get ahead of your buyer.

3. NERVOUSNESS.

It is normal to expect that at times, particularly when you are starting out in sales, you will find yourself quite nervous over an upcoming sales call. At times like this, you should shift your thoughts away from the customer and focus on thinking about your strengths and what you bring to the table. With all your preparation and product knowledge, shift your focus to the other person and think about why they want to hear from you. This shifting of focus and not worrying will naturally relax you, and you will find it much easier to be genuinely sincere, and also easier to project enthusiasm and confidence in your presentation.

4. FAILURE TO SEE YOUR CUSTOMER'S "WORLD" AND PROBLEMS.

One of the worst mistakes a salesperson can make is to get so wrapped up in their product that they fall in love with it and forget

> Let your customer do the talking!

> Plant yourself in your customer's shoes!

THE TWELVE BIG SALES MISTAKES

Plan for every sales call!

to see that they have lost the recipient of the presentation along the way. Salespeople can easily be caught up in telling the world about their great product or service when no one really cares. Often this sales pitch ends up being to someone who is not a real buyer or to someone who doesn't have a need for your product. Selling is rarely about convincing someone they need what you have. *Selling is really about identifying who needs what you have and being the one to get it for them.*

5. FAILURE TO DO ADEQUATE PRECALL PLANNING.

Being poorly prepared is the number one reason why salespeople don't get the sale. Your competition outsells you because they know more about the client situation than you do, and they do a better job. If it's really at the end of the sale, in many cases it might be too late. If you've developed the right relationship along the sale, then sometimes you can have a conversation with that buyer and say, "What have I done wrong?' And they might tell you outright, "You messed up. If you do X, Y, and Z, then you're still in the running."

6. ASKING FOR A COMMITMENT TOO SOON.

Asking for a commitment before the buyer has conceptually bought into your product or service is another big reason why you lose sales. *If you're getting objections, that's a big signal you're going too fast.* They're saying, "We have no money, we have no time, we want to think about it." This means you goofed, but it's not over yet. Hang in there. Work the process and help the customer over the objections.

7. BECOMING COMPLACENT.

Sometimes experienced salespeople get lazy. When you've been in sales a long time, there're two things to watch for. One is that you plateau because you're successful and happy, and you're having a great life. The problem is that you really can't stop in selling. You're either going forward or you're going backward. Also, you can get overconfident, which is again discounting all the things you did right

THE TWELVE BIG SALES MISTAKES

in the beginning. Many times I've heard people say, "I used to do this and it worked." Ask yourself, "When did I stop doing this?" Many times all you may need to do is rebuild the good skills and discipline you once had.

8. OVERREACTING TO OBJECTIONS.

When you encounter objections, don't go into a reactionary mode, which is what many salespeople do. What you should do is listen. This is where you need major control over your facial expressions. Don't look like you're being sucker-punched. Don't look like it's the end of the world. Look like you're interested and curious about how they feel. Then you ask a question. The question has to be extremely open-ended, very investigative: "Could you explain a little bit more?" "Share with me?" "Explore with me?" "Describe to me?" When an objection comes up, get them talking to hear the rest of the story. And then you'll want to acknowledge or summarize, "If I'm hearing you correctly, you're concerned about . . . This offers proof to the other person that you're listening. It also gives them the opportunity to add more if you didn't get it correctly. Now, when you go to answer them, answer them from the information you just got. For each objection, there's a way to respond by interpreting the objection, not at face value, but in the context of what they really want from you and from your product or service.

> Don't be knocked out by objections!

9. INABILITY TO ARTICULATE VALUE

A big sales trap is talking about your products or services strictly in terms of features—that is, what the product or service is. By focusing on features you miss the opportunity to articulate value. *Value articulation comes from being able to discuss your product and service from the customer's perspective rather than yours.* You must be able to bridge the gap between what your product or service is and what it actually does for customers.

> Emphasize value in terms of "solutions," not features.

10. TRYING TOO HARD TO SELL

Overselling is a big turnoff and enters the picture for many reasons. You might be under a lot of pressure to meet a quota, you might really want this one, you might be rushing this one to go sell the next one, in each case your tendency of trying too hard won't help. The real test is to ask yourself when it feels like you're selling too hard, "Whose agenda am I coming from, mine or the customer's?" Customer-Focused Selling keeps you out of the trap of selling from your agenda.

11. MISTAKING BUSY FOR PRODUCTIVE.

When you are busy all day long, it feels great! However, at the end of your day it doesn't matter what you did, it matters if you did the right things! Don't mistake busy for productive. Don't let the business run you; you must run the business. Don't hope for sales to happen; make them happen. Don't be reactive; be proactive. Real productivity comes from a well-designed strategy and day-to-day implementation.

12. LACK OF SALES FOLLOW-UP.

Research has shown that 70 percent of all sales are made after the fifth contact. However, most salespeople stop selling efforts after the second contact. See the problem? Just when the customer is beginning to warm up, most sales follow-up has been tossed aside. Obviously you are missing sales opportunities, but even more so, you aren't getting paid appropriately for the time you have invested! Don't let go of a prospective customer until you both decide it's not a good fit!

> Are you being productive? Or just busy?

H A P T E R

25

DRESS
TO
SUCCEED

Just because most businesses are allowing more casual dress in their workplace, doesn't mean that you're going to succeed in sales by dressing as casually as you can. Buyers expect sales people to dress professionally. And they do appreciate and respect a salesperson who dresses well—no matter how casually dressed they are themselves. Stand out from the crowd with immaculate grooming and superior business dress and you'll be that much closer to getting the sale even before you arrive at your appointment!

DRESS TO SUCCEED

The subject of appropriate dress often comes up in sales, for selling is a profession that puts you constantly onstage, in front of your customers. Many people, unfortunately, take this to heart and dress as though they really are onstage and develop a persona that supports this image.

Others, just as unfortunately, think only one-dimensionally, focusing solely on their product or service. They forget that they are also part of the sale, that they are perceived by the potential customer as the cornerstone of a customer service system that potentially may be providing service or products to them. In this sales process, both your appearance and your actions play strong roles in helping the client make their decision regarding purchasing from your firm.

Your dress code won't make the sale, but it can prevent it!

When it comes to appropriate dress, there are no hard-and-fast rules. However, there are guidelines that define what should be the intent of your dress code, and that, if followed, will serve you well throughout your career.

YOU SHOULD APPROACH SALES FROM THE CUSTOMER'S POINT OF VIEW.

Remember that your intent in Customer-Focused Selling is to link your product or service features with the customer's needs or problems. More than ever before, today's customers are only interested in what your product or service can do for them. This is more than a cliché, for business has become very serious, and with the current downsizing and increased responsibilities everyone is facing, there is little patience or time for anyone who is other than all business. This means that your presentation should be very pragmatic and customer-focused.

> You and your dress are part of the sale.

DRESS TO SUCCEED

LET YOUR PRODUCT OR SERVICE BE THE BRIGHT SPOT.

Never dress to detract or distract from your product or service. Customer-Focused Selling is focused on the customer, not on you.

For years, IBM held the reputation of being all business and number one in customer service. They also became known for their professional white- or blue-shirt look. By maintaining a clean-cut, all-business image they were able to let their product and service be the most noticeable thing about their sales presentations.

Although times have changed, the concept of not dressing so as to overpower the attention you want focused on your product or service remains an important factor in your sales effort.

The more you divert the customer's attention from the solution being offered, the less your chances of developing that critical linkage between your potential client and your product or service. You must realize that for your customers, as well as for yourself, time is money, and that they want to get right down to business. Rather than trying to get their attention, you want the answers your product or service provides to take center stage.

RELATE YOUR DRESS CODE TO YOUR CUSTOMER'S LEVEL OF DRESS.

In considering appropriate apparel, it is important to be aware of both your customer's and your industry's unwritten dress code. When defining your personal level of wardrobe sophistication, you should never be too loud or too low in your clothing choice.

You should never dress to be the center of attention, nor should you ever be the worst-dressed person in the room.

Strike a happy medium with your dress and strive to look like a solid citizen of the industry or service you represent.

For example, following this advice for someone selling in the building trades might mean wearing khakis and a nice, casual shirt with a collar, rather than worn jeans with a T-shirt. Conversely, wearing a suit, no matter how casual, would likely lead to your being

> Never dress to detract or distract from your product or service.

> Be aware of both your customer's and your industry's unwritten dress code.

> Strive to look like a solid citizen of the industry or service you represent.

DRESS TO SUCCEED

perceived as someone who doesn't get their hands dirty, someone who might not know what they're talking about when it comes to construction sales.

SAVE FLASHY DRESS FOR AFTER-HOURS

Within any generally defined level of dress, care should be given to avoid creating an image that customers will have trouble identifying with. Using our construction sales example from the previous section, think about how the potential customer would react if the salesperson arrived not just in khakis but in expensive, labeled designer khakis, and with an obviously expensive designer shirt and imported shoes. Can you just imagine how hard it would be for the field foreman to listen to the sales presentation when he's wondering to himself, "Where the heck did you get that outfit?"

EMPHASIZE QUALITY, NOT STYLE, IN YOUR WARDROBE.

For women, this problem can be even more prominent if they let the social pressure to dress fashionably overrun their common sense. It is far better to invest in a few high-quality outfits that are understated, than in more noticeable and stylized clothes that garner too much attention and that perhaps lead the customer to pay more attention to your dress than to your sales presentation.

Of course, for every rule there is an exception, and you should not adhere blindly to this guideline. The fashion industry, for example, expects you to be a walking billboard for your wares. Similarly, anyone from a top-flight ad agency in New York City is expected to project an image just as creative as their work. But, in general, it is usually the best approach to present yourself dressed to reflect the competent, dedicated professional you are. Just as you wouldn't want to present shoddy or inappropriately gaudy business literature, you want to present that same theme in your dress code. Let your product or service garner the customer's attention!

> It is far better to invest in a few high-quality outfits that are understated.

DRESS TO SUCCEED

USE YOUR WARDROBE GUIDELINES TO SELECT YOUR CAR.

When buying or leasing a car, you should use the same care and values that you use in choosing your wardrobe. Whatever mistakes you might make in choosing a wardrobe are amplified when they are represented in your choice of automobile.

In Customer-Focused Selling we always start with the customer's sensibility, and once again, with this in mind, it should be obvious how to approach this issue. What customer isn't going to be put out when a potential vendor arrives in an automobile far more expensive than the customer could purchase. And similarly, who isn't going to taken aback when picked up at the airport in a real clunker?

In the United States after World War II, there was an unwritten rule that salespeople should drive only American, not foreign, cars. For many years there was reasonable logic behind this, as it was not uncommon to come across someone with lingering, bitter feelings stemming from the war. On a more current theme, the intense foreign competition now experienced by almost all marketplaces has developed a keen awareness of, and predisposition for, goods made in the buyer's country.

Of course, this concept continues to blur, with Toyotas being manufactured in Kentucky, Chryslers being produced in Canada, and all automakers striving to develop more "world-class" cars. However, the concepts of staying attuned to your customer's value system, and reflecting this in your dress and working values, remain valid.

NIX ON THE ROLEX.

This awareness of what is appropriate should extend to many other related areas. For instance, when buying a new watch or briefcase, you can't go wrong in selecting solid, mainstream products. For instance, traditional American values, when selecting travel luggage, are far better represented in American Tourister than they are in Louis Vuitton. Similarly, you might have just acquired a great raccoon coat, but realize it's too controversial and too noteworthy for business occasions.

> When buying a new watch or briefcase, you can't go wrong in selecting solid, mainstream products.

DRESS TO SUCCEED

When renting cars, this logic would dictate a midsize car in preference to a full-size Lincoln or a subcompact Mazda. Think of the statement you'd make arriving in an expensive rental car—money to burn (translate that into big margins/high prices). Or conversely, can you hear "cheapskate" muttered under your customer's breath when they squeeze into your subcompact? You can almost hear them thinking, "Will this company really spend what it takes to provide us with adequate service support?"

Be careful that what you do, and how you do it, leave the right lasting impressions.

THE HALO OF IMMACULATE GROOMING.

Everyone knows that keeping your car washed and clean sends an important message about how you do business. Similarly, you would not wear a tie or blouse if it had an obvious stain. Unfortunately, pressured salespeople can fall into the trap of becoming too busy to maintain their possessions or themselves.

Getting the car washed frequently is as important a habit to develop as is taking care of your personal hygiene. And it makes similar sense to maintain your wardrobe or anything else that starts to look shabby, and that may need a trip to the dry cleaner's, or even replacing. Maintaining a positive image that doesn't detract from, but that only enhances the services you provide, can be one of the biggest hidden helpers in your sales arsenal.

Extend this concept of building a positive image more broadly to include other activities that also can benefit from this added attention and reflect positively on you.

For instance, don't just drop off samples in a loose envelope; add a typed note that reiterates their features that are particularly important to the account. Don't just drop off a one-page quote for your building cleaning services; take the time to place it in a binder with visually attractive collateral materials, and add a cover letter summarizing how your service best addresses their particular needs. You don't know where it may end up, but wherever it is, someone will be sure to notice your extra efforts in a positive light.

> Your image can make the sale.

DRESS TO SUCCEED

> Almost everything you do is a reflection of yourself, and by extension, the product or service you represent.

Remember, almost everything you do is a reflection of yourself, and by extension, the product or service you represent.

Always keep your customer in mind. Throughout all your actions, not just in how you dress, you should remain focused on the customer and their likely response to and interpretation of your activities. Continually build their confidence in your abilities by sending them the quiet signals that will make them both comfortable and confident in their choice of you as a vendor.

26

SELLING TO MULTIPLE DECISION-MAKERS

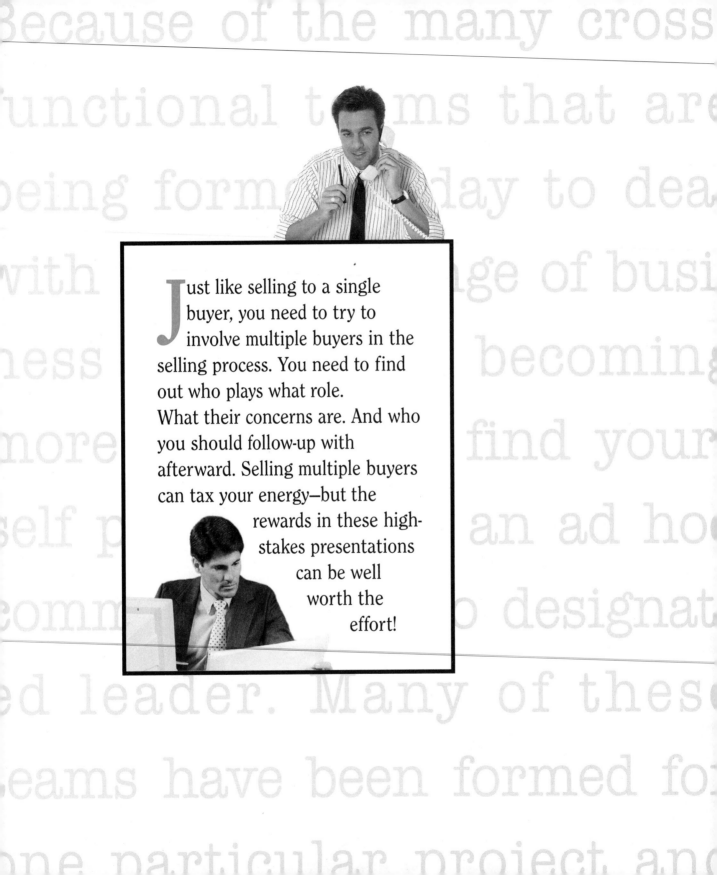

Just like selling to a single buyer, you need to try to involve multiple buyers in the selling process. You need to find out who plays what role. What their concerns are. And who you should follow-up with afterward. Selling multiple buyers can tax your energy—but the rewards in these high-stakes presentations can be well worth the effort!

SELLING TO MULTIPLE DECISION-MAKERS

W hen you enter any sales situation where there are a number of people present, you are going to have to modify your sales presentation to take the group dynamics into account.

There are several key differences when selling to multiple decision-makers instead of to an individual. You will likely often find yourself presenting to three to five people at a boardroom table. And whenever you face multiple decision-makers, your approach is going to be different in several ways.

UNDERSTAND THE DIFFERENT PLAYERS AND THEIR ROLES.

The first thing you must do is figure out the different personalities and roles in the room. Pay attention to body language. You'll do that with an individual, but even more so with a group.

There may appear to be someone who is the leader, who's managing the meeting, and whom you address in most of your conversation. But you've got to be very cautious not to direct all your attention to that person, as you'll alienate the other people in the room, who probably also have a huge influence on the decision, but just don't appear to at that moment.

The best way to manage this is to be cautious and include everyone in the room in your conversation. You want to respect them and make them all feel part of the sales process, just as you've done with the whole Customer-Focused Selling process until now.

DETERMINE THE DECISION-MAKING PROCESS.

To be effective with any group of multiple decision-makers, it is imperative, before you begin your presentation, that you understand the unique decision-making process the group will use.

> The first thing you must do is figure out the different personalities and roles in the room.

SELLING TO MULTIPLE DECISION-MAKERS

And understanding the process that will be used, you'll want to tailor your presentation to take it into account.

The easiest way to understand the decision-making process is simply to ask directly how the team will function in its decision-making. Of course, there may be more going on than meets the eye, but if you don't feel you have a clear picture, follow-up with additional clarification questions until you feel you fully understand their process.

Of course, there are any number of leadership and group dynamics that can emerge from this unknown group, so let's look at some of the more common group structures you'll likely encounter.

Strong Leader with Weak Followers

If you convert this strong leader to a champion of your services, you've got the sale made.

Strong Leader with Strong Peers

Make a special effort to take everyone's issues into account. Any one holdout who is unconvinced can ruin the deal.

Weak Leader with Weak Peers

Make friends with everyone and take the time to educate and move ahead slowly.

Weak Leader with Strong Peers

Make sure you address everyone's questions because the leader will be looking for the others to make his or her decision.

Information Gatherers for Unavailable Decision-Maker

When the decision-maker is not in the room, you'll have to educate the group on how to sell your product or service. More on this special case in a minute.

TAKE CONTROL OF THE MEETING.

It is almost impossible to gain the consensus of a group if you don't take control of the agenda.

Take control of the meeting, and the agenda, by first establishing everyone's role, issues, and expectations for the meeting. A

> Ask questions, if necessary, to clarify the roles of different people.

SELLING TO MULTIPLE DECISION-MAKERS

clever way to do this is to turn the introduction spotlight on them before the ball gets passed to you.

If you've just come in or are completing the review of their decision-making process, you need to take control and say, "Before I start, I'd like to take a minute and, if I could, just hear briefly from each one of you what it is that you do and what you'd like to get out of this program." Or if they've already invited you to begin your presentation, you need to say, "I'd be happy to, but before I do that, could I ask, from each of your perspectives, what your objectives are for this program."

Each of them will now state their own agenda, and whether it's the CFO, the VP of sales, the VP of customer service, or the operations department, they each have their own agenda for that decision, and you need to uncover and understand it before you start to present your services.

> Each decision-maker has their own agenda.

FIND THE BUYING "TRIGGERS."

It is key that you make note of all of the issues each person would like addressed. You must make certain that you use the introduction round table to pull out everyone's objectives for the program. You'll want to be certain to address each item individually when you get around to reviewing concerns and issues.

Don't make the big mistake of forging ahead with your sales presentation and falling victim to an onslaught of questions.

If you haven't taken the time to get all the issues on the table before you begin, you'll find yourself with real problems. All of a sudden you'll be fielding questions from all areas of the company, and the meeting will be out of control. The group's confidence in your presentation will drop accordingly. And your performance will drop as you find you can no longer relate to the group.

You avoid this by being proactive. Ask for their perspectives, and their objectives, first.

Then, when it's your turn to present your services, articulate value by referencing the key bullet points that each of them gave you, and describe how your product or service addresses them.

SELLING TO MULTIPLE DECISION-MAKERS

It is imperative that you use the information you uncover from the group in the sales presentation. You incorporate it by saying, "George, as you mentioned . . . here's how that would work in the Customer Service Department . . . " And, "The new technology reduces risk by . . . "

You've got to make sure that you're inclusive of all issues as this is the point when you are putting their concerns to rest and building confidence in your product or service. If you don't fully address these concerns, then new questions will likely arise after your presentation, you'll lose control of the meeting, and your presentation will suffer dramatically.

DEALING WITH NO DESIGNATED GROUP LEADER.

Because of the many cross-functional teams that are being formed today to deal with a diverse range of business issues, it is becoming more common to find yourself presenting to an ad hoc committee with no designated leader. Many of these teams have been formed for one particular project and have little organization and no defined decision-making process.

This can be a very difficult situation for the unprepared salesperson.

When faced with just such an amorphous group, ask outright, "Who's the lead person on this?" And if they say, "We're really going to discuss it as a committee and agree together," then ask them to embellish their answer. "What is your process on this?"

Then listen for the key information. Is the decision actually made by all the people in the room and nobody else, or is this a committee that's gathering information and then taking it to the real decision-maker?

That's the critical distinction, and you need to know the difference when you're selling to a team. Just because it's a group does not necessarily mean that all the decision-makers are in that room. If they say, "Well, as a committee, we're going to decide," then you just forge ahead and ask, "What's your time frame? What else do you need to know? How can I be helpful to you on this?"

> It is becoming more common to find yourself presenting to an ad hoc committee with no designated leader.

SELLING TO MULTIPLE DECISION-MAKERS

On the other hand, if they say, "Well, this team is then going to take our recommendation over here to XYZ, who really holds the decision power," you need a different strategy.

Again, you first need to identify all the issues and challenges. *Then you need to coach them on selling.*

You should say to them, "Okay, tell me a little bit about how you will proceed from here." And they'll say, "We're going to take it next week to Tuesday's meeting." Then you can say, "Great. Could you tell me a little more about the process and describe how this group will present the program to that team (or to that committee, or that person)?" They'll say, "Oh, we'll probably go over this." Or else they'll look really puzzled and say, "We're not sure. We haven't thought about that yet."

It is important to realize that they're not going to sell your product or service nearly as well as you could.

Your job is to coach them on how to sell your product.

Find out how the process will proceed.

Perhaps you can give them a prepared, one-page handout and review it with them, saying, "Most people have found this analysis of our product benefits and cost savings to be really helpful when presenting the pertinent background information to others." And what you usually see is that look of tremendous relief because these people are in the role of delivering information and you have just made their job easier and more organized.

Their responsibility is to provide accurate information to the decision-maker or makers. Your responsibility is to assist them in this effort.

DEALING WITH TOUGH QUESTIONS.

How do you address tough questions from the group? Be careful; don't overreact.

Again, a mistake that many salespeople make is reacting too quickly, very much like in the objection-handling process. When someone asks you a question, don't be afraid to ask them to elaborate if you're not clear on what they really want to know. Or when you answer, make sure you're concise and very clear about how your product or service can directly answer their concern.

SELLING TO MULTIPLE DECISION-MAKERS

If people are asking questions because they don't understand your product, slow down or back up. Ask them if there's a specific area they'd like more information on. Always take the responsibility. Say things such as, "Maybe I wasn't clear on this particular area" or "Let me give you a little more information in that area." So embellish, but don't make them feel stupid for asking the question.

BE A FACILITATOR WHEN FACED WITH CONFLICTING DEMANDS.

Conflicting interests is another dynamic that often comes up in groups, particularly with teams that don't get along well. If you've got one person who doesn't want to spend any money, and somebody else who wants to buy whatever you have, then you have conflicting values, which must be dealt with: protecting a budget versus delivering some kind of result. Team members should be coming from the same place, but in reality it doesn't work that way.

DON'T TAKE SIDES.

When groups start to disagree among themselves, don't take sides. Try to engage those with conflicting points of view in a discussion of priorities so that a full understanding of their different needs can be reached.

You need to go right into a facilitation role, which is, again, flushing out all the issues. So use an approach such as, "From what I'm hearing, you have concerns with some of the budget constraints. But what I hear over here is that you are responsible for reaching this kind of result. Are there any other concerns?" So get them all on the table. You can eliminate the arguing and take control of the meeting by answering the issues all at once, rather than one by one.

If you start to get on either side, or are perceived as taking sides, remember that the one who may be hesitating may have just as much influence over the buying decision as the one who wants to go forward. So from a sales perspective, it serves you best to stay right in the middle, very convinced and very confident that your product or service is right for them. And then make sure you are including

> Try to facilitate the discussion so the process moves ahead.

SELLING TO MULTIPLE DECISION-MAKERS

and answering all the objections at once so you can work toward mutual agreement.

. . . .

MULTIPLE BUYERS EXAMPLE: TAKING CONTROL OF THE MEETING

In this example, Sam Hunt is making his second call on Telecall. Sam's company, Williams T&D, has been included in the final selection process by Telecall as one of three competitors. There are several members of Telecall present in the meeting, including George Pinkston, the VP of finance; Marty Fineman, the VP of sales; Beverly Nunn, the senior manager of customer service; and Marilyn Hoffman, the internal training director. Sam must include all those involved in the purchasing process, identifying each individual's objective and gaining each person's agreement. Up to this point he has only met with Beverly Nunn.

THE INEFFECTIVE APPROACH

Beverly: Hi, Sam. Welcome back. As I told you, I've asked some people from our organization to join us.
Sam is a little uncomfortable with all these people. A couple make eye contact.

Sam: Hi, everyone. [*He nods to them.*] I'm glad I could do this. I brought a slide presentation with me to give you a sense of Williams T&D's capabilities. It will take just a minute to set up.

Beverly: Sure. Go right ahead. Let us know when you're ready.
Sam opens up his laptop computer.

Sam: It'll only take a second. [*He starts his laptop*] Okay, I'm all set. Before I begin, are there any questions?
No one says anything.

Sam: As Bev may have already told you, Williams T&D has specialized in customer service training for nearly ten years. Now, as this first slide shows you. . . .

> Sam starts the presentation right off, without learning anything about the people at the meeting.

SELLING TO MULTIPLE DECISION-MAKERS

People in the room watch him, some take notes, a couple stare off into space or look at the walls

THE EFFECTIVE APPROACH

Beverly: Hi, Sam. Welcome back. As I told you, I've asked some people from our organization to join us.
Sam looks around the room. He makes eye contact with everyone.

Sam: Good seeing you again Beverly. I'm delighted that I can talk to all of you about some of the ways that Williams T&D can work with Telecall to significantly increase your customers' satisfaction using our training system.

Beverly: We're ready whenever you are.

Sam: Before I begin, however, I'd like to take a couple of minutes to meet everyone. Can we go around the table and have each of you tell me a little bit about yourself and about your objectives for this program? I'd really appreciate it.

Beverly: Sounds like a good idea. Why don't you start, Marty.

Marty: I'm Marty Fineman, vice president of sales. I started here about three years ago. Naturally, I've got a sales perspective on this. Since my job is to bring in new business, I've got to make sure any company's first experience with us is perfect. We can't promise results if we don't treat our own customers right.

Sam: That's helpful.

George: I'm George Pinkston, vice president of finance. I'm the money cop here. [*Everyone laughs.*] My objective is simple: I want to get the most bang from the buck.

Sam: Now, there's an objective that everyone can relate to. Next?

Marilyn: I'm Marilyn Hoffman, the internal training director. You and I met briefly. [*Sam acknowledges this with a nod.*] I'll be the one you'll be working with most directly. I guess my primary objective is to get a program that really works. We've tried some customer service programs before—off-

Sam first learns the objective of each individual at the meeting.

SELLING TO MULTIPLE DECISION-MAKERS

the-shelf stuff—and were disappointed. I'm hoping you have something new to offer.

Group looks attentive, interested to see how Sam will answer their needs.

Sam: Great. That's very helpful. I'd like to show you now how Williams T&D will help you meet each of your objectives . . . and train your employees effectively. Let's get started . . . [*Sam opens up his laptop.*]

COMMENTARY:

As you can see, group dynamics are very different from selling to an individual.

The key to managing this situation included three important factors:

1. *Set the tone of the meeting with introductions to acknowledge all present parties.*
2. *Uncover each individual's objectives.*
3. *Tailor your presentation to effectively meet the needs of each person in the room.*

Keeping this in mind will give you the ability to get all the heads nodding in the right direction . . . saying yes! Include all parties when presenting your product or service. Avoid the pitfalls of preconceived notions, assumptions, or discounting people's input. By addressing all parties in your presentation, you will be best positioned to gain the group's consent and make the sale.

> Be sure to connect on an individual level with as many decision-makers as possible.

MAKE A CONNECTION WITH EVERYONE IN THE GROUP.

As with an individual decision-maker, use this process to make a connection with each individual in the group.

Remember that groups don't make decisions; people within groups make decisions.

So on some level, business or personal, you want to make a connection with everyone in the group. This can be through a

SELLING TO MULTIPLE DECISION-MAKERS

handshake, eye contact, or uncovering individual objectives. All contribute to developing a connection between you and that person. Only when you've made these individual connections with all in the group will they say, "Yes, we want that person's services."

FOLLOWING-UP THE GROUP PRESENTATION.

Usually salespeople make the mistake of assuming the person who talked the most is the lead. And even if they are the lead, they're probably the least likely to want to get bogged down on the details of the follow-up. So ask, "How should I proceed?" "Who would like me to interface with on this?" "I'd be happy to submit a proposal to you; whom shall I direct it to?"

Let them all look at each other and indicate, "I don't know. Do you want it?" "No, I don't want it. Do you want it?" Let them decide who should be the lead person. Undoubtedly, whomever you might have picked would have been the wrong one.

If you've asked them to designate the person, then you're much more likely to get this person's support in following-up with your efforts. If you get an agreement on your contact person, look that person in the eye and you say, "I'll have that application information to you in two days." And they'll say, "Great," for they don't want to be left alone holding the bag. Expect to get a warm reception when you do call back in two days and deliver as promised.

REMEMBER, IT'S A GROUP OF INDIVIDUALS.

When presenting to more than one person, remember not to lose sight of the individuals in the group. If you are to be successful when presenting to multiple decision-makers, it is key to stay focused on meeting the individual agendas of everyone present. To be most effective in your sales presentations, never forget that you must win over the members of your audience one at a time.

And you do this best by focusing not on the group, but on making individual contact and addressing individual concerns.

> Determine in advance who you should follow-up with.

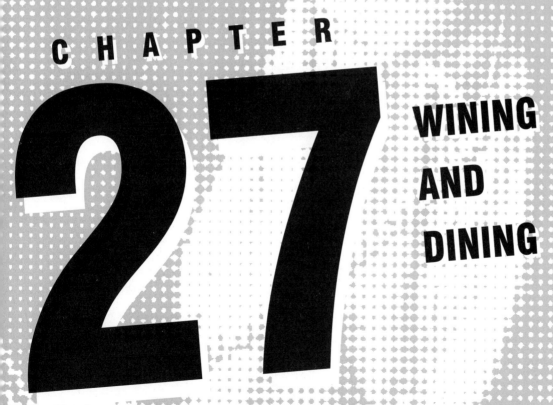

CHAPTER

27

WINING
AND
DINING

You can go a long way to building positive working relationships with your customers by interacting in non-business ways. But you need to be very careful to have the right mix of business and non-business conversation—not getting too familiar too quickly nor being too cold or narrowly business focused. You can also build relationships by sending gifts, cards, and relevant books or press clippings—but make sure any activity you do is appropriate.

WINING & DINING

Cultivating customers means building relationships beyond the scope of your services. You might find that you click quite well with some customers, while others seem harder to connect to. Wining and dining gives you the opportunity to slowly bring your relationships to the next level. Many great business deals have come about on the greens of a beautiful golf course or in the cocktail lounge of a fine hotel. So what can you do? What's the real business etiquette of wining and dining as a sales tool? First and foremost, remember the following guidelines:

Guideline	Reasoning
Be professional.	Seems obvious, but it's easy to forget when you feel comfortable!
Don't overindulge.	The client will remember in the morning, and you can't erase it!
Don't spill your guts.	Do they really need to know the details of your personal life?
Listen more than you talk.	Getting connected to customers means letting them feel "heard."
Keep the counseling alert.	Be cautious about giving advice on personal matters; get them help rather than advise.
Respect confidentiality.	Remember the saying "Loose lips sink ships." It's true!

Generally, when dining with a customer, it is appropriate to touch upon a non-business topic—such as favorite hobbies or sports—but don't get too familiar too fast.

Wining and dining with customers will help you get to know them better, understand who they really are, see beyond their external "business persona," and assist you in building their loyalty. As you begin to analyze your wining and dining activities, start by

WINING & DINING

identifying your objective. Are you trying to gain new business, keep old business, rejuvenate an existing account, or leverage an account into referrals? All of these are great reasons to take the extra measure with your client. Let's take a look at how.

The coffee generation: Many business meetings take place over a cup of coffee. The popularity of today's coffee houses reflects businesspeople's need for a gathering place outside the office. The attraction boils down to the fact that the coffee house tends to be comfortable and the meeting very efficient. Most businesspeople today are extremely stretched with their time; the coffee meeting is a great alternative to lunch.

The best use of a coffee meeting is for times when you might have some "real" business to attend to and would also like a short amount of time to discuss other things. For example, maybe you have to get something signed by the customer and at the same time you'd like to find out more information about another branch where you could sell your products or services. A smart use of your time is to get the paper signed first, then chat for a bit and get to know them a little better. Once you've listened for a while, you've earned the right to ask for the information you're after. Keep the meeting short, under one hour, to respect the time of your customer. Remember to establish next steps before you leave.

Today's business lunch: Be selective about how you spend your lunch time. Reserve lunch meetings for your best accounts, the best referral sources, and accounts with the most potential for growth. These are the ones you need to get better connected with. They're worth your investment of time to position yourself for the future. If you're suggesting the restaurant, make sure to select one with excellent and efficient service, a professional atmosphere (no fast food here!), and a noise level that allows conversation. Whenever possible, make a reservation in advance. Always be there first; a sales manager I once had always said, "If you're not early, you're late!" I believe that's still good advice.

The key thing to remember about the business lunch of today is that you are being analyzed on several levels at once. You are being

> "Coffee cup" meetings mean less time committment for you and for the buyer.

analyzed on how professional you are, how prompt, how you present yourself, your manners, your conversation, and your comfort level in business. All of the subtleties contribute to the customer's overall impression of you. Each lunch is an opportunity to bring your image to greater heights or to hurt it. Make sure you manage your behavior, and the impression will take care of itself.

Quick advice on who pays: In most cases, you pay for the customer.

An exception is if they absolutely insist; however, they may be testing your commitment to them. Use the business lunch as a great place to do business and get to know your customer better.

Social dining: Whether it's an out-of-town business trip or a local get-together, social dinner engagements with customers are common. What are the do's and the don'ts? Make sure you are dressed appropriately for a dinner event; if you're not sure of the required attire, call the hotel or dinner spot and ask! Better to be more conservative than flashy; save the fashion statements for friends.

If you are hosting the evening, take into consideration any dietary restrictions your client might have to avoid making them feel awkward. I have a wonderful client with very strict dietary restrictions due to religious commitments; he appreciates that I keep this in mind whenever I make reservations. If I'm unclear about a choice, I always ask for his approval of a restaurant. Attention to the small stuff tells the client that you use your head and think of their well-being.

Social dining by nature infers that you will be "socializing" more than talking business. In fact, there needs to be a gentle balance. If you simply chat all evening, the client might not think you care about their business; however, if you come on too strong about business, they'll surely feel that you have no clue when to turn it off! The balance you're looking for should come from the client; let the client guide the conversation. Ask good questions that get them talking: "John, I noticed you are quite a golfer . . . What are the courses like around here?" or "What do you do with yourself when you're not at the office?" or better yet "What do you do for fun?" The key is to give them the freedom to talk about things they enjoy: family,

> All of the subtleties contribute to the customer's overall impression of you.

> You need to balance social topics and business topics.

WINING & DINING

sports, hobbies, personal interests. Then listen. Be interested. You will learn about the total person, which will help in business dealings. Look for the clues: Are they competitive, very active, busy with small children? Do they prefer to relax, love to travel? All this information will help you "talk" directly to them, sell to them down the road with a better understanding of who they are.

Holiday cards: Holiday cards are often a source of confusion. Send them? Don't send them? What should the greeting say? Holiday cards are a terrific tool; it's a good idea to keep in touch with you prospects and clients as much as possible. Just remember, don't do what everybody else is doing. Many companies and sales reps send "Christmas" cards. The best approach is to keep the greeting nondenominational. "Happy Holidays" or "Season's Greetings" are effective and safe. Better yet, why not wait a week or two and send a "Happy New Year, best wishes for a prosperous new year" and keep your card out of the crowd of the flurry of Christmas greetings? Another alternative is to pick one or two other holidays that might be relevant to your business or your customers' business. For example, I have a friend who owns a graphic design company, and he always sends out Valentines to his clients, prospects, and networking associates. He certainly separates himself from the crowd; this is the only "work-related" Valentine that comes to my office. How about Halloween? Or Groundhog Day? Or even the first day of summer? A colleague of mine was responsible for creating "International Moment of Laughter Day." You could certainly have fun with that one! So yes, holiday cards work. The magic comes from letting your clients know you are thinking about them and that they are important to you; the success comes from doing something unique.

Gift giving: Gift giving continues to be an important custom for sales reps to follow; however, you must proceed with caution. Many companies have instituted policies that restrict gift acceptance and state the value of an acceptable gift (a $25 limit is quite common). What do you do? Step one is to find out the policy of your clients and then work within their guidelines. The secret to impactful gift giving is to keep the gift thoughtful and appropriate.

WINING & DINING

Occasions that are likely to warrant gift giving include the following:

- Thanks for your business
- Completion of a great project
- Thanks for the referral
- Congratulations on a promotion
- Holiday gift giving
- Personal celebration (new baby, new house, birthday)
- Personal tragedy (death in the family, car accident, injury, or illness)
- Reached a personal or professional goal (ran their first marathon, learned French, etc.)

Gift ideas for "thank you" or "happy" occasions might include gift baskets, plants, flowers, motivational posters or sayings, business or occasion-related books, a monogrammed pen/pencil set, a humorous mug, golf balls, etc. The more you know your clients, the better off you are; think "different" and have fun. Ask yourself, "When I think of John, what do I think of?" Develop a gift around that idea.

Gift ideas when a client is experiencing a problem (personal or professional) should be conservative and respectful. Best bets are food gift baskets or flowers. Keep the message simple; just let them know that your thoughts are with them.

The personal touch: Small gestures on your part are interpreted by customers as signs that you know them, understand them, and care about them. These are good relationship builders. For example, one of my clients is a golf addict. He just loves the game and enjoys everything about it. Golf balls, tees, a nice towel for his golf bag might be okay, but no doubt he already has plenty of these items. Every summer a "seniors" golf tournament comes to our area. Through casual conversation, I asked my client if he had ever had a chance to attend a seniors tournament, and he said no but that he'd love to. Through a connection I was able to get six admission tickets to the event. I sent them to my client with a "no special reason" note, just a simple "thought you'd enjoy these." The client thoroughly

> Small gift gestures can be good relationship builders.

WINING & DINING

enjoyed the tournament, and he has never forgotten the gesture. The personal touch is always appreciated. Take the time to think about your customers, what they like, and how you might be able to bring some joy into their day.

Articles and Books of Interest: Another great way to build rapport and develop your customer relationships is to keep them in mind when you come across an interesting book or article. The book or article should be relevant to your customer on either the business or personal level. One of the clients I work with is the director of training and development for a worldwide organization, and through a dinner conversation I discovered that he was quite interested in launching a consulting practice in the next five years. I have a friend who authored a fabulous book on starting a consulting practice, and I quickly bought my client a personalized copy. He appreciated the support of his dreams and loved the fact that it was autographed. Once again, you can demonstrate through your thoughtfulness that you listen to and support your clients. Another client of mine was interested in expanding her networking activities, and when I received an invitation to a wonderful conference I quickly faxed her the information so she also might attend. She was delighted that I thought of her. The key with articles, books of interest, or faxes is to keep them targeted entirely to the pleasures, interests, and development of the client. Both of you will enjoy the benefits of an enhanced business relationship.

In summary, customer relationships need to be honored and cultivated. Go beyond the scope of your work and get to know your customers as people. The wining and dining lets you build friendships as you build business. People do business with people they like and trust. Strategic wining and dining will increase your sales and your enjoyment.

A highly relevant book or newspaper or magazine article may be greatly appreciated.

Harnessing the power of electronic media is increasingly important in sales today. The internet can offer you access to limitless accounts of information; e-mail can speed your communication and help you find leads; and your own web site can pull qualified customers directly to you!

USING ELECTRONIC MEDIA TO BUILD SALES

No one can afford to be in sales today and not be aware of, if not using, electronic media in support of their business. By electronic media I simply mean using your present PC to its full potential as a tool for communications and information gathering, not just simply as a word processor or spreadsheet generator.

The latest generation of PCs and software has made available to everyone the ability to become a New Age communicator with virtually instant access to vast databanks and information never before so readily available. It also offers the possibility of inexpensive, twenty-four-hour access and interactive communications with an unlimited number of people and businesses.

And because Customer-Focused Selling is information-based, requiring in-depth knowledge of customers and industries, electronic media offer a perfect fit with this approach to sales.

For a variety of reasons, Internet use has been going through a period of explosive growth, and all bets are that this will continue for some time to come. Usage is such that businesses are not perceived as contemporary if they do not have an Internet address in their literature.

Over and above the cost of your PC, the cost of a modest Internet presence is almost nil, with the average Internet service provider now costing between $15 and $30 per month. And this commonly includes up to 10 megabytes of space to put up a modest Web site. Finding a service provider is quite easy; just look in the phone book or use the Web itself, at www.webweek.com, to help you locate a local server.

The bottom line is that everyone, from single-person offices to larger businesses, should consider having an Internet address. All it takes is a little time to set up, very modest monthly charges, and you're ready to get started building your electronic media presence.

> A simple web site can add to your professional image.

USING ELECTRONIC MEDIA TO BUILD SALES

USING THE INTERNET.

Information! Information! Information! If there's one main point that everyone agrees on about the Internet, it is that it's fantastic at searching out all kinds of information. This is done through the use of a browser, such as Netscape™, which you can purchase or even download for free off the Internet. The new generation of Microsoft Windows 97™ even comes prepackaged with one. Using them is simply a matter of entering the Internet site address, commonly called the URL (Universal Resource Locator), and seconds later the home page is up on your screen.

If you don't have a specific address you're seeking, then it's simply a matter of using one of the many excellent search engines to track down possible sites after you've entered key search words. Alta Vista™ and Yahoo™ are two of the most popular search engines, the former being well known for its word search capabilities, the later for its business search index.

To use these most effectively, it might be wise to purchase one of the many "how to search the Internet" books now on the market. They contain many tips on how to search out all types of information, and they have addresses of many useful sites.

In line with our focus on understanding your customers and their industry, dig right in with searches on specific accounts, your competitors, industry and trade organizations, government regulations, and related news events. Whatever the topic, you'll likely be astounded at the depth of information available.

And to stay current on a particular topic or industry, try joining a related list service, which will E-mail you topic updates periodically. You might even find yourself joining a chat group for ongoing topical discussions.

DEVELOP YOUR OWN WEB SITE.

Using the Web to gather information is only half the fun. Using it as a sales tool is where it can really begin to pay dividends.

Most people are in agreement that sales through the Internet are only in their infancy, but even if this is the case, there are numerous ways in which it can be used to augment your sales efforts or to

The internet is a great information source.

USING ELECTRONIC MEDIA TO BUILD SALES

generate qualified leads, *and it's at work twenty-four hours a day, seven days a week.*

Setting up your own Web site and home page has become quite easy and no longer requires that you hire an expensive outside consultant. Larger businesses, which can afford a real pro and have the budgets to go after impressive graphical interfaces, are, of course, free to do so. For the others with modest budgets, consider purchasing one of the numerous Web site software start-up kits now on the market. For free "how to" advice and links check out the Netscape site. Within one to two weeks you will likely have developed competency with the task.

With a little planning before you begin, your site can become even more useful. Remember these tips when you're planning yours:

> A little bit of work can greatly increase the effectiveness of your web site.

WEB SITE TIPS.

1. Make Your Site Interesting

   Don't put people to sleep when they visit your site. Pages of text, figures, and lists will turn anyone off very quickly. Make an effort to incorporate interesting graphics, illustrations, pictures, even humor to keep people interested in pursuing further levels of information at your site.

2. Give People a Reason to Come Back

   Plan a format for your site that gives timely information and requires that people revisit your site from time to time. Incorporate new product releases, applications information, upcoming trade show times and places, special news and PR events, whatever you can think of that would be of ongoing interest to your potential clients.

3. Incorporate a "Request for Information" Form

   If someone has made the effort to track down your Internet site, chances are they would be interested in receiving further information on some of your products or services. Designing a "request for information" form is a good way to track down potential leads, as you now have their E-mail address, and hopefully their business address and phone number for follow-up.

USING ELECTRONIC MEDIA TO BUILD SALES

4. Use Contests to Create Some Fun

   Challenge people on related trivia facts, add frivolous questions, reward every hundredth person who registers. Have a little fun with your format, and let people know you are not just there for the sale, but that you enjoy what you do and you're not afraid to show it. Remember, all work and no play make Jack a dull boy.

5. Update Your Site at Least Every Two Weeks

   Nothing is older than yesterday's news. Keep your site current to keep people interested and coming back. Old or abandoned Internet sites have become extremely common on the Web. News of past events becomes a real turnoff when outdated, so commit to an ongoing effort to keep your site "fresh."

6. Register Your Site with the Major Search Engines

   All the major search engines offer you the ability to register your site address. Make sure to include the use of key search words in your html code, which will pull up your URL address when people specify them in their searches.

7. Cross-Market Your URL Address

   Even the best Web site will do your business little good if people aren't aware it exists. Beyond the occasional visitor who finds you through a topic search, most people will want to visit your site when they are seeking further information on your product or service and want to avoid any sales pressure. Be sure to put your URL address on all your literature and let them discover the useful features of your site. If they fill out the "request for information" form, they'll likely be receptive to a follow-up letter or phone call.

ELECTRONIC MAIL.

If anyone needs evidence that communications in sales are changing radically, the tremendous volume of electronic mail (E-mail) being exchanged daily is most convincing. You can almost instantly follow-up on meetings and phone conversations where you want to confirm points or send data that customers are waiting for before proceeding.

> Updating a web site is crucial for getting people to come back again and again.

> Tell everyone imaginable your web address.

USING ELECTRONIC MEDIA TO BUILD SALES

Personally, I still like to send out a crisp, formal thank-you letter or itemized action list after important meetings. But for more casual requirements, nothing beats the speed and efficiency of a prompt E-mail response.

For the small business, using E-mail can also constitute a significant cost savings. After the monthly user fee, there is no cost for use of this feature. Sending letters at no cost feels great and encourages you to be even better at following-up with potential customers.

QUALIFIED LEAD GENERATOR.

Sales leads on your doorstep! If you've done a good job of developing an interesting Web site, chances are that many of the people who have made the effort to seek your site out are going to sign up for more information. If you've designed your questionnaire consistent with the Customer-Focused Selling focus, then it will request considerable background material and an explanation of the potential customer's needs and problems.

Your response to this qualified lead should be to contact the potential customer to gather more information, not an invitation to sell. If you don't want to scare this lead away, keep the relationship at the information-gathering stage while you build credibility.

Don't just use your Web site only for the obvious advertising and cataloging. Insert a list of frequently asked questions, or include some broad applications information that is aimed at building your image as a knowledgeable source. This gives you a positive image and motivates them to file away (bookmark) your address for future use when similar needs arise.

A side benefit is that you will find your catalog (and postage) expenses decreasing as people are able to immediately print out any product or business information of interest.

And think of the cost savings in advertising and promotion. Local paper and trade advertising expenses add up quickly for the small business and are often deemed successful if they bring in a handful of interested potential customers. To be successful, you don't need a large volume of leads. Any you do receive are prequalified, and it may only take closing one or two to pay great dividends.

Get qualified leads from your web site!

USING ELECTRONIC MEDIA TO BUILD SALES

BROADCASTING: DIRECT MAIL ELECTRONIC STYLE.

If you've been collecting E-mail addresses with your information requests, then you'll want to treat them like the valuable commodity they are and use them judiciously for sending out product announcements, news releases, or even newsletters.

For whatever purpose you choose, don't put all the relevant information in the communication. Keep back the more in-depth details, which will require them to return to your Web site for more information. Announce that new product, but require them to come to your site for exact performance specifications. Announce the lead to a story, but get them back to read the full article.

And again, other than your invested time and monthly provider fee, this form of mail costs you nothing.

As with phone and fax soliciting, you may also find that there are unique E-mail address lists you'll want to purchase. If they're the right lists for you, this may be a very cost-effective approach, as the traditional printing and mailing costs don't exist.

INTERNET/E-MAIL NEGATIVES?

Not many. The service and cost are great. But, of course, expect your competition to visit your site when they get wind of it. So be sure to keep this in mind when developing content for your business Web pages.

Don't give away your proprietary tricks or services; make your content more of a general service, and save the unique extras and special services for sales-closing sweeteners.

For those who do request additional information, make sure you send it out promptly. This brings up a potential negative in that all Web sites require constant attention and upkeep.

Seek out customers with E-mail.

USING ELECTRONIC MEDIA TO BUILD SALES

Not only is there the pressure of constant incoming E-mail, but as we've noted before, the site should be updated at a minimum of every two weeks. It is all too easy to let this slip; don't. For anyone visiting your pages infrequently, they will notice this immediately.

As with any of your work, attention to detail sends a subtle message to your customer base about the quality and execution of your work.

TOMORROW ON THE WEB.

There comes a point with any new technology where you just have to get on board or risk missing the boat entirely.

Anyone who held back too long in becoming familiar with the PC for everyday business use likely came to the point where they had to scramble to catch up. The general usage and applications that rapidly followed gave early adopters a competitive advantage.

Today, use of the Internet is much the same case. Its power as a communicator is only now being discovered and developed. The use of its information-gathering power is just now being understood and applied in business. And it's anticipated that its net business applications will continue to evolve for years to come.

If you're not using the Internet now to support your sales efforts, I strongly recommend you do. Don't wait until doing business on the Web becomes a necessity. With the cost of admission so low, get in early on the learning curve and find out for yourself how best to use the Internet to build your business leads and sales.

Keep your focus on reaching and servicing your customers. And send the message to them that you are a contemporary business offering the latest in products and services.

> Get active on the web as soon as you can!

In sales everyone has days when insurmountable roadblocks and problems seem to be cropping up everywhere. Here are sixty tidbits of advice, offering possible solutions to common selling obstacles that you are likely to encounter. Beyond offering solutions to individual sales issues, taken as a group, they show that there are usually plenty of other courses of action you can take when the sales process seems to be slowing down.

1. ADVANCING THE SALE.

I'm stuck and I'm having trouble advancing the sale. What can I do next?

Ask probing questions to further assess the situation.

This is a great approach, as probing for information will accomplish several objectives. First, you will discard assumptions of why the sale is stuck and gain clarity from the prospect's perspective. Second, it allows you to make the sale a collaborative effort between you and the buyer. It allows the buyer to participate in the planning and problem-solving, with new information or ideas based on what you learned from the buyer. This is most often the best approach to advance the sale.

2. PRICING.

The customer has a problem with our pricing. How do I come up with a solution that satisfies both my customer and my company?

Articulate value and separate yourself from the crowd.

This is a winner! When you focus on the product or service value, you steer the customer away from any questions about price. When you are getting questions about price, it means that the prospect doesn't feel that what they are getting is worth what they're thinking of spending. In other words, they don't see the value. Concentrate on their business objectives and articulate the value of your product or service as it relates to their goals. By the way, if you are not sure about the value of your product or service, ask some of your satisfied accounts, and get them to tell you how your product or service adds value to their business. Value includes all the tangibles and intangibles. Make a list, articulate value, and you will separate yourself from the crowd.

> Pricing issues are among the most common and difficult obstructions.

3. STEEP COMPETITION.

The competition in my market is increasing fast. What can I do to deal with it?

Know your fit in the marketplace.

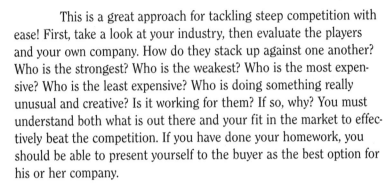
SALES COACH

With mounting competition in every industry, you need to understand your peculiar product features and benefits.

This is a great approach for tackling steep competition with ease! First, take a look at your industry, then evaluate the players and your own company. How do they stack up against one another? Who is the strongest? Who is the weakest? Who is the most expensive? Who is the least expensive? Who is doing something really unusual and creative? Is it working for them? If so, why? You must understand both what is out there and your fit in the market to effectively beat the competition. If you have done your homework, you should be able to present yourself to the buyer as the best option for his or her company.

4. MAKING QUOTA.

I'm having problems making quota. What can I do to turn things around?

Seek help from a mentor or manager.

Great approach. When sales quotas are slipping, it is too easy to blame yourself. Don't waste the energy focusing on how bad the situation is. Look for alternatives. A mentor or a manager can be an excellent facilitator in getting you out of your slump. Some of the key questions they might ask are: "Describe to me your best sale ever. What made it good? How can we re-create that in another sales situation? How do you see the market? The competition? Your product or service? What do you like about selling?" A manager or mentor will help you filter out the negatives, focus on the positives, and identify whether you need skill-building or a confidence booster.

5. SALES ROLLER COASTER.

I've been experiencing lots of ups and downs in my sales volume. What should I do about this sales roller coaster?

Create a gas pedal.

This can be a winner! Don't accept the ride; take control and manage it. The roller coaster ups and downs are directly related to your prospecting. Always prospect! This includes asking for referrals, repeat business, networking, cold calls, newsletters, writing, speaking, and PR efforts. When you are really busy with sales, that is the time to put the proverbial pedal to the metal and keep prospecting. That will make the roller coaster go up and stay up.

6. SKILL DEVELOPMENT.

I've been in sales for some time now and I'm afraid of losing my edge. How do I keep the momentum going?

Invest in a seminar or workshop.

A great approach for every person in sales. You deserve to invest in yourself. You spend it on clothes, cars, or a house, why not take the time to invest in your sales education? You have already started by purchasing this book and taking the time to study the various sections to see what you can do to improve your selling ability. Why not go even farther and sign up for seminars, workshops, or even a sales retreat where you can exchange ideas and strategies with other salespeople? You'll use what you need, when you need it. The investment in yourself will pay off for everyone—your company, your customers, and, of course, YOU! Continue the commitment to invest in yourself.

7. LOSING CONFIDENCE.

I had a bad response from my last few sales calls and I'm losing faith in the sales process. How can I get it back?

Focus on long-term goals.

This is the best way to "keep the faith." Say to yourself, "I'm going to give it some time. I'm going to do the right things, and it will work out." Focus comes from two places. One is focusing on the moment—the skill of being fully present. You also need a broad picture focus, which is goals. Have some goals and objectives—not just financial goals, but also personal goals . . . lifestyle goals. This will help you realize the larger purpose. It's not just do or die in these five minutes or whatever happens here today.

8. SALES APPROACH.

What is the best approach to selling?

Shift your focus to the buyer.

> To really excel in sales, you must constantly be stiving to improve your skills.

SALES COACH

This is a good approach to naturally relax you because you're not thinking about yourself but really thinking about the other person. The intangible benefit of shifting your energy to the buyer is that he or she will sense that genuine sincerity and relax enough to start trusting you.

9. NERVOUSNESS.

I've been getting nervous before a sales call. How can I overcome it?

Don't try to overcome it; face it head on.

It's okay to be a little nervous. The best way to overcome fear of a sales call is to practice, practice, practice. After you meet with enough people, your nervousness will diminish. So acknowledge that you are afraid and it's okay. Sometimes if people are not nervous it means that they don't have enough invested in it. So nerves can be looked at as a sign of positive commitment.

10. RESCUING SALES.

I'm losing a sale. How can I rescue it?

Slow down the sales process to work on your relationship with the buyer.

This is the best approach because if you're getting objections, that's a big signal that you are going too fast. You're ready to close and they haven't decided if they are going to do business with you yet. When you're in the selling process, there is some point, and it may be hard to recognize, when conceptually the person has decided that they like you and you know your stuff and they're going to do business with you. So if you think you may be losing a sale, slow down, work the process, and help the client over the objection.

11. PRODUCT FIT.

I just lost a sale where my product didn't seem to fit the client. How should I determine where it does fit in?

Ask the client what the criteria were for the decision against it.

This is an excellent way to learn about your product and the marketplace. Don't be outright. Ask a bunch of other questions such

> Many seemingly "lost" sales can be saved if you don't panic and you keep enthusiastically working the sales process.

as "I would have loved to have done this project. What were some of the contributing factors to it not making sense at this point?" This will tell you how they are perceiving you and your product, as opposed to your own assumptions of what happened.

12. VOICE MAIL.

I am getting a contact's voice mail. How can I get them to call me back?

Leave a brief message with a thought-provoking reason as to why he or she should call you back.

A solid reason for the person to call you back is the best approach. Don't leave an impersonal sales pitch, though; personalize it as much as possible. Request that you would like to meet with them to talk about how your product might fit into their situation. This should get them thinking about how your product will help them, and that they should call you back to find out. Then leave your name, number, and a good time to call you back.

13. NOT TAKEN SERIOUSLY.

I feel that some prospects think of me as "just a salesperson" and don't take me seriously. What can I do about it?

Be a business expert.

Don't approach sales as a sales expert. Approach sales as a business expert. Read the top business papers, the top business magazines, study how business is done. The way businesspeople think is the way your prospects and clients think; study the methods and understand what they need.

14. OVERPREPARED.

I prepare very carefully for all of my sales calls, and it's not helping. What's wrong?

Beware of assumptions.

Planning for a call is critical, but make sure you add a healthy dose of flexibility and let go of all your assumptions. The best sales calls include preparation and then a focus on strategic questioning and intense listening. You'll uncover the true reasons why people will do business with you and avoid letting assumptions get in your way.

> Sometimes you have to earn the respect of buyers who don't appreciate your salespeople.

SALES COACH

15. MOTIVATION.

What is the best way to motivate myself to make more sales?
Figure out what you like.

The best way to motivate yourself is to identify the part of your work that you enjoy most. Focus your energy on these areas and view all other areas of your work as necessary pieces that allow you to do what you enjoy. Finally, link your work to personal rewards. Your accomplishments should contribute to your desired lifestyle and a sense of well-being to ensure a high level of self-motivation.

16. NEGATIVITY.

How do I handle prospects who react negatively to me just because I'm in sales?
Don't act like a stereotypical salesperson.

People react negatively to sales reps because of previous negative experiences with less than professional reps. The best way to deal with preconceived notions is to do the opposite of what they expect or fear. Don't be pushy, and don't pitch. Rather, invest your time in listening to the client's concerns and needs. Sell through involvement, and the prospect will be more willing to advance the sale.

Be particularly cautious about hard-selling prospects who seem to have stereotyped all sales people.

17. PROSPECTING TIME.

Should I allocate a set amount of time to prospecting?
Always be prospecting.

You should be prospecting at all times! Make sure that prospecting is a regular part of every week. Make it a way of operating rather than a "thing to do." Schedule networking meetings, schedule cold-calling time into your week, and most of all, keep your eyes peeled for any potential contact that has a good chance of turning into a sale.

18. WHEN TO GIVE UP.

When is it time to stop pursuing a prospect?
It depends on the potential return.

You stop pursuing a prospect when you've decided the potential return is not worth the investment of time necessary to capture the sale. The bigger the sales potential, the longer the time frame is likely to be. The key is to know where you are at all times in the sales dynamics process and know what it will take to advance the sale. If you are spending a lot of time trying to move the process along or if the client seems indifferent or a tire-kicker, it is time to move on. In either case, determine the sales potential as early as possible.

19. SALES TYPES.

Is there any chance I'm just not the right type of person to be in sales?

There is no "right" type of salesperson.

Top-producing sales reps are made up of all types of people. The qualities they share include personal commitment, superb interpersonal skills, client focus, and continuous learning. Unless you have an aversion to dealing with people or a lack of commitment to quality and excellence, there is no reason why you can't be a top performer by learning to hone these valuable skills continuously.

20. HIGH-IMPACT PRESENTATIONS.

How can I increase the impact of my presentations?
Focus on the prospect's point of view.

For more impactful presentations, make sure to focus your language from the prospect's point of view. Translate your service or product attributes into the client's desired results. Combine detailed descriptions of your capabilities with big-picture client goals. Always use questions to check in during the presentation to make sure your ideas are being accepted.

21. PRESENTATION OVERKILL.

How do I avoid presentation overkill?
Keep the prospect involved.

You must be an astute observer of body language and keep the prospect involved. Present a few key points, then watch for a reaction, and ask questions to get them talking. Let them guide you by their interests rather than using anything you might have preplanned. Flexibility and client focus are musts to avoid presentation overkill.

> Improve your presentations by getting closer to the prospect's needs—not by adding more presentation "jazz."

SALES COACH

22. NEW COMPETITION.

Competitors are moving into my territory. How do I protect my turf while increasing sales?

Keep in close touch.

Communication and persistence are the keys. You must be diligent in following-up with clients on a regular basis and always be on the lookout for new prospects. Raise your own bar and let the competition try to match you instead of you trying to fend them off. Find out from your existing base of customers how you can serve them more effectively. Then take action and give them what they need and want—before your competition figures it out and beats you to the punch.

23. BURNOUT.

How can I avoid burnout?

Take time away from selling.

Take time for yourself. A well-rounded individual is a more innovative thinker and a better sales rep. Keep commitments to family and friends. Engage in recreational activities, pursue hobbies, or join a social club where you can get away from business and enjoy the company of others who share your interests and pursuits. Salespeople are always frightened of taking time away from selling, but in fact your sales will increase if you give yourself breaks regularly.

> Regular participation in non-business activities helps you for sales.

24. SALES SUCCESS.

What is the biggest factor is making sales?

Focusing on the prospect.

The biggest factor in making sales is your ability to understand the prospect's business situation and your ability to articulate your product or service as the best solution. Focus on increasing your questioning skills, listening skills, and personal judgment skills.

25. IDENTIFYING VALUE.

How can I make my "value add" clear?

When selling products or services, make sure you articulate value. Value means results. Help your prospects understand exactly how you provide results with your product or service. This will get you off selling commodities and on to articulating value. To identify the value you offer, make a list of ten to twenty by-products of working with you. Now ask your clients how they see your value. You'll probably be delighted at their response and you will have the information necessary to truly articulate value.

26. PLANNING.

How important is planning to sales success?

Run yourself like a business.

You must be extremely organized to be a top producer in sales. Use a calendar system that shows you a day at a glance and a month at a glance, and keep at least six to twelve months in a book, updating it regularly. Build in planning time to keep on top of it all. In addition, write yourself a personal business plan and review it at least once every six months.

27. EXPERTISE.

How much expertise do I need to have about a potential customer's business before I can try to sell to them?

Be an expert in your product

Many people work across all industries. You need to be an expert in your product, and you need to be an expert in understanding what problem your product solves.

28. KNOW YOUR COMPETITORS.

How much do I need to know specifically about my competitors before I talk to potential customers?

It depends on the sophistication of your product or service.

The degree and amount of information that you need to prepare before you talk to a client depends on the sophistication of your product or service, and how competitive your product or service is. If there are ten people like you calling on this person every day, then you'd better do a little extra homework so you can position yourself differently from the others.

29. PROSPECT LIST.

How do I get a prospect list?

> Adding value means adding results.

SALES COACH

There are always creative ways to develop better prospect lists.

Start by trying to develop your own.

You should usually try developing your own prospect list before you consider buying one. In developing your own list, you want to start to think about who the buyers of this product are, how you get their names and numbers, and where you get them. Now, don't ever underestimate your local library, your local town hall, or your local chamber of commerce. There are various places where you can find people. Here's an example of how to approach this: In the alarm industry, people who are building a home are good prospects because the walls are open and they can put in the wires easily. How could I ever find out about these people early on? Well, guess what? Everybody doing building has to get a building permit from the town or city hall. That's public information. There's some legwork to be done. But you're building a list of customers that have a need in a particular market.

30. HOT PROSPECTS.

I've generated a list and have a number of customers. How do I sort through them to know who is really hot and where I should invest the majority of my time?

Develop need-based lists.

You know "hot" is determined by biggest need. You need to have some criteria built into your products or services that are signals that you know when people need you. Always try to develop lists that are need-based, not hope-based, and try to segment them into different groups or tiers. Some of this can be done through gut. In most cases in selling, it's going to take getting on the phone with three or four good qualifying questions that introduce who you are and that gather information on whether these potential customers are hot or not.

31. CUSTOMER'S PRIORITY.

Are there any questions or tricks I can use in trying to pull out from potential customers what their sense of priority is?

Use open-ended qualifying questions.

There are a couple of keys to that. One is to know your own time frames. In other words, know what the key drivers are, how people make decisions for your product or service, and then ask questions that are not intrusive. "Do you have a need for this?" does not work. "When do you want to do this?" usually does not work. What you want to do is ask something like, "What's your process on this? What's your perspective on this?" You just want to get them talking. The problem with too many qualifying questions is that they tend to be closed-ended. Keep the qualifying questions open-ended because you don't want to set up their answer. You don't want a "yes" or a "no." You want information so you can position yourself for today, tomorrow, or down the road with that client. Everyone's a potential customer, and you really want to go with that attitude: It may not be today, this second, this minute—but it's a potential customer for me.

> Establish customers' sense of priority by asking open-ended, qualifying questions.

32. GOOD QUESTIONS.

What if the questions I ask don't produce a nice, free-flowing conversation?

Don't ask yes-or-no questions.

Try to make sure the questions you ask can't be answered with a "yes" or a "no," which gives you nothing. Turn everything into an opportunity for growth.

33. SEMINARS.

Do you think that trying to develop my own lead lists by offering information at a seminar is a good idea?

Okay, but no hidden agendas.

It can be a very useful approach. The key is never to have a hidden agenda. You don't want to surprise people, so at the seminar you should say, "As part of our service, we will be contacting everyone here today to just see if you have any individual questions." Now, if somebody comes over to you and says, "I don't want a call. I don't want to be on the list," you should respect that request. People don't want to be used. Be up-front with what you're doing.

SALES COACH

34. NOT PLANNING.

What is an indicator that I'm not planning enough? What happens to people who don't plan?

You're uncomfortable from the outset because you don't know what to expect.

The way you know you're not planning enough is in the first two minutes of the interview. You're extremely uncomfortable because you don't know what to expect, and you don't know or you're not sure what you're going to say. Preparation reduces anxiety, so excessive nerves always indicate that you're not prepared. The second situation is when the client is asking you questions that surprise you. It means you didn't do enough research. It should be a red flag if they're either asking you unexpected things or are frowning when you ask them, as if you should know the answer.

> Preparation reduces anxiety.

35. SETTING THE TONE.

Sometimes I have trouble getting the ball rolling in a first meeting. Any suggestions?

Be confident, fully present, and genuine.

From the minute, from the *second* you see your buyer, you need to be setting a tone. Body language is critical. People believe what they see even more than what they hear. So first of all, you want to exude confidence. A great way to do that is with a nice, strong handshake, and direct eye contact. And don't be afraid to pause. Your primary focus should be right on the customer, and that means being fully present. There is not one perfect approach. One traditional method is to look around their office and comment on things you see. Those items wouldn't be in their office if they didn't want to be able to talk about them. The key is never to be phony. Don't say, "Oh, I love fishing!" if you've never gone fishing. Instead say something like, "Oh, you're a fisherman. I've never tried it. What's it like?" So again, come from a foundation of honesty and truth.

36. SMALL TALK.

Is small talk always the right way to get started?

Take your cues from the buyer.

If you have a fast-paced buyer, they're going to have little if any time for this. This will be a half a sentence. "How are you today?" "Fine." That's your clue that says, "I don't want to chat with you. I don't want to be your buddy. I want to do business." So you respect that and go with it. You will find that your approach varies from customer to customer.

37. Dress.

How do I know how to dress if I've never been to the company before?

Dress the way the customer expects you to dress.

To a certain degree your garb, your dress is a little bit like an actor and actress, part of the role. It's part of who you are, however, so don't compromise your personal taste, but be the professional at the highest level. If you want to be perceived as a professional, dress as a professional. Your real gauge is your customers. What do they expect to see when you walk in the door? How can you enhance and not diminish from that image?

38. Dress-Down Day.

How should I dress if I'm meeting a client at their site on their dress-down day?

Dress professionally.

Ninety percent of companies have adopted casual day. But that doesn't mean you should. It's their casual day, but you should say, "I dress professionally so I look like what they expect me to be, the most professional in my profession."

39. Dress for Women.

Are the rules for dress different for women in sales than for men?

Yes. But the focus must still be on business.

Men have much more leeway. My main advice is to dress so the focus is on the business, not on you. Women need to ask: "What is the message I'm sending?" If your focus is anywhere but business,

> Dress the way the customer expects you to dress.

or if your mouth says business but the rest says "What are you doing later?", you've got a problem. It's confusing your buyer. I highly recommend using a professional wardrobe consultant.

40. HANDSHAKE.

I'm not sure what to do when I'm first getting started and the customer doesn't get up to initiate a handshake.

You should take the initiative and extend your hand with confidence.

People don't necessarily get up and observe all the social graces, for a wide variety of reasons. But that doesn't mean you shouldn't. The idea is that you're coming in to be an ally to this business in some way. The first thing you can do is set the tone for that by extending your hand with confidence. If you just let the status quo exist, you've made a mistake. Take the time to take the initiative. By that little gesture, you will separate yourself from the crowd, because if that person has behaved like this all day, chances are the three people before you have walked in and sat down and the three people after you will walk in and sit down, thinking that's what that person wants. In that instance, you need that personal connection, you need the touch to break down the barrier in what's gone on in that person's day until now.

41. TRUST.

How do I know early in a new sales relationship that I'm beginning to establish some trust?

Look for signals.

Always think of yourself as building a platform for communication. Trust comes from somehow resonating with you, so I'm constantly looking at you for signals that you're with me, signals that you trust me. You start to be more forthcoming with information, your body language relaxes, your palms open up. Eye contact is a good sign; leaning in is a good sign. What you can do to really facilitate that process, first of all, is make sure that everything you say is honest, candid, and from your heart.

> If the customer hesitates to shake hands, you should take the initiative and extend your hand anyway.

42. NO SMALL TALK.

What if a customer lets me know that he or she doesn't want to make small talk at all? Doesn't that make it harder to begin developing trust?

You picked up the signal and respected it.

No. You can build trust and credibility with that person by showing that you understood, that you picked up on the signal, and that you respected it. You honored his criterion for a good meeting. The next way of doing it is by stating clearly and concisely what your agenda is and inviting him to participate. You have said, "I'm organized, I'm prepared, I respect your time." Again, all of these build trust and credibility. You've also to some degree stopped him in his tracks and said, "You're not rushing me out of here. These are the three things I'd like to do. What else would you like to accomplish?"

43. WON'T TRUST SALESPEOPLE.

Aren't there some people who'll just never trust salespeople?

Most of the time, they're just busy or skeptical.

There are some very skeptical people out there. You don't have to like everybody. You won't necessarily feel like you have this, "Great, I want to have you over for dinner Saturday night" relationship with every client, and probably not with most. However, don't misinterpret the pace of business for "I don't like salespeople" nearly as much as "I'm a busy person. I need my time spent well." Don't project your own fears onto this situation. If you truly can impact this person's business, you will gain their respect, and your value is heightened in their eyes.

44. BAD PREDECESSORS.

What about situations where my predecessor created bad feelings?

Let the customer vent, then turn to the future.

That's a very real-world question. Oftentimes the sales rep going out the door has not necessarily left on the best terms, has not necessarily done a good job servicing his or her accounts, so there

> Don't engage in small talk if the customer doesn't want to.

SALES COACH

may be disgruntled feelings. When you take over, guess what? The customer wants to vent. So when you go in, your introduction or your agenda would reflect that. "I'm here to introduce myself, but also to get an update of your account and find out what were some of your frustrations, what are some of the hopes for the future, how We can work together effectively." Give them the opportunity to clear the path, because right now, you are the company, and the key is to empathize without sympathizing. That's a critical distinction— empathy, not sympathy. Say something like, "I can understand how frustrating that must have been," and then stop. You don't agree with them. You don't say, "That's nothing. You should have seen what happened to such-and-such customer down the road." You don't jump on the bandwagon. You're role is to take it. That's it. Give a little bit of empathy and then ask them, "What would you like to see done differently?"

> Let the customer vent if you're walking into a bad situation.

45. BETTER PRODUCTS.

What do I do when my competitor has a better product?
Find out why people are buying from you.

That is a very good question. Today the reason the skill set of the salesperson is so critical is because the differences in products, in pricing, in technology are shrinking—which means you are likely not to have a better mousetrap. If your competitor down the road has a much better mousetrap, now you've got a little bit of a problem but your job is to say, "How do I position myself? Who are my buyers? Why would they buy what I have instead of what the competition has?" In other words, you need to understand why people buy from you if there's a better version down there. In most cases, that gets you off the commodity sale. Commodity is let me match my thing against your thing, and the better thing wins. Don't do that. Don't even play the game. Get off of that and say, "I don't really care. What I'm concerned with is my customer and how MY thing is going to increase their business."

46. GOOD DIALOGUE.

When I try asking questions, I have trouble keeping a dialogue going. What am I doing wrong?

Don't ask closed-ended questions.

The typical questions that salespeople ask are product-related: How many do you use? What kind do you usually order? How many? Such questions go on and on and on. They tend to be closed-ended questions with specific answers. That's the worst approach. A much better approach is to get a broad-picture perspective on their business so you say to them things like, "Tell me a little bit about what you see out there. What's affecting your business right now? Tell me a little bit about your company."

47. RAMBLING.

What do I do when the person just keeps rambling on when I ask questions?

Interrupt to summarize what they said.

You need to stop them periodically. You'd rather have them more talkative than not talkative, but the challenge is that information can get lost. So as they are going on and on, you just interrupt and say, "Let me just jump in here for a minute." And you summarize what they said so far and you get them back on track. Now, if you feel like they've really exhausted their real issues and they're just kind of babbling, you say, "Tell me a little bit more about that one," if you want more information. Or you say, "Sounds like those are the biggest ones. Is that right?" "Yes." "Well, no, there are two others that are bigger." So again, you're always summarizing and gaining agreement that you were accurate in what you heard.

> Yes, it's okay to tactfully interrupt a rambling buyer.

48. NOTES.

Is it okay to take notes during client meetings?

Yes, but ask permission.

A good sales rep takes periodic notes. It's always important to say, "Do you mind if I take a few notes?"

SALES COACH

Use the "ping-pong" technique to get quiet buyers talking.

49. BRIEF ANSWERS.

If I ask a nice, open-ended question but get a very brief closed answer, does that mean I should stop asking questions?

No. It means you should explain why you're asking.

There are two reasons why you get brief answers. One is that the person is extremely skeptical, very withholding, and thinks it's none of your business. In that case the setup of the question may not have been appropriate. In other words, the only reason why a very reserved buyer is going to give you information is if they perceive that it will benefit them. So the setup needs to be an explanation: "To tell you about what I do effectively, it would be helpful to me if I knew a little more about what you do." If you ask a good question and they give a brief answer, they're testing you to see if the stock answer will make you go away. And if you just wait, hesitate, and keep quiet for three extra pulses, that person is likely to continue. In communication, it's like Ping-Pong, and our cue to the other person is when I'm quiet, you're supposed to start. If you don't start, I think it's still my turn. There are very few people who will be quiet through that pulse.

50. ENOUGH INFORMATION.

How do I know the point when I've gathered enough information?

Let the customer end it, not you.

The best gauge for you is who's talking more. If the customer's talking more, that's a good sign. Let them end it, not you. Go back to the summary and make sure that your last question is always, "Have I got that correctly? Is there anything else?" And maybe you even say, "Is there anything else critical to this discussion?"

51. BAD QUESTIONS.

Are there any questions I should never ask?

Be careful of the question "Why?"

That's a dangerous question in sales. If someone is telling you information about their business and you ask, "Why did you do that?" the question is heard negatively. It is heard as an accusation.

A better way is to give them some of the open-ended investigative questions that tell me, share with me, explain to me, explore. "Could you explain to me some of your objectives in that?" "Could you describe to me a little bit about what you were trying to accomplish with those things?"

52. LAPTOPS.

I feel more confident when I can use a presentation from my laptop. Any problem with that?

Save it for last.

It's called a crutch. Throw away the crutches. I would save the dazzle tools and things for last. Again, if you've got something on your laptop that is really, really attractive, use it. But use it as a crescendo, at the end, not at the beginning. Don't focus all your energy on what you're selling; focus your energy on how it's going to solve that customer's problems.

53. SELLING TO OTHERS.

What do I do when I've sold to one person in the company, and now that person has to sell to the other relevant parties?

Coach them through the whole presentation.

First of all, try whenever possible to avoid that situation. No one is going to sell your products as well as you do. But in the real world there are situations where you have to present and they have to go back to the committee and you cannot go there with them. Always try to get in by offering to make yourself available to answer any new questions that may come up. But let's say you just can't; your next-best approach is to say, "So, what will you do on that meeting on Thursday?" Let them talk through how they're going to sell it. Go through the whole presentation, doing the prep work. The last point is to ask, "What else can I do to help you prepare?" Try to flush out their weak point or points so you can coach them through that meeting before they have to go through it.

54. NEED MORE TIME.

What do I do when the customer says okay to everything, but won't close because they say they need more time?

> Avoid presentation crutches like computer graphics and slide shows.

SALES COACH

When the customer says they need more time, find out why.

Ask questions to find out what's really going on.

Don't push it, but get them to talk. And through talking, they're going to say things that are going to cause you to ask other good questions. You're trying to find out what's really going on here. In most instances the stated objection is the opposite of what's really going on or is unrelated. It was just a way to kind of put you off. "I want to think about it" means "I don't want to make a mistake, I don't want to take a risk. I'm not comfortable making this decision now." It means "I need my comfort level raised." So you need to apply comfort. Maybe it's in the form of proof. Maybe it's testimonials, guarantees, warranties. There's a variety of ways in which you could answer, but you need to work on their comfort level with making this decision.

55. TIME TO CLOSE.

How do I know when it's time to close?

Lead them through the business process.

The sales rep's mindset should be, "We're going ahead with this. The process on this is . . ." Those are the words that work. "Our process on this is, you and I need to take a look at our calendars, schedule it out. We'll be here two weeks from that date at that time." Lead them through how you do business together. That's one way to do it. Another way that works well is to say, "Does that make sense to you at this point?" The customer has not necessarily said, "Yes, I'll buy," but is saying, "I let that objection go. I'm okay now." So I would say, "Let's take a look at next steps," which means we're going forward, right?

56. WAIT FOR COMPETITION.

I'm not sure what to do when the customer says they need to wait and hear from my competition before making a decision.

Try to contact them again right before or right after the competition.

If this comes up as a surprise at the end, you need to know if it is merely an objection, or if they really cannot proceed until they've interviewed everybody. Let's say it's true; then you just very

SALES COACH

simply say, "How would you like me to proceed from here? Would you like me to call you, you to call me?" Let them be in the driver's seat. It's a good idea to see if you can think of any other reason why you have to contact them one more time, either right before the competitor or right after. Find another way to get in there.

57. REFERRALS.

What's the right time to start trying to generate referrals?
After you've proven yourself.

One of the best ways to generate referrals is to look for them from your first interaction. On the first sale, be thinking of the third sale and the fifth sale and the tenth sale down the road. Look at this not as a single event but as a series of opportunities this company could lead you to. You always need to be thinking that way. However, there's a difference between when you see it and when you say it. Identify it earlier, say it later. And what I mean by that is you have not earned the right to ask for referrals until you have proved yourself to this client. You need to have done a good job. You need to have created some results for this client already. The more appropriate time to ask is any time after the business, after you have already proved yourself.

58. FOLLOW-UP.

How should I follow-up a first meeting?
Be sure to thank them for their time.

The follow-up could take a couple of forms. In some way you need to say, "Thank you, I appreciate your time." It's good to produce a custom letter that you send out to the president or someone in the company who's appropriate. A couple of people should receive thank-yous. Thank-yous are something everyone knows they should do, but very few people actually do it. Your consistent objective with building business is to separate yourself from the crowd. You *want* to thank them. Make sure you do it.

59. NO PLANNING TIME.

What if I don't have the time for good precall planning?

> Don't ask for referrals too early.

SALES COACH

> Even a couple minutes of pre-call planning can make the difference.

Do it in the parking lot.

When you're at your appointment and haven't invested the time necessary in a good precall plan, do it in your head in the parking lot. Make a quick mental note of the four essential categories: the prospect's business climate, the client, the product, and yourself—and mentally answer the questions. Make sure the areas you cover are "Why are they meeting with me?" and "What are my three primary objectives for this call?"

60. PUBLIC SPEAKING

How should I approach public speaking opportunities?
Educate, don't sell.

Networking is not selling. Save the pitch. The way to get business from networking is to educate yourself about what others do. Find common ground and then educate them about what you do. Educate through examples. Provide clear examples of the type of business results you provide for your clients. Cultivate relationships with education.

30

SUCCEED WITH
CUSTOMER-
FOCUSED
SELLING

If you really use Customer-Focused Selling, you can become a top producer in your industry! Customers want solutions. And they want a salesperson they can trust to help them find those solutions. You *can* find those customers. You can *win* their trust. You *can* help them find *solutions*. You *will* succeed with Customer-Focused Selling!

SUCCEED WITH CUSTOMER-FOCUSED SELLING

The world is your laboratory; go test these principles. You can't learn to swim in a seminar, you can't learn to ride a bike from the sidelines. Now that you've covered all the principles, ideas, and tips in Customer-Focused Selling, get out there and test them in your world, your marketplace, with your customers. The quicker you get to work, the quicker you'll be delighted with the results.

You can expect many shifts by putting Customer-Focused Selling into action. You'll notice the first shift within yourself: You'll replace skepticism with a healthy dose of hope, as you've finally discovered a selling process that lets you be you. Customer-Focused Selling in the real world gives you confidence, knowledge, structure, and a methodology to advance any sale. The biggest shift: You'll raise the bar on yourself, you'll develop a higher level of expectation in your sales capabilities and performance. You can be a top producer in your company, your market, and your industry.

The next shift to watch for is the impact you'll have on your customers. With all you hear today about putting the customer first, you'll be one of the few who actually know how to do it. Customers are screaming to be heard; most often the competition isn't listening. You now have the ability to understand what your customer truly needs, make the link to your product or service, and articulate how you and your customer can work as business partners to create business solutions. The impact on your customer is profound. You're viewed not as a sales rep but as an ally, a business expert, a resource, and a secret weapon for your customers' success. And as they succeed, you, too, succeed with Customer-Focused Selling.

The real benefits? Everybody wins, everybody enjoys the process, and everybody makes more money! As you invest the time to understand your customers, you build a foundation of rock-solid trust and credibility. When you are able to translate

> **Everyone wins with Customer-Focused Selling!**

SUCCEED WITH CUSTOMER-FOCUSED SELLING

your products or services into business solutions, you cultivate a customer for life. And as you continue to provide outstanding service, follow-up, and additional products and services to your customer, you grow a wealth of continuous business in the form of referrals. Everybody wins.

Business gets easier as you use Customer-Focused Selling to honor and assist your customers in their business growth. The world of business today is desperate for principle-based selling. Your customers need you as much as you need them. Customer-Focused Selling provides the bridge for exceptional communication and increased sales.

To succeed, "results" are the name of the game. The world is your laboratory, and you must be hard on yourself. Don't settle for mediocre performance, don't take the quick fix, don't resort to traditional tactical sales approaches; invest the time in using Customer-Focused Selling. You deserve to have fun, you deserve to feel the joy of selling from your heart and winning sales day after day. Selling isn't magical; you are the magic. Your ability to understand your customer, ask questions, listen, interpret, articulate value, and provide solutions—that's the real magic. You can do it with Customer-Focused Selling, and the more your practice in the real laboratory, the better you get and the more you succeed.

I remember as a young child my father teaching me in ten minutes the essence of Customer-Focused Selling. Back then we had one television in our home, and on this particular evening at age six I was watching one of my favorite shows. My father, king of the house, came into the room and abruptly changed the channel. Now, in my

> Your customers need you as much as you need them.

SUCCEED WITH CUSTOMER-FOCUSED SELLING

house you didn't talk back to my father. Instead, I got up to leave the room, aggravated that I missed the ending of my show. "Stop right there!" I heard thunder behind me. As I slowly turned around, my father had a dead stare on me. "Are you leaving the room because you're done watching TV or because I changed the channel?" Fearing only slightly for my life, I stood tall and answered, "I'm leaving because you changed the channel." My father took a long pause. I held my breath and refused to speak or move. After what seemed like an eternity, my father gently responded, "You sit back down here and you explain to me why I might enjoy your show; then we'll decide which one to watch." I rambled on for five minutes nonstop about why my father would truly adore my show, exuding every ounce of genuine enthusiasm, giving all my examples of enjoyment from his perspective. And so we watched my show that night. Looking back, I realize that at six years old I learned the principles of Customer-Focused Selling: Understand the other person, identify what they need, articulate from their point of view, and be genuine. End result: Everybody wins. My father was the national sales manager of a nationally known company, I often wonder if he practiced all of his sales meetings on his kids first! My guess is yes.

I share this story with you to help you see that you, too, understand these principles. You may have learned them many years ago or just the other day, but knowing them and using them are two very different things. Value yourself and your customers enough to put these principles into action. Final thought: Trust the process, and the result will take care of itself. Customer -Focused Selling is for you. Now it's time for you to make it your own.

> Understand the other person, identify what they need, articulate from their point of view, and be genuine.

APPENDICES

CUSTOMER DATA

CUSTOMER DATA

There are two kinds of data you need to be on top of with customers: hard data (facts and figures) and soft data (feelings and opinions). In addition, you need to collect information from two perspectives: the customer as a company and the customer as an individual. Look at the following customer data sheet to see how you can apply this to your customer fact-finding.

CUSTOMER DATA SHEET

Company name:_____   Date:_____

Company Information

Age of business: _____
Annual revenue: _____
Structure: _____
Number of employees   _____
Number of locations: _____
Products/services: _____
Current situation: _____
Future focus: _____

Individual Information

Current position: _____
Years with company: _____
Background with company: _____
Prior experience: _____
Likes/dislikes: _____
Business community involvement: _____
Description of work style: _____
Other observations: _____

Personal Information

Born/raised: _____
Family: _____
Interests/hobbies: _____
Weekend activities: _____
Likes/dislikes: _____
Food/restaurants favorites: _____
Description of personal style: _____
Other observations: _____

TELEPHONE SCRIPT: SCHEDULING AN APPOINTMENT

Open

Objective: Greet and identify yourself to the prospect

"Hello [prospective client's name], this is [full name] of [company name]. How are you today?"

Body of the Call

Objective: Set expectations

"I noticed we're both members of the chamber of commerce and realized that we've never had an opportunity to talk. I work in [your company's market] and the reason for my call is to find out more about what you do. Do you have a few minutes?"

Objective: Investigate, qualify, and decide on next steps

"Tell me a little bit about your business...."

Let the prospect respond, then prompt with key questions to qualify the prospect. For example:

How old is your company?

What types of products or services do you provide?

How long have you been with the company?

Objective: Schedule appointment

"That sounds great. I'd like an opportunity to sit down and hear more about your business and to tell you a little bit about some of our new business products. Are you available early some morning next week?"

Close

Objective: Summarize and establish next steps

If they say "yes."

"Sounds great [prospect's name], I look forward to seeing you next Thursday at 9:00 am at your office. See you then."

If they say "no."

"[prospect's name], it sounds like you're tied up for the next few weeks. Can I try you back at some future date? Thanks. When would you like me to call? Great. Then I'll call you the beginning of June and look forward to meeting you then."

LETTER OF INTRODUCTION

Date
Name
Title/company
Address

Dear [name],

[Personalized attention-grabber]

Congratulations on reaching your fifth year in business. What a milestone! Although I've seen your name around town quite often I realize that we've never really had the opportunity to sit down and talk.

[Statement of purpose]

The purpose of this letter is to introduce myself and let you know in advance that I'll be calling you next week to schedule a time to get together. As the [title] of [company] here in [location], it's my goal to personally connect with all local business owners such as yourself.

[Call to action]

I look forward to talking with you next week and setting up a time to meet.

Sincerely,

Name of sales rep
Title

[Added value]
P.S.: Enclosed is a recent article I thought you might find interesting!

SAMPLE PROPOSAL

Date
Name
Title/company
Address

Dear [name],

It was a pleasure meeting with you yesterday and learning more about [prospect's company name]. Based on our conversation, you are looking for [state product or service] to meet the following three objectives:

Increase [state prospect's desired result]

Enhance [state prospect's desired result]

Develop [state prospect's desired result]

As we discussed, to best accomplish your goals, our [product or service] will best suit your needs. Enclosed are the specifications tailored to your situation. The financial investment for this [specific product or service being proposed] is [state the total dollar amount]. This investment includes all [list related value-added items—e.g., research, materials, labor]. I look forward to talking with you further about this project.

Sincerely,

Name of sales rep
Title

LETTER OF AGREEMENT

Date
Name
Title/company
Address
Dear [Name],

This letter confirms our agreement for [state product or service] to [state what is to be done] on [date]. We further agree that [your company name]'s fee will include:

A. [State terms agreed upon]

B. [State terms agreed upon]

C. [State terms agreed upon]

For this work [their company name] shall pay [your company name] in the amount of [state the fee] per [product or service item], a total of [state total investment required by prospect]. A deposit of [money amount] is due upon signing this agreement. The balance of [money amount] is due within [number] of days of the completion of [product or service].

Please sign both copies of this agreement. Return one copy to [your company name] with your check for [deposit money amount], and retain one copy for your records. I look forward to working together on this project.

Sincerely,

_____   _____
Name of sales rep/date   Prospect's name/date

_____   _____
Title   Prospect's company

THANK-YOU LETTER

Date

Name
Title/company
Address

Dear [name],

Thank you for the opportunity to work together on [state the product or service]. It's been a pleasure assisting you with [state the business objective].

Enclosed are [added value—e.g., articles, notes regarding the project, additional information, testimonials from people involved in the process], which I thought you'd enjoy seeing. I appreciate your business and will give you a call in a few weeks to check in.

I look forward to working together again soon.

Sincerely,

Name of sales rep
Title

THANK-YOU FOR THE REFERRAL

[Handwritten is preferable]

Date

Dear [name],

Just a quick note to thank you for the referral to [state prospect's name]. As a result of your referral, I [state a result or the current status—e.g., scheduled an appointment, met with them], and I will keep you posted on the outcome.

Thanks again for thinking of me and please let know how I can be helpful to you.

Regards,

Name of sales rep

SPEAKING ENGAGEMENT REFERRAL FORM

YES, YES, YES . . . I WANT TO INCREASE MY BUSINESS!

_____ Yes! Please add me to your mailing list at the address below. Send me your free quarterly newsletter immediately so I may learn more about how your products and services can help my business grow.

_____ Yes! Please call me at the number below. My company is interested in your products or services and would like to talk directly to you.

_____ Yes! Please call me at the number below. I know of another organization that would be interested in a speaker on this subject.

Name: _____

Title: _____

Company: _____

Address: _____

_____

Telephone: _____

Fax: _____

INTRODUCTION LETTER

Date

Mr. Jonathan White
Vice President
First National Savings Bank
496 Main Street
Super City, U.S.A. 00001

Dear Mr. White,

Computer software programs play a key role in the efficiency of your branch managers, your internal staff, and the bank as a whole. However, struggling through manuals and learning a system can be time-consuming as well as frustrating. That's where we come in!

Software Teaching Pros (STP) is a software consulting firm dedicated to teaching your staff in the most efficient manner possible. Your branch managers, CSRs, and tellers learn only the programs they need, in their office. Since 1992, STP's trained staff of fourteen software experts has been helping companies leverage their software systems to raise internal productivity and deliver higher levels of customer satisfaction.

I look forward to talking with you in regard to the types of programs your staff may currently be using, or may wish to use in the future, and how we can assist you in that process. Enclosed is a brochure with some additional information on our company. I look forward to talking with you early next week. If you have any immediate questions, please feel free to contact me directly at 1-800-111-1111.

Sincerely,

Ross Jones
Senior Account Executive

INTRODUCTION LETTER

COMMENTARY ON INTRODUCTION LETTER

Sales letters are a valuable tool in prospecting. You have the opportunity to grab the prospect's attention and deliver a powerful message, but you must do it fast! Research has shown that adults barely read letters. They look at the opening and the close and then decide if they will read the body of the letter–much like they would read a newspaper, skimming the headlines and then deciding if they want to read an article.

If you have only few seconds to grab their attention, the letter has to be good. "Good" means clear, concise, with a thought-provoking opening and call to action at the close. You want that reader to feel as if you wrote that letter directly to him or her. The focus of the letter should be from their "world," not from yours. The letter should immediately reflect that you understand their issues and you have a unique solution. Don't make the mistake of overselling! The objective of a prospecting letter isn't to sell products or services; a well-designed prospecting letter will get you lots and lots of sales appointments to sell products or services. Let's take a moment to dissect this sample prospecting letter.

Name and address: Always address an introduction letter to the most appropriate person you can find in the organization. You'll probably need to make a preliminary phone call to gather an appropriate name. The person may not be your ultimate decision-maker but should have a direct interest in purchasing and using your product or service, and have responsibility for the results. In this example, the letter is written to Jonathan White, the vice president for retail lending at a midsize bank. We know in advance that Jonathan has direct responsibility for the results of all the branch managers, customer service reps, and tellers; he's a perfect prospect for this software training company.

First paragraph: Focus on the prospect. Talk directly to the person you're writing the letter to. What's their problem or issue? When they read this letter you want their head to be nodding "Yes, that's exactly my problem." You want them to feel like you know them, you understand them, and like you've worked in their industry forever. Most people respond to positives better than to negatives, so the tone of your letter should be upbeat, direct, and to the point (even if your grabber is extremely negative).

Second paragraph. Focus on your company. Once you've outlined the challenge, you must present your company as the solution in a succinct and powerful manner. Even though you are talking about your company in this paragraph,

INTRODUCTION LETTER

keep the language focused from the reader's perspective and articulate the end results you can create for them. In this paragraph the reference to ". . . raise internal productivity and deliver higher levels of customer satisfaction" is exactly what a bank needs in today's competitive business environment. The statement was made in language that the vice president will "hear" and relate to. To increase your credibility in the letter, add some facts and figures, such as the date you started, how many employees, or even some "name brand" companies you have done work for. In this letter we referenced "Since 1992 . . ." and ". . . staff of fourteen software specialists" to add depth, strength, and impact.

Third paragraph: The third paragraph of your letter should be a call to action and state the next steps. Remember that most prospects are very busy doing their job and have very little time to call you back. Keep the responsibility of follow-up on your shoulders. In this prospecting letter, for example, "I look forward to talking with you early next week". . . lets them know that you will be contacting them and lets them know when they can expect to hear from you. Prospects will call if they have an immediate need, and it works well to provide your direct phone number in the final paragraph to make it easy for them.

Closing: A rule is to be conservative with first contacts. Sticking to the basic "sincerely" will always serve you well. For your name, spell out your proper name and sign it with any nicknames you use often; for example, "Edward" signed as "Ed," or "Richard" signed as "Rick." Use your title; the reader wants to know who you are in this company—sales representative, senior account executive, sales consultant. Whatever title you use, it should be reflected under your name.

Enclosures: If you have a short collateral piece you'd like to enclose with the letter, go ahead. A basic brochure or descriptive cut sheet on products or services can work well. One caution: Less is often more with prospecting. You don't want your prospect making a buying decision about your product or service based on one letter and a brochure; your objective is to get them interested enough to see you! You can qualify them on the phone call, but don't let any enclosure rule you out before you have a chance to talk to them. Before you put anything in with the letter, ask yourself one simple question: "Will including this piece help or hurt my chances of seeing this prospect?" You decide which way to go. If you're not sure, test it out. Send ten letters out with no brochure and ten letters with a brochure, and see which one yields more sales appointments!

COLD-CALL FOLLOW-UP NOTE

Date

Name
Company
Street
City, state, zip code

Dear Jennifer,

Thank you for your time today. During our brief meeting it was interesting to learn more about your company. Enclosed is the additional information you requested on our products and services for you to review.

I will give you a call early next week to schedule a time to get together to further discuss your company's situation and how I may be helpful to you.

Sincerely,

Your name
Your title

P.S.: Enclosed is an article on skiing that made me think of you and that I thought you'd like to see. Enjoy!

Objective. *The purpose of this follow-up note is to prove three things: your attention to detail, your listening skills, and your follow-up skills. "Actions speak louder than words" is true. Rather than telling them you are great at servicing your customers, you have already demonstrated it with this follow-up note. Take the time to send the follow-up note, and your odds of getting a true sales appointment will go way up.*

NETWORKING FOLLOW-UP LETTER TO AN INITIAL CONTACT

Date

Name
Company
Street address
City, state, zip code

Dear Terry,

It was a pleasure meeting you at the chamber of commerce event last night. I've already thanked Richard for introducing us. Based on our conversation, we are both talking to the same buyers.

I work as a resource for my customers and from time to time I may have a customer with the need for your services. I'd like to get together to learn more about your company and fill you in about the scope of my services. I'll give you a call at the end of the week to set up a coffee meeting.

I look forward to talking with you soon.

Regards,

Your name
Your title

Objective: The objective of this letter is to make a second connection, separate yourself from the crowd, and clarify that you are requesting a "networking appointment" rather than a sales appointment. You'll find that this letter builds good will, makes the recipient feel important, and sets the stage for a great networking coffee.

SAMPLE AFTER-THE-SALES-CALL LETTER

Date

Name
Company
Street address
City, state, zip code

Dear Ruth,

Just a quick note to thank you for your time at our meeting today. It was quite interesting to learn more about [state the prospect's company name] and your specific objectives.

To clarify next steps, you'll be faxing me the specs for this project and I will be sending you a formal proposal by the end of the week. I'll give you a call early next week to make sure you've received the proposal and to answer any questions you may have.

I look forward to working with you on this project.

Sincerely,

Your name
Your title

Objective. The purpose of this letter is to make sure the prospect under-stands what to expect from you and what, if anything, you expect from them. In addition, you have made another immediate contact, which provides an example of excellent follow-up and superior customer service, two of the very things your prospect is likely to evaluate. Make sure that whatever time lines you commit to in this note . . . you honor!

SAMPLE E-MAIL TO EXISTING CUSTOMER

Hello, Gary.

Just a quick note to follow-up on our meeting today. As always, it was great to see you. I really enjoy working together. Here's the brief punch list with time lines for you about the upcoming Time & Territory Management program for your senior sales staff:

Item	Requirements	Date of Completion
Sales staff names	Gary will provide list to Nancy	August 1
Sales staff interviews	Net-Works will make calls	August 15
Program customization	Net-Works design	August 31
Materials shipped	Gary will give contact	September 5
Program delivery	Net-Works will present program	September 15

I look forward to working together with you on this project! I'll give you a call in early August to check for any changes in your marketplace.

Nancy

Objective. E-mail messages should be concise, contain all the details necessary to the message, and be clear on any required next steps. Be careful about sending chatty messages—your customers don't have time to be reading unnecessary E-mails. Customers who use E-mail respect salespeople who use it as a business tool to pass information in an efficient manner. Use it for what it's designed for!

Streetwise

NetResults

A Quarterly Publication

Networking and Sales Ideas for Business

Net Works
Make the Connection
Summer 1995 Vol. 2 Issue 1

Welcome

Ola, buen dias! Net-Works training programs are now available in Spanish throughout Mexico through an affiliation with Management Resources-Mexico. In a recent trip to Mexico City I was delighted to complete negotiations and meet several of the trainers. What countries next? Argentina, Chile, Peru and Columbia!

Business continues to expand and the list of satisfied clients grows steadily. The past several months have opened up a rush of public relations opportunities including six published articles, one cable TV show and 3 radio spots. The results of all this exposure? Several new clients and many audio cassette tape sales. Yes, P.R. pays nice dividends.

Please call me at 1-800-371-2264 with any questions or comments. Services include professional speaking, custom training and consulting, all focused on new business development, networking and sales!

Warmest regards!

Nancy J. Stephens

Uncover Your Hidden Sales Force

by Nancy J. Stephens

We all recognize our sales people, right? How many other employees are consistently in touch with our customers and would never consider themselves in sales? Customer service representatives, telephone support staffs, front line people? Their biggest fear is that you'll ask them to sell! After all, the reason they got into customer service is so they'd never have to sell.

The best way to assist your service staff in developing their selling skills is to help them understand that superior customer service is sales. The following three fundamentals are key:

1. Clarify Sales and the Sales Process

In order to sell, recommend, or refer, front line staff associates must understand the dynamics of sales and the sales process. They need product training, but as important they need to know what to do with the product knowledge and understand how to sell in a service environment.

2. Enhance Listening Skills

Effective selling requires a higher level of questioning and listening skills to "hear" a customers needs, leads and clues. Customers are constantly sending

(Cont'd on page 2)

Plant Seeds Where You Want Them to Grow!

by Nancy J. Stephens

Where should you be investing your networking time? An important question. The best advice is to be selective. In every business our most valuable asset is our time, the way you invest yours is crucial to your success. In networking, less is often more. Choose one to three organizations that make the most sense for you.

"In every business our most valuable asset is our time..."

1. Industry Related

One of the associations you attend should be industry related. You must keep the "pulse" of your industry as well as cultivate relationships for information and referrals.

(Cont'd on page 2)

This issue...

Uncover Your Hidden Sales Force (cont'd)

messages and signals for additional opportunities. The customer service staff member needs to be able to identify those "triggers" and feel confident to address them.

3. Build Customer Relationships

The customer service staff is perfectly positioned to build long term customer relationships. They build the trust which is fundamental to the sales process. Help them to realize that taking this relationship to the next level includes anticipating needs and providing solutions...otherwise known as sales!

Uncover the hidden sales force in your company with customer service reps, telephone support staffs, and front line people, and you're likely to increase morale, job satisfaction, and sales!

Based on Net-Works Enhanced Customer Service Program, call for more information.

INFONET
QUESTIONS AND ANSWERS

During speaking engagements throughout the U.S. and Canada, I find that many people ask the same questions. This column addresses those most commonly asked. Please FAX your sales and networking questions to Net-Works InfoNet at (508) 369-3816. Answers will appear in upcoming issues of Net-Results.

Q. What's the best level to network your way into a corporation?

*A. Target your networking towards the top. It is always easier to be referred down an organization than up an organization. At lower levels the key responsibility is for a **budget**, not where you want to be as a service provider. At upper levels the key responsibility is for **results** - exactly where you want to be. This positions you as a value provider not a cost, as an investment not an expense. Always network at the highest level possible.*

Q. How can I help my people to close more sales?

A. In order to close more sales, help your people to do an outstanding job up front. The bulk of sales are made in the early stages of the sales process not at the "close". Consistently work on questioning skills, listening skills, and the ability to assess situations accurately. When your sales associates enhance these skills, they will close more sales.

Q. How is Networking different from Prospecting?

A. Prospecting is the activity of looking for clients. Networking includes a small portion of prospecting but is primarily an activity which creates referral sources. Prospecting will give you one sale from one contact, networking creates many sales from one contact. Both are important but distinct business building skills.

Q. How can I get my people to "think on their feet" more effectively?

A. To help your people increase their ability to "think on their feet" you need to enhance their ability to "hear" with depth and apply judgement. They need to be able to interpret and respond to information on two levels - the surface words and the meaning beneath. For example, if a customer asks "You're with what company? Who are they?", what they are really saying is... "Educate me, make me feel comfortable, show me that you have confidence in your ability to service me, show me you're a player." Thinking on your feet includes the ability to hear both, apply judgement, and respond with confidence.

Make The Connection with International Networking (cont'd)

happen. Educate yourself first and others second.

4. Leverage Your Audience for Information.

At a recent program for a worldwide company I had an audience which represented about 22 countries. During my program on networking skills I took the opportunity to ask one simple question..."What would need to be altered for this networking methodology to be effective in your country?" From Japan to Germany, Taiwan to the UK I received an overwhelming response that, with slight alterations respecting cultural differences, this would "work" everywhere...YEAH! And how come? Networking is building long-term mutually beneficial relationships, the essence of good business. Interesting enough, our international connections figured this out a long, long time ago. This kind of information from an audience can help build future international business. The bottom line, make the connections, utilize international networking and you'll find yourself wherever you wish to go!

> *"Networking is building long-term mutually beneficial relationships, the essence of good business."*

Note:

Watch for an in-depth up-coming article on effective selling. To request an advance copy, call (800) 371-2264 or FAX (508) 369-3816.

INDEX

INDEX

INDEX

INDEX

Streetwise Customer-Focused Selling is also available as a software product!

Designed for Microsoft Windows 95 • CD-ROM • 3.5" DISK • Mac OS

Designed for Windows®3.1, Windows®95, and Macintosh®

SUCCEED IN SALES BY PUTTING YOUR CUSTOMER FIRST

CUSTOMER-FOCUSED SELLING

Customer-Focused Selling covers it all! You'll learn proven cold calling techniques, how to build rapport, gain trust, ask the right questions, overcome objections, and gain agreement. You'll see on video how the pros sell and you'll find interactive tools and exercises to help you sell better too! Here you will:

- ▶ See How the Pros Handle Each Step of the Sales Process;
- ▶ Learn Cold Calling Techniques That Work;
- ▶ Learn Plenty of Ways to Find New Accounts.

Customer-Focused Selling presents a new sale technique that involves the client every step of the way and will show customers that you really care and that your product can help. Distinguish yourself from the masses and get in touch with Customer-Focused Selling today!

SPECIFICATIONS

CD-ROM (Win/Mac Multimedia) Version: CD-ROM drive
3.5" Disk (Win Lite) Version: 3.5" disk drive

Windows: Windows 3.1 or higher, Windows NT, or Windows 95 • 386 PC (486 or Pentium recommended) • Sound Blaster or compatible audio • 4 MB RAM (8 recommended) • 5 MB free hard disk space

Macintosh: System 7.0 or higher • Performa, Quadra, Centris or Power Macintosh • 4 MB RAM (8 recommended) • 5 MB free hard disk space

MADE WITH M MACROMEDIA

Also available at software retailers nationwide:

500 BUSINESSES YOU CAN START

DO-IT-YOURSELF ADVERTISING

HIRING TOP PERFORMERS

MANAGING PEOPLE

SMALL BUSINESS START-UP

How to order: If you cannot find this software at your favorite retail outlet, you may order it directly from the publisher. Call for price information. BY PHONE: Call 1-800-872-5627 (in Massachusetts 781-767-8100). We accept Visa, Mastercard, and American Express. $5.95 will be added to your total order for shipping and handling. BY MAIL: Write out the full title of the software you'd like to order and send payment, including $5.95 for shipping and handling to: Adams Media Corporation, 260 Center Street, Holbrook, MA 02343. 30-day money-back guarantee.

ADAMS MONEY-BACK GUARANTEE 30-DAY

Visit our exciting job and career site at http://www.careercity.com

Nancy J. Stephens, international speaker and consultant, is the founder of Net-Works, a sales consulting firm specializing in new business development. Since 1991, she has trained sales representatives, senior executives and business owners throughout North America and Europe on how to gain new business with a unique set of networking and sales methodologies.

She is the author of an audio cassette program, an instructional video series, and numerous magazine articles. Prior to Net-Works, Nancy was a national trainer for a computer service bureau, a member of the Leader's Forum in the Insurance Industry, and a top-producing Sales Manager for a regional security alarm company.

Nancy Stephens can be contacted at:
Net-Works
Carlisle, MA 01741
(508)371-2268 or (800)371-2264